Edward Albee:
Playwright In Protest

Edward Albee:

PLAYWRIGHT IN PROTEST

by Michael E. Rutenberg

DBS PUBLICATIONS, INC.
DRAMA BOOK SPECIALISTS
NEW YORK, NEW YORK

39353

PS
3551
.L.25
Z87

Published in the United States
DBS PUBLICATIONS, INC.

DRAMA BOOK SPECIALISTS

Library of Congress Card Number: 69-15670

Printed in U.S.A. by
NOBLE OFFSET PRINTERS, INC.
NEW YORK 3, N. Y.

In memory of John Gassner

Contents

Introduction   3

CHAPTER 1 / The Zoo Story   15

CHAPTER 2 / The Sandbox   41

CHAPTER 3 / Fam and Yam   51

CHAPTER 4 / The American Dream   61

CHAPTER 5 / The Death of Bessie Smith   79

CHAPTER 6 / Who's Afraid of Virginia Woolf?   95

CHAPTER 7 / Tiny Alice   119

CHAPTER 8 / A Delicate Balance   137

CHAPTER 9 / Adaptations

        The Ballad of the Sad Cafe   167

        Malcolm   179

        Everything in the Garden   185

CHAPTER 10 / Box-Mao-Box   201

CHAPTER 11 / Two Interviews with Edward Albee   229

Chronological List of Premieres   261

Notes   263

Selected Bibliography   273

Edward Albee:
Playwright In Protest

Introduction

EDWARD ALBEE was born in Washington, D.C., on March 12, 1928. Two weeks later he was adopted by Reed and Frances Albee, heirs to the famous Keith-Albee vaudeville chain. The two-week-old infant was taken to the Albee Tudor mansion in Larchmont, New York, and quickly surrounded with nurses, servants, and eventually tutors, all of whom later doubled as Edward's playmates. By the time he reached his fifth birthday, the family had already begun sending him in the family Rolls-Royce to see Broadway plays on matinee days. In spite of this rather luxurious upbringing, Albee admits that he was a problem child, and at the age of eleven he was sent to Lawrenceville in the hope that boarding school would straighten him out. In retaliation he cut classes, refused to do assignments, would not participate in sports, and generally behaved so incorrigibly that he was expelled in a year and a half. Back home, his defiant attitude only worsened the situation, and Mrs. Albee promptly shuffled him through a series of fashionable Eastern preparatory schools, including one military academy, and then on to Trinity College in Hartford, Connecticut, where he stayed slightly more than a year. Unwilling to attend chapel, and still dissatisfied with a rigid curriculum, he finally abandoned his formal education and returned to Larchmont. For a year he lived at home mingling with the country club set while commuting to Manhattan to work as a script writer for a New York radio station.

In New York he had begun to meet and become friendly with a group of artists and young intellectuals whose lifestyle Mrs. Albee could not tolerate. Finally, at the age of twenty, after one too many family squabbles, Edward took his books and his records and left home permanently. The young Albee started Manhattan life rather well, renting a lower Fifth Avenue apartment with a boyhood friend. He was receiving two-hundred and fifty dollars a month from his paternal grandmother, so he could be free to continue his early interest in writing. But within a year, the allowance ceased, and Edward had to find employment and a cheaper place to live. He then slipped through a succession of jobs as record salesman, waiter, copy boy, counterman, and Western Union messenger.

At about this time he met composer William Flanagan, and spent the next nine years sharing a variety of inexpensive apartments with him. These cold-water flats were not only damp and cold, but reeked of cat food because Edward was always picking up strays.[1] It soon became impossible to write in that depressing atmosphere, and Albee took to leaving the apartment at night to become involved in literary and philosophical discussions in some coffeehouses on Macdougal Street. Emotionally stimulating as these encounters were, Albee soon realized they were a pretext to avoid writing. In an effort to break the cycle, he began to dissociate himself slowly from the Village crowd, but instead of sending him back to his writing, this self-imposed isolation only succeeded in depressing him further.

It was at the peak of despair that one night, in a last-ditch effort to make something of his life, Edward Albee sat down to write about a pathetically lonely young man, orphaned at an early age by the premature death of his parents, and later shunned by society because of what psychiatrists have referred to as a case of borderline sanity;[2] a totally alienated failure bent on making contact with someone of the establishment—even if it meant dying in the process. It was Albee's first serious attempt at writing a play—an act of desperation after having failed to produce anything of merit in either the novel, short story, or poetry, in the nine years since he left Larchmont. He called the play *The Zoo Story*. What followed was an outpouring of such extraordinary plays that Edward Albee is often considered the most important playwright of the contemporary American theatre. His playwrighting, which now spans a decade, has brought him the New York Press Association's Best Plays Award, the Lola D'Annunzio Award, the New York Drama Critics Award, and the coveted Pulitzer Prize. In appreciation of his distinguished literary career, the National Academy of Arts and Letters elected him to membership in 1966.

Why has Albee been embraced as the single hope for an almost ossified Broadway theatre? Unquestionably it is his supreme ability to present plays of shocking social protest which reflect present-day thinking. These plays, rich in verbal texture and poetic rhythms, display his uncanny genius for theatricalizing human conflict and speak to a modern generation determined to break through the deadly apathy of the fifties. It is a television generation that has been horrified by the assassinations of John and Robert Kennedy, Martin Luther King, Malcolm X, and Medgar Evers; a generation of dissidents appalled at this country's intervention in Vietnam, and angered by a war budget of thirty billion dollars a year while Congress quietly cuts back federal funds for the maze of domestic poverty programs to a token two billion dollars a year; a generation that has read the President's *Report of the National Advisory Commission on Civil Disorders,* and agrees with its indictment of our historically irrational and inhuman racist credo.

Albee speaks to these dissentients who are united in their fervor to churn up a social cataclysm that will bring about needed reforms. He speaks to those who have stood up to the huge, previously unshakable urban Boards of Education, and are now forcing them to decentralize in order to give

more community control over ghetto schools. He appeals
to those kindred youth who have watched their elders dissociate themselves from the plight of the American Indian
and the migratory farm worker and look the other way
while ten million people in this wealthy nation suffer the
effects of malnutrition because they are too poor to buy
the proper food. Albee relates to a new student generation
that has seen first-hand evidence of CIA subversion of the
National Students Association and recognizes the *faux pas*
Congress made when it exempted this undercover agency
from normal legislative surveillance and the General
Accounting Office;[3] a student generation that is beginning
to question those institutions of higher learning that advo-
cate the right to teach *in loco parentis* and disallow students
a voice in campus administration or shaping curriculum—
a rationale that has also punished male students for long
hair and fanciful clothing.

Until the 1960's, writers committed to socio-political involvement still feared blacklisting in the aftermath of the
almost hysterical red-menace scare of the McCarthy hearings
in the mid-fifties. During that period—not yet easily forgotten
—thousands of important careers were ruined when the nation believed the senator's trumped-up tale about a mono-
lithic Communist takeover.

A social drama, which Harold Clurman has said ". . . attempted to make the stage an instrument of public enlightenment through a passionate involvement with the national
scene,"[4] emerged briefly in this country in the thirties and
then died; partly because its leftist views mistakenly carried
the taint of party Communism; partly because the plays, with
few exceptions, were mediocre and one-dimensional, drama-
turgically propelled by naive enthusiasm toward simplistic
conclusions. The public quickly tired of these works of protest as soon as the wartime boom had reversed the effects of
the Depression. The populace saw a rosier life ahead with

new opportunities to make money in either the black market or defense plants.

After the war, continuing to act under the Truman doctrine, this country entered the Korean conflict and the economy continued to soar. Writers, deluded into believing that no social problems existed in this land of plenty, or frightened by the power of blacklisting which still associated leftist thinking with Communist doctrines, withdrew further and further from what Sartre referred to as "literary engagement." Gerald Rabkin, author of *Drama and Commitment,* tells us that *Partisan Review* sent a questionnaire to a number of established writers in 1948, asking about the artist's relationship to the growing tension between the Soviet Union and the United States: " 'Do you think a writer should involve himself in it (as a writer? as a person?) to the point of commitment?' " Professor Rabkin informs us that "the response affirmed the necessity of the writer's detachment."[5] He also notes that as late as 1960, *Anvil,* a socialist publication, asked another group of prominent writers if the artist has an obligation to political commitment. All agreed that "there is an inherent conflict between artistic integrity and any commitment."[6] An erosion of spirit had carried over from the McCarthy era and remained with the establishment; it became more potentially threatening than a drop in the Dow Jones average or gross national product.

But with the advent of Sputnik, which shook this country out of its escapist complacency, and because of John F. Kennedy, a whole new generation refused to accept tradition without change. In pre-election campaign speeches he stressed his "New Frontier," and urged the country not to "shrink from that new frontier [and] look to the safe mediocrity of the past." His famous inaugural address carried within it a *lietmotiv* applicable today:

> . . . let the word go forth from this time and place to friend and foe alike, that the torch has been passed to a

new generation of Americans born in this country, tempered by war, disciplined by a hard and bitter peace, proud of our ancient heritage, and unwilling to witness or permit the slow undoing of those human rights to which this nation has always been committed, and to which we are committed today at home and around the world.

The revolution had begun. A different generation, grown up with· the bomb, nurtured in affluence, highly mobile, better informed than their pre-electronic-age predecessors, moralistic, was now dedicated to the overthrow of social, political, religious, and economic oppression in American life. Participation in freedom rides, sit-ins, teach-ins, marches, demonstrations, and outright civil disobedience to certain laws held immoral and untenable to one's own conscience, changed the entire life of this country. "Make love not war," has now become the poster-theme, and gentle, powder-faced Tiny Tim, playing his battered ukulele, singing falsetto songs from a forgotten age, embodies this new love-generation's belief in the right to do your own thing.

Contemporary writing turned about and soon began to reflect this new surge of social commitment. The *New American Review* (of fiction, essays, and poetry) devoted its summer 1968 edition to a socio-political dialogue between writer and reader. National magazines and scores of paperback books whose main themes examine the domestic and foreign scene have entered bookstores and newsstands across the country. In the theatre Edward Albee writes reformist plays of social protest which unflinchingly reveal the pustulous sores of a society plagued with social ills. His first decade of playwrighting has consistently displayed an unyielding social commitment as he experimented with varying dramatic styles and playwrighting techniques. Realism served admirably for the shocking events of the *The Zoo Story, Who's Afraid of Virginia Woolf?,* and *A Delicate Balance;* surrealism provided the form for the socio-political didactics of *The Sandbox* and *The American Dream;* impressionism was the major style of social protest in *The Death of Bessie Smith;* symbolist mysticism permeated the theological metaphysics of *Tiny Alice;* and theatrical revolution prompted the polyphonic, non-narrative design of *Box-Mao-Box*.

Albee's early plays from *Zoo Story* through *American Dream,* though vastly different in theatrical form, are all protests in defense of those outcasts of society who have been victimized by the stupidity and bias of the successful elite. In *Virginia Woolf* his sociological vantage point changes, and he attacks the hypocrisy and corruption in some circles of the intelligentsia of our society, stripping all comfortable illusion from the protagonists in an effort to make them face the truth of their barren lives. The later plays, *A Delicate Balance* and *Tiny Alice,* continue the destruction of individual illusion, but go further into an exploration of modern man's very real sense of isolation and estrangement from society and his God. The adaptations, *Ballad of the Sad Cafe* and *Malcolm,* though certainly not up to the level of his indigenous works, support his defense of the misfit—society's outsider—while the last of these, *Everything in the Garden,* continues his assault on an affluent society gone amoral. His newest theatre piece is actually two short but highly original plays of The New Theatre. The first, *Box,* a post-holocaust requiem for the dead, performed in monodic fashion, is carefully interwoven into the second, *Quotations from Mao Tse-Tung,* a contrapuntal score for voices whose main theme is man's impending doom.

Albee's plays of social protest work because they touch the pulse of change in our time. He is into what is happening. The anti-realistic revolution going on in today's New Theatre had its start with men like Jarry, Artaud, Beckett, Ionesco, Genet, and Pinter, but its social commitment was influenced by Edward Albee and his English counterpart, John Osborne.

Young American playwrights such as Rochelle Owens, Sam Shephard, Paul Foster, Megan Terry, Leonard Melfi, Lanford Wilson, Jean-Claude van Itallie, LeRoi Jones, Rosalyn Drexler, and many, many others, came out of Albee's Playwrights Unit and other Off-Off Broadway hostels, notably: Joe Chaiken's Open Theatre (which is an outgrowth of the Beck's Living Theatre), Ellen Stewart's Cafe La Mama, Al Carmine's Judson Memorial Theatre, Ralph Cook's Theatre Genesis, and the late Joe Cino's Cafe Cino. These innovative artists have in part helped to create the mixed-media play—a genre more stirring and more raucous than its prototype, The Living Newspaper of the Federal Theatre.

It is apparent in any historical overview of dramatic writing in this country that it has been Edward Albee (though Miller should be included, but to a lesser degree) who has shown the new theatre writers that they can no longer remain aloof to social and political commitment as their predecessors did for more than a quarter of a century after the demise of social drama in the late thirties.

The commitment of today's new theatre people is real and it is vital. Yale University recently held a symposium on "The Theatre in American Political Life," and panelist Robert Mandel, a first year Doctor of Fine Arts candidate, said it like this:

> I think the crimes being committed now are just so great that moral conscientiousness has its logical result in political action. I don't think you can divide the two anymore. We can't tell ourselves any more that we know that war, racial prejudice and economic oppression are immoral and yet cop out by saying we are not cut out for politics . . . if we don't do anything . . . we are not withdrawing from politics, we are withdrawing from life . . . politics is part of that experience you bring to bear on your work. And if you don't bring it to bear . . . then you are just copping out. You will never succeed. You will dehumanize your art, you will kill the theatre.

> Of course, a lot of people think that the theatre can
> never be an effective political weapon . . . but if it's true,
> I think we should all get the hell out of here.[7]

Some *have* dropped out, frantic to induce an LSD psychosis or narcoticize themselves into vegetative oblivion, rather
than admit to the boredom of an uncommitted life. But
Edward Albee has not left the scene. Unwilling to accept the
perpetuation of a *pastiche* theatre, he refuses to compromise
his personal vision, vindicating this new generation's belief in
him. All across this country, with the sole exception of
Shakespeare, he is the most produced playwright in colleges
and universities. It is because Edward Albee has never believed—as do his European contemporaries—that man is a
helpless pawn caught in the capricious grip of an absurd and
indifferent universe. Writing out of the social ferment and
societal unrest which surrounds his very existence, Albee has
given a resurgence to the history of social protest in the theatre, a tradition that has its roots in Aristophanes' criticism
of the Peloponnesian War. Albee is, and has always been, a
social protester, deeply moral, and committed to the cause of
human dignity in an ethically moribund age. He has
said of the artist's work, ". . . the responsibility of the writer
is to be a sort of demonic social critic—to present the world
and people in it as he sees it and say, 'Do you like it: if you
don't like it change it.' " As Alan Schneider has declared,
Albee "speaks and feels for the American moment that is
now, and he's a talent that has only started."[8]

CHAPTER 1

THE ZOO STORY

The Zoo Story was first produced in Germany, having its premiere in Berlin on September 28, 1959. It seems rather odd that the first play of an indigenous American writer should have to be performed outside of his own country, but Albee, like so many other unknown writers, had had the play politely refused by a number of New York producers, who, afraid of presenting a new writer, quietly returned his manuscript. In the preface to his first play, Albee states that the initial rejection of the play was natural and to be expected. It was a "short play, and short plays *are* unfortunately anathema to producers and—supposedly—to audiences." Perhaps it is for this reason that Albee never refers to his plays as one-acters; instead he calls them plays in one scene or short plays. The play was read by friends of Albee and circulated unsuccessfully from New York, to Florence, to Zürich, to Frankfurt, and finally to Berlin for its belated world premiere. The response in Germany caused enough of a stir to enable it to be produced four months later Off-Broadway at the Provincetown Playhouse on January 14, 1960. Friedrich Luft wrote in *Die Welt:* ". . . it is highly talented and, in its dialectic of absolute evil, it has often a ghastly lustre."[1] *The Darmstädter Echo* was a bit more prophetic when it stated: "This monologue of a desperate man, imploringly looking for human contact and friendship, is an experiment and perhaps a discovery for the theatre."[2]

The "players" as Albee refers to them, are only two. Peter, a man in his early forties, is "neither fat nor gaunt, neither handsome nor homely." His suit is tweed and his demeanor unobtrusive, suggesting the conformity of William H. Whyte's organization man.[3] Peter works for a firm that publishes textbooks. Ironically Albee has given this unseeing (the stage directions call for him to clean his glasses at the start of the play), complacent, middle-aged man a job as an executive for textbook publishers. He is probably one of those well-paid, successful individuals who can edit college and high school texts to give the impression that the book was designed and executed by a computer. The standard approach to textbook writing seems to delete any evidences of the writer's personality in order to achieve subject matter objectivity. Peter fits his job well. His personality is, as he himself puts it, ". . . normally . . . uh . . . reticent."[4] He will never own his own business. He does not have the drive. A beautiful touch in terms of characterization is Albee's remark that Peter smokes a pipe. According to Vance Packard's exposé on pyramid climbing in business, the perfect executive type doesn't smoke a pipe because it gives the impression to the organization that he is not a "decision-maker."[5] Peter's unobtrusive personality allows him to do his work without ever disturbing the well-ordered society of the textbook publisher.

The other man in this play is named Jerry. Jerry, according to Albee's description, is a man in his late thirties, "not poorly dressed, but carelessly. What was once a trim and lightly muscled body has begun to go to fat; and while he is no longer handsome, it is evident that he once was. His fall from physical grace should not suggest weariness." Albee's description subtly prepares his audience for Jerry's ultimate retreat from life at the end of the play. According to most studies of mental patients confined to hospitals, the initial breakdown is graphically shown by a neglect of the body. Patients also become careless about their clothes, showing a marked disconcern over their general appearance.[6] Jerry is becoming careless about how he looks. He is not psychotic, however, though there are signs throughout the play that point to his being a borderline case. Albee has said that Jerry "is not insane. He is over-sane."[7] Nevertheless, his personal cares and concerns with the everyday routines of life have already begun to disintegrate into a form of self-exile from the society that has not allowed him to succeed. We soon sense that this man is one of society's outcasts. Professor George E. Wellwarth calls Jerry "an outsider—rootless and aimless."[8] Harold Clurman makes a similar reference to his "estrangement from society," but quite properly adds that along with his rootlessness it is his utter poverty that forces him to remain alone in the largest city in the world.[9] He has not succeeded in the American tradition as Peter has.

Harold Clurman has incorrectly described Peter as society's "average representative,"[10] which would hardly be the case, as Peter's executive salary is way beyond the average American's annual income. Jerry doesn't make $18,000 a year. In fact, Jerry doesn't do much of anything. He has become the alienated failure, the bad luck sign with whom successful people never want to mix. And so this is the start of our play. Two men, one a success, the other a failure, meet one Sunday afternoon in a public park.

From the beginning of the play when Jerry arrives on the scene, he is immediately drawn to Peter who represents his antithesis. It is difficult making contact because Peter is totally unaware of Jerry's presence; he complacently avoids life's stream of passersby, preferring to hide behind a book. Professor Rose Zimbardo recognized this prevailing theme when she wrote the following: "Contact is from time to time made, but always with great difficulty and never with any assurance that it can be sustained. . . ."[11] Jerry, however, is persistent. He repeats his opening remark three times, each time just a bit more boldly, until Peter is forced to emerge from behind his book and confront the world:

JERRY: I've been to the zoo. (PETER *doesn't notice*) I said, I've been to the zoo. MISTER, I'VE BEEN TO THE ZOO!

PETER: Hm? . . . What? . . . I'm sorry, were you talking to me?

Peter's well-ordered life has now been interrupted, never to return to its original calm. Jerry asks directions; he has lost his way. Jerry probably lost his way much before this play began. Perhaps it happened soon after he arrived in New York. He is not a native New Yorker. His intuition tells him to seek help from Peter who appears to know his way around the city:

JERRY: . . . Have I been walking north?

PETER: North? Why . . . I . . . I think so. Let me see.

Peter is momentarily puzzled; it had never occurred to him that a man speaking English could lose his way in Manhattan. Jerry continues asking questions in an effort to get his bearings:

JERRY: Is that Fifth Avenue?

PETER: Why yes; yes, it is.

Parts of Fifth Avenue are categorically the mark of style and taste, dealing in items designed for the more affluent of our society. Peter knows exactly where it is. A few more lines of dialogue establish that Jerry has not been walking "due north." Jerry is off his course as he trespasses into Peter's world, but the action already begun, Jerry presses on. We soon learn that Peter's intellectual achievement has reached the level of *Time* magazine which, he feels, is the magazine for mature-thinking Americans:

JERRY: Well, *Time* magazine isn't for blockheads.

PETER: No, I suppose not.

Jerry maintains the conversation, mentioning his dislike for the west side of the park. For the first time Peter is slightly interested and asks, "Why?" Jerry avoids the subject with, "I don't know." As the play progresses, however, he will eventually tell Peter about himself, and we will then understand his seemingly casual remark. Peter, by this time, would like to end the colloquy and return to his book, because society teaches its metropolitan members not to strike up conversations with strangers in New York City—it is dangerous. Jerry will not be put off and asks rather bluntly:

JERRY: Do you mind if we talk?

PETER: (*Obviously minding*) Why . . . no, no.

JERRY: Yes you do: you do.

PETER: (*Puts his book down, his pipe out and away, smiling*) No, really; I don't mind.

JERRY: Yes you do.

PETER: (*Finally decided*) No; I don't mind at all, really.

Peter has given in to Jerry, but their "talk" assumes the form of an interrogation with Jerry as the inquisitor. Jerry's tactlessness unnerves Peter and he comments, ". . . you don't really carry on a conversation; you just ask questions. . . ." Peter's evaluation is valid because Jerry is incapable of the relaxed, spontaneous flow associated with friendly conversation. While it is true that these two men are not friends—and this would in itself produce a somewhat awkward atmosphere —there is a strong suggestion that because of Jerry's estrangement and subsequent desperate need for friendship, he has lost the ability to accept another person's attention in his fervor to spill out his own lonely feelings. Peter, then, is only an emotional sounding board for Jerry who is not, until the end of the "dog monologue" (through his confessions), psychologically ready to accept Peter as a newly found friend. Walter Kerr talks about this very problem in referring to the play's structure. He says: "It sags in the center because it is a soliloquy rather than a play; the isolation that is talked about separates the contestants so ruthlessly that they cannot ever lock horns dramatically."[12]

Jerry's utter need to talk and talk so overpowers Peter that for three quarters of the play Peter is nothing more than a convenient dramatic foil for Jerry. Peter's character clearly suffers as a result. One critic noticed the unevenness of character delineation when he wrote that "the bench sitter is less a character than an idea (Mr. Square . . .) so *The Zoo Story* lacks a convincing antagonist."[13] Nevertheless, this question and answer technique does give us expository background material very quickly so that the audience, having had the facts, will be able to respond to the shocking ending. It would be impossible to have this data appear more subtly unless the play were a full-length drama which Albee, I believe, realized would dilute its final impact. Consequently, using this interrogative approach we very quickly learn much about Peter's business and home life. Within three and a half pages we are told that Peter is married and has two girls, although he wanted a boy because "every man wants a son," and his wife will give him no more children. They have two television sets, two parakeets, and cats; Peter makes around $18,000 a year working for a publisher, and they live between Lexington and Third Avenues on Seventy-fourth Street.

Let us examine this conglomeration of information more closely, seeing how Albee neatly fits Peter into the American success mold. Peter has two television sets. He has accepted and believes that life can be beautiful when one has two of everything. He is upper-middle-class America, convinced by Madison Avenue advertising that an expanding economy is a sure road to happiness. The problem, of course, lies in expanding further when we are now dangerously over-producing. The answer, as reported by Vance Packard in his recent book *The Waste Makers,* is to convince every American that it is utter desolation to be without that second car, that second home, and above all that second TV set.[14]

Peter has two girls and stoically accepts the fact that he will never have a male child to carry his name. It is interesting to note that it is not the seeming sterility of their marriage (a theme to which Albee devotes much of *Who's Afraid of Virginia Woolf?*) that bothers Peter, but rather his inability to conform to what most people want:

JERRY: But you wanted boys.

PETER: Well . . . naturally, every man wants a son, but . . .

JERRY (*lightly mocking*) But that's the way the cookie crumbles?

PETER (*annoyed*) I wasn't going to say that.

JERRY: And you're not going to have any more kids, are you?

PETER (*A bit distantly*) No. No more.

His girls both have their own parakeets—a tribute to his misapplication of modern child psychology which states that parents ought to treat all the children equally, lest "sibling rivalry" appear.[15] It occurs neither to Peter nor to his wife that one family parakeet can be enjoyed by both children. What is perhaps more illuminating is the fact that there are cats in a household of birds. Curiously enough, the idea of cats in the household was his wife's. Apparently she enjoys this predatory situation. Jerry is by no means unaware of the cat-bird implication as is Peter:

JERRY: Do they carry disease? The birds.

PETER: I don't believe so.

JERRY: That's too bad. If they did you could set them loose in the house and the cats could eat them and die, maybe. (PETER *looks blank for a moment, then laughs*)

At this point in the play we have learned quite a bit about Peter's life, but almost nothing of Jerry's except that he says, "I don't talk to many people. . . ." He seems, however, to show a great desire to talk to Peter because "every once in a while I like to talk to somebody, really talk; like to get to know somebody, know all about him." It does not occur to Jerry that getting to know someone is a reciprocal arrangement. What Jerry wants now is not a friend but a sympathetic listener. Jerry needs to talk, not listen, and now that Albee has given us enough of Peter's background to enable us to concentrate on Jerry, the next major portion of the play is virtually a thirteen-page monologue with periodic interjections from Peter. Peter has been conditioned enough not to be too demanding or original. He is not used to voicing his opinion, taking the initiative, or exerting pressure on those around him. It is not too difficult, therefore, for Jerry to keep him listening. Peter is both fascinated and repulsed by Jerry's life, yet bulldozed enough by the display of histrionics to hold his seat until the performance is over.

Up until the present moment there has been mention of the zoo eight times in as many pages. Obviously Jerry is deeply concerned with what he experienced there, and has trouble repressing the experience from his consciousness. All we can understand at this early juncture is that the thought of the zoo cues Jerry's question to Peter concerning the dividing line between "upper-middle-middle-class and lower-upper-middle-class." The question, surely, is ridiculous, but it begins to shed light on his observations at the zoo, for we know that whatever happened there has made him think of society's strata.

As the play progresses, we learn that Jerry has walked along Fifth Avenue to the zoo. He has undoubtedly seen chic hotels, replete with aging dowagers with French poodles, busy business men, overly polite doormen, and the very expensive dress shops—all gathered to pamper and please the most discriminating tastes of the wealthy. Jerry is not part of this world, and his estrangement is made more glaring as he encroaches upon a society that shuns him much as Yank was shunned as he walked along Fifth Avenue in O'Neill's *The Hairy Ape*. Nevertheless, he continues his walk, vicariously absorbing the bustle and excitement. Finally, he reaches the zoo and another society is thrust at him. Here in the Central Park Zoo he sees the primitive, savage, brutal society of the jungle. Jerry has run the gamut in one day from the most so-phisticated to the most primitive world, exposing himself to each, and he ends the journey having learned that both soci-eties bar him from entrance much the same way that his land-lady's dog tries to keep him out of his own dwelling.

What Jerry actually went through at the zoo is not yet known to his audience and is, at this point, barely intelligible to Jerry, though there have been critics who have felt that Jerry's behavior in the play is premeditated. One in particu-lar has gone on record as saying that in *The Zoo Story*, it isn't until the suicide-murder is effected that it goes back to become Jerry's aim throughout the play.[16] There is no sub-stantial evidence to support this point of view, especially if we look to the very ending of the play when Jerry says, ". . . could I have planned all this? No . . . no, I couldn't have. . . ." Assuredly in this early segment of the play we should realize that he has not had time to verbalize his feelings. He needs to talk about where he has been and what he has seen before he can view his life with some semblance of true perspective. Jerry begins by telling Peter why he chose the walk:

> JERRY: . . . It's one of those things a person has to do; sometimes a person has to go a very long distance out of his way to come back a short distance correctly.
> PETER: (*Almost pouting*) Oh, I thought you lived in the Village.

Jerry's philosophical explanation of his motives goes right by Peter who is upset because Jerry is not a Village bohe-mian. If he were a Village resident, then Jerry's atypical beha-vior would be understandable to Peter because he considers all people who live in the Village *demimondes* of society. Peter's stereotyped view of Village life angers Jerry into tell-ing him exactly where he does live:

> JERRY: . . . I live in a four-story brownstone rooming

house on the upper West Side between Columbus Avenue and Central Park West. I live on the top floor; rear;
west. It's a laughably small room, and one of my walls is
made of beaverboard; this beaverboard separates my
room from another laughably small room, so I assume
that the two rooms were once one room, a small room,
but not necessarily laughable. . . .

Jerry's blatant confession marks the beginning of a series of
grotesquely pathetic pictures of one kind of very real life in
New York City. It is a vivid portrait of society's outsiders,
trapped in dwellings of oblivion, quietly seeking refuge in
cheap rat-infested hovels in order to survive another day in a
society that does not want them. We find that the other inhabitants of this rooming house are also outcasts from society.
Next door to him on the other side of that beaverboard wall
lives a Negro homosexual whose entire existence revolves
around constant trips to the hall bathroom. The Negro has
no friends, or at least he never has visitors. The two front
rooms are occupied by a large Puerto Rican family forced to
live in crowded squalor by prejudice which also keeps them
from competing with the better educated and specially
trained mainland-born American. This problem of racial
prejudice is taken up by Albee more fully in *The Death of
Bessie Smith,* but the seeds of his ensuing plays of social
criticism begin here in *The Zoo Story.*

Mary Lukas, critic for the *Catholic World,* quite correctly
labeled Albee as a social critic when she wrote: "Albee and
the generation of new American dramatists who are just beginning to appear understand themselves as its [society's]
critics and its foes. They have not made the world they live
in; they disapprove of its phony mores and demands. Unlike
some of his European colleagues, Albee's outlook has nothing
in it of despair. His argument is less with life than with society. . . ."[17] Albee, through Jerry, continues describing the
sordid conditions that house the outcasts. In the other front

room there lives a mysterious person he has never seen. Except for the landlady, the only other inhabitant of this four-story building that Jerry is aware of is a lady who constantly cries from behind a closed door. No one makes contact with anyone else. Each remains in his own little cubicle, isolated from the rest. For Albee this rooming house symbolizes our hellish metropolis. It is a city of indifference, apathy, and isolation, where man is so disengaged from his fellow man that thirty-eight people in New York recently witnessed a murder and no one offered help. Not one person picked up his telephone to call the police.[18] It is a world in which violence rules the city's streets. This is what Albee is writing about as he allows Jerry to open his life to Peter who, since he helps write books which will educate, should logically be the man to consult for a better world.

Jerry continues his pleas for understanding as he lists his complete possessions for Peter. They comprise a few clothes, some kitchen utensils, a pack of pornographic playing cards, a Western Union typewriter, and a strongbox without a lock containing rocks picked up on a beach during childhood. Jerry uses the stones to weight down a batch of "please" letters. This meager collection of both personal and utilitarian items is a crushing indictment of Jerry's failure in the big city. Jerry also keeps two picture frames without any pictures, suggesting his deep longing for parents, family, or anyone he can remember with love. But he has no one; both parents are dead, and the frames remain a constant reminder of his orphaned life. Jerry denies any feeling for his parents, but he has carried those frames with him for more than twenty-five years, belying his rather flip attitude toward them:

JERRY: But that was a long time ago, and I have no feeling about any of it that I care to admit to myself. Perhaps you can see, though, why good old Mom and good old Pop are frameless.

25

Albee will have more to say about Pop and Mom in *The American Dream* and *The Sandbox*. Yet it should be pointed out that Albee's dissatisfaction with parents as a major theme in his later plays first emerged in Jerry's confession to Peter.

As we continue to examine Jerry's personal properties, the unlocked strongbox containing his most intimate remembrances informs us that his entire past life is open for inspection. No one, of course, is interested—least of all Peter. Jerry wants friendship desperately and will reveal himself completely in an effort to get it.

The sea-rounded rocks Jerry tells us are in his strongbox represent a desire in Jerry to return to the time when the rocks were originally found. He has kept them with him far too long for the rocks to be nothing more than a forgotten remnant of childhood days. The rocks are an ever-present sign that he wishes to return to a time prior to the death of his parents, a time of innocence. The rocks, worn clean from the eroding sea, cover a pile of special letters:

> JERRY: . . . sea-rounded rocks I picked up on the beach when I was a kid. Under which . . . weighed down . . . are some letters . . . please letters . . . please why don't you do this, and please when will you do that letters. And when letters, too. When will you write? When will you come? When? These letters are from more recent years.

This reference, though at first sight quite vague, nevertheless is the beginning of a series of references to Jerry's homosexuality. Some critics have gone so far as to label the entire play as nothing more than "an unsuccessful homosexual pass";[19] consequently, this should be examined and analyzed further, in order to determine its validity within the play's framework. The next allusion comes when Peter asks about the picture frames:

> PETER: (*Stares glumly at his shoes, then*) About those two empty picture frames.

JERRY: I don't see why they need any explanation at all. Isn't it clear? I don't have pictures of anyone to put in them.

PETER: Your parents . . . perhaps . . . a girl friend.

JERRY: You're a very sweet man, and you're possessed of a truly enviable innocence . . .

Obviously Peter has missed the subtle implication of the letters when he asks about a girl friend. This naivete endears Peter to Jerry. He realizes he has nothing to fear from this man's superficial scrutiny. Later, however, Peter's inability to understand will infuriate, frustrate, and finally depress Jerry to the point of suicide. For the moment Jerry is disarmed enough to ask Peter his name. Peter replies, and their relationship takes on a more intimate quality. In his effort to make Peter understand why there isn't a girl in the picture frames, Jerry reveals that it has been impossible for him to make love to the same girl twice. But in trying to explain his actions, the female love partner changes:

JERRY: I wonder if it's sad that I never see the little ladies more than once. I've never been able to have sex with, or, how is it put? . . . make love to anybody more than once. Once; that's it . . .

The important word here is "anybody" because now Jerry is equating his expressions of physical love with either sex. To make the point even clearer, we have only to continue to quote a bit more from the same speech:

JERRY: Oh, wait, for a week and a half, when I was fifteen . . . I was a h-o-m-o-s-e-x-u-a-l. . . . And for those eleven days, I met at least twice a day with the park superintendent's son . . . I think I was very much in love. . . .

What is perhaps even more interesting than this disclosure of adolescent homosexual behavior is that he returns again to the park in his mature years in search of the very same kind of love and compassion. Their talk continues as Jerry expresses his surprise that Peter is more interested in the picture frames than in the pornographic picture cards. Peter boastfully explains he is no longer in need of dirty pictures now that he is older, and Jerry delivers a trenchant retort to Peter's growing insensitivity:

> JERRY: I wasn't trying to plumb your post-adolescent sexual life and hard times; what I wanted to get at is the value difference between pornographic playing cards when you're a kid and pornographic playing cards when you're older. It's that when you're a kid you use the cards as a substitute for a real sexual experience, and when you're older you use real experience as a substitute for the fantasy.

Jerry considers adult sexual behavior, his own certainly, as post-adolescent. That is, a continuation of fantasy activity simply taking on a new and perhaps more subtle form. To Jerry, childhood sexual experience is primarily concerned with fantasy, for the real experience is more difficult to obtain. Yet, when maturity comes (even marriage) the same fantasy continues. The only difference is a periodic departure from it in the form of the real thing. As far as Jerry is concerned, we never lose our adolescent need for those dirty pictures or, in his case, the homosexual partner. Tom F. Driver of *Christian Century* supported this theory when he wrote: "The suicide in *The Zoo Story* was a ... lad unable to outgrow the homosexuality of adolescence...."[20] Albee has made another blistering social comment about our seemingly adult society. Note the tremendous growth of "girlie" magazines, and even more recently the advent of magazines geared toward the homosexual—all now to be found in the most respectable book stores and newsstands. Obviously these publications are selling well.

Peter, embarrassed, prefers not to discuss the matter, and Jerry quickly complies by describing his hatred and repulsion for his landlady, which is slightly reminiscent of Raskolnikov in Dostoevsky's *Crime and Punishment:*

> JERRY: . . . But the one I'm getting to, and all about the dog, is the landlady. I don't like to use words that are too harsh in describing people. I don't like to. But the landlady is a fat, ugly, mean, stupid, unwashed, misanthropic, cheap, drunken bag of garbage. And you may have noticed that I very seldom use profanity, so I can't describe her as well as I might.
> PETER: You describe her . . . vividly.

Peter is right; Jerry can create a vivid picture for his audience. He has ability with words.

Perhaps it might do well to mention a basic problem inherent in the script. Jerry is "not a beatnick,"[21] as Albee has said. Yet Harold Clurman has gone so far as to call him a "derelict."[22] If he is presented as worthless, then his death will not shake our complacency. The potential in the man must be allowed to come through so that the audience can see a glimpse of what this man might have been had his intelligence and overly sensitive personality not worked against him in the jungle environment of New York City. Jerry senses rejection much sooner than Peter does, making it easier for Peter to go through his daily activities. Peter misses most of what is happening around him. Jerry absorbs, analyzes, and digests whatever he comes into contact with—an emotionally exhausting practice. Jerry's extreme sensitivity to ugliness will not allow him to use filthy words or expressions in a world where the four-letter word has become commonplace as a means of expression. No matter how provoked, Jerry will avoid the common, the vulgar, and retreat from life until the wound is healed. He cannot compete in a society geared to jungle conditions. Anyone who has ridden the New York subways during the rush hours will attest to the conditions herein described. Jerry must not be allowed to appear to his audience as an itinerant bum; his inherent intelligence and compassion must stand out as the high points of his personality. If he is maladjusted to his society it is because, according to Albee, society is sick—not Jerry.

Jerry continues his tirade against the landlady and her dog, reporting that she spies on him to insure that he brings no visitors to his room. His one room has then become a prison with the landlady his warden, and her dog the instrument of her power. Ironically, Jerry's dwelling is not that different from the animal cages in the zoo. Neither allow society to come into the environment, nor do they permit interaction between the inhabitants; each little cubicle is closed off from the other. Jerry, as one of society's outcasts, is forced to live like an animal, neatly placed away out of reach in some small sordid human zoo, only to be thought about when his dead body presents a problem to the park or police officials.

One aspect of Jerry's character has not been explored by the critics. It is his sense of humor, or what is left of it. In his attempt to escape from the landlady's sexual advances, he has learned to use his rapidly depleting sense of humor:

> JERRY: But I have found a way to keep her off. When she talks to me, when she presses herself to my body and mumbles about her room and how I should come there, I merely say: but, Love; wasn't yesterday enough for you, and the day before . . .

In all likelihood, this pretense of acceptance is enough to placate the landlady's lust, sending her hebephrenically giggling back to her room, accompanied by her monstrous dog. Yet, Jerry's sense of humor is almost extinct. Rarely does it emerge again except perhaps for a brief moment or two during the "dog monologue." Jerry is deadly serious. His diminishing sense of humor is further warning that part of him has begun to die. Just the act of going through each uneventful day has become such an ordeal for him that he no longer sees anything comic in his miserable existence. Still, his wit has remained and is very much in evidence, though it has turned inward in a self-destroying way.

Be that as it may, his brief mention of the landlady's dog has cued his remembrance of whatever it was that happened to him at the zoo. Again he promises to tell Peter what happened there, but first Jerry feels the need to explain his relationship to the landlady's dog so that Peter will better understand why Jerry made the trip in the first place. Jerry begins his eight-page monologue by further describing the animal as an emaciated, possibly infected, sexually misused dog, with an over-sized head poised ready to attack him whenever he enters the building. He implies that there is a possibility of sodomy existing between the landlady and her dog and then quickly shifts from this revolting thought to the unhappy statement that dogs, like people, are indifferent to him, with the exception of this one particular dog. The symbolism, unmistakably, is that the dog represents that vicious aspect of society which attacks whenever Jerry tries to gain entrance. The dog never attacks when Jerry leaves the premises, only when he enters. Later in the play Peter "will respond to the invasion of his 'property' with the same ferocity the dog has shown,"[23] clearly illustrating this animalistic reaction to an invasion of one's private thoughts.

Because society's members refuse to become involved with each other, Jerry has gone through life making periodic superficial and meaningless contracts which have left him frustrated and lonely. He craves closeness, concern, any form of recognition. He is then suddenly faced with a situation which is the exact opposite of that to which he has been accustomed: His landlady's dog dislikes him enough to try to bite him. The dog is anything but indifferent, and Jerry is beside himself trying to figure out what to do about it. He does not understand why the dog should have such antipathy toward him. It never impresses Jerry that the dog's aversion to him might stem from the animal's jealous reaction to his mistress's lewd interest in her boarder. Whatever the reason, the dog's attitude is so upsetting to Jerry that he promptly tries to win its favor through bribery. For more than a week he offers sacrificial hamburger meat in an effort to appease the animal's wrath. When the dog's anger is not abated, Jerry decides on a new approach. In order to gain passage to his room, he decides to kill the dog by mixing rat poison into its hamburger meat. The situation here is clearly a modern parallel to Theseus' mythological descent into Hell, as seen by Rose Zimbardo who writes: "The description immediately identifies the dog as Cerberus, the monster, all black with flaming eyes, who guards Hell. . . . Theseus throws drugged honey-cakes to Cerberus to gain entrance to the Underworld. The West Side rooming house then is Hell and Jerry's adventures with the dog symbolize the mythical hero's . . . descent into Hell."[24] The dog gulps the bait and shortly thereafter becomes deathly ill. Jerry passes through a temporary respite, but the dog eventually recovers. Jerry then explains to Peter that the outcome of his sordid death plot has produced in him a feeling of friendship toward the dog: "Yes, Peter; friend. That's the only word for it. I was heart-shatteringly et cetera to confront my doggy friend again."

To all appearances, friendship and attempted destruction are somehow equated in Jerry's mind. Finally, he feels contact has been achieved with the beast, regardless of how pathological the method. The result of his encounter produces in Jerry a feeling of love for the dog: "I loved the dog now, and I wanted him to love me." Love, then, is the hoped for result after repeated patterns of violent behavior. Love assuredly does not develop, and Jerry comments on the consequences of his conflict with the dog: "Whenever the dog and I see each other we stop where we are. We regard each other with a mixture of sadness and suspicion and then we feign indifference. We walk past each other safely; we have an understanding." Henry Hewes says of the state of compromise reached between Jerry and the dog that "this state—the basis of so many relationships in modern adult society—is what has driven Jerry into his present pilgrimage . . . to the zoo."[25]

The analogy is unmistakable. In Albee's terms our dog-like society is coolly indifferent. We each go our own way, careful not to involve ourselves too deeply with other people. Contact is made solely on the most primitive levels of thirst, hunger, and lust. Only in these areas is there total commitment. And when this bestial interaction explodes, and we are forcibly jolted out of our vegetative state by violence and are touched and possibly hurt, immediate uninvolvement must take place if we are to survive this onslaught. We must make a sudden and complete break from the experience. And in its place, at a safe distance from one another, create a more protective shielding future relationship. A clinical, rather antiseptic understanding, cleverly established, keeps everyone painlessly apart. Richard Kostelanetz, in his article on Albee entitled "The Art of Total No," comes close to the same conclusion. He advises us "that all relationships that should be founded on love are cemented by either hate or habit. . . ."[26]

It is true that Albee bases his argument on one man's relationship to one dog, but the dog is symbolic. According to Albee, we are all animals. Even Peter, drawn into making violent contact with Jerry, is an animal. Jerry announces to Peter after the assisted suicide that "it's all right, you're an animal. You're an animal too." Jerry has turned quiet Peter into a frightened, raging animal because it is the only way to break through Peter's complacency. But Jerry had not planned to kill himself—at least not consciously. Prior to the suicide he had tried to make Peter understand and feel compassion for his plight. But Peter, Albee's representative of a rather placid conformist, neither understands Jerry nor cares to try:

> PETER: (*numb*) I . . . I don't understand what . . . I don't think I . . . (*Now, almost tearfully*) Why did you tell me all of this?
> JERRY: Why not?
> PETER: I DON'T UNDERSTAND!
> JERRY: (*Furious, but whispering*) That's a lie.
> PETER: No. No, it's not.
> JERRY: I tried to explain it to you as I went along. I went slowly; it all has to do with . . .
> PETER: I DON'T WANT TO HEAR ANY MORE. I don't understand you, or your landlady, or her dog. . . .

Peter is telling the truth. He really cannot comprehend or empathize with Jerry's situation. Yet this is precisely what Jerry wants—sympathy; someone who will be able to feel the loneliness and isolation.

Unfortunately Jerry's tale has not succeeded in arousing Peter out of his complacency, and so, Jerry must begin the final step toward bolting this vegetating organism into action. He begins to attack Peter physically, hoping that on this lowest level of behavior he will not be rejected again by this symbol of disinterest. Peter's demeanor is temporarily changed as he begins to lose control of himself; it seems that he is terribly ticklish. Noting this reaction, Jerry starts to tell Peter why he made the trip to the zoo: "I went to the zoo to find out more about the way people exist with animals, and the way animals with each other; and with people too. It probably wasn't a fair test, what with everyone separated by bars from everyone else. . . ."

As the last section of the play unfolds, Jerry, in his hatred for Peter's complacency, begins punching him as he tells of the lion cage at feeding time. This is the world to Jerry—the lion cage as the animals rip and tear at the raw hunks of meat thrown to them. His frustration and anger, at Peter and Peter's society, is now so strong that Jerry practically pushes him off of the bench. Peter, dismayed over Jerry's rising fury, shouts for a policeman, but Jerry comments: "You won't find a policeman around here; they're all over on the west side of the park chasing fairies down from trees or out of the bushes. That's all they do. That's their function. . . ." Ostensibly Jerry has had some dealing with the police on this matter as he appears to speak from first-hand knowledge.

As already stated there are other references in the play that point to his sporadic homosexual activities—all tinged with the suggestion of guilt. Earlier in the story was his episode with the park superintendent's son whom he felt he loved. Later, however, his attitude changes to bitterness as he refers to the possibly homosexual "please letters" which he declares are of more recent vintage. There *is* evidence for critics to write of *The Zoo Story* that a "masochistic-homosexual perfume . . . hangs so heavily . . . that Mr. Albee's love-death . . . yields more readily to clinical than theological analysis." [27] The allusion to theology is actually an answer to some critics who have evaluated the story as a modern morality play. The most outspoken of this group is Rose Zimbardo who has written an article on symbolism and naturalism in the play. She writes: "What Albee has written . . . is a modern Morality play. The theme is the centuries old one of human isolation and salvation through sacrifice."[28] Albee, however, has said on various occasions that he did not have Jesus in mind when he named the character Jerry. The play deals essentially with human outcasts in a savage society.

Let us, however, return just briefly to Jerry's much-alluded-to deviant sex life. Toward the end of the dog speech there are rather distinct suggestions of abnormal sexual behavior. The most blatant is Jerry's hysterical confession concerning the "little ladies" of his acquaintance. He shouts,

". . . with love, with vomiting, with crying, with fury, because the pretty little ladies aren't pretty little ladies, with making money with your body which is an act of love and I could prove it . . . with God. How about that? WITH GOD WHO IS A COLORED QUEEN . . ." It would appear from this speech that Jerry has been able to survive by making money with his body. The thought is revolting to him, however, and with this motive, as well as the squalid conditions he must face every day of his life, the suicide ending does not appear as melodramatic as Brooks Atkinson has made it. He has said: "It ends melodramatically as if Mr. Albee has lost control of his material."[29] On the contrary, given what we know of Jerry's background and present state of mind, his death would seem the logical escape for him out of the brutal, degenerate world he knows.

And so we come to the end of this sordid story. Jerry has so shaken up Peter's self-assurance that, trembling with fear, he has picked up Jerry's knife in an effort to defend himself from what he now considers to be a madman. Jerry has finally succeeded in making contact, but the price has been too great. Peter has been reduced to a very frightened man and is in no condition to feel compassion for anybody. Peter has only one objective: to get away from Jerry as fast as he can, defending himself as he begins to retreat. But it is too late; Jerry hurls himself at Peter, impaling his body on the outstretched knife held defensively in Peter's hand.

It is difficult to know explicitly why Jerry chooses suicide. John Gassner has felt that it is the only way Jerry can make Peter admit to his existence. During an interview with me, Mr. Gassner said: "The final impression I came away with and the one that was most meaningful to me, was that the young man was so eager for contact, and so desperate, that he committed suicide; and the suicide takes the particular form of forcing another man to recognize him, even if it means killing him."[30] Yet Albee has said that the ending is

"neither nihilistic nor pessimistic. . . . My hero is not a beatnick and he is not insane. He is over-sane. Though he dies,
he passes on an awareness of life to the other character in the
play; the play, therefore, is obviously not a denial of life."[31]
Still, in spite of Albee's comments, there hovers over the ending a feeling of the utter waste and uselessness of Jerry's life
before he met Peter. His suicide is a denial—at least of his
own life. And ironically the only time he has made any last-
ing contact is at the price of his life. Walter Kerr put it this
way: "Death, it would seem, is the only event staggering
enough and personal enough to bring two entirely isolated
souls in touch with one another."[32] Paradoxically, as Peter
unwillingly helps Jerry out of his morbid world, he is at the
very same instant shocked into the thick of it.

The final scene shows Jerry relaxed for the first time in the
play as the knowledge of his actions finally becomes clear to
him. The world is a zoo, and he wants no part of it. He
thanks Peter for helping him end his tortured life. The dazed
executive wanders away, knowing he will never forget Jerry's
personal anguish. Jerry then carefully wipes away any trace
of Peter's fingerprints from the knife because the terminating
action of the play is a suicide, and only the victim must be
held responsible.

CHAPTER 2

THE SANDBOX

The Sandbox was originally written to satisfy a commission from the Spoleto Festival of Two Worlds, in Italy, which needed a short dramatic piece for its summer program. Mr. Albee was at the time preparing a longer play (still within the one scene framework) called *The American Dream,* and subsequently had to cease work on it to fulfill his obligation to the Festival. This was done by extracting several of the characters from the half-finished *American Dream,* which takes place in an apartment, and transferring the people to a new but related outdoor environment. The play was never performed at the Festival, and instead opened at the Jazz Gallery in New York along with a collection of other short works by new authors on April 15, 1960.[1] The title page states that this fourteen-minute playlet is "in memory of my Grandmother (1876-1959)." Grandma is the heroine in this terse, sardonic comedy which reflects what sociologist David Reisman calls "the elimination of . . . grandmother from . . . the home . . ."[2]

The action takes place near the ocean; Albee describes the setting:

> A bare stage, with only the following: Near the footlights, far stage-right, two simple chairs set side by side, facing the audience; near the footlights, far stage-left, a chair facing stage-right with a music stand before it; farther back, and stage-center, slightly elevated and raked, a large child's sandbox with a toy pail and shovel; the background is the sky, which alters from brightest day to deepest night.

An examination of the stage directions gives us some insight into this surrealistic tragicomedy. To begin with, the placing of what few set pieces there are suggests a more presentational approach than Albee had used in *The Zoo Story.* Three chairs, a sandbox, and a musician's stand on an otherwise empty stage, to all appearances isolated and unrelated, will in the course of the play all come together as closely interwoven symbolic devices sharply illustrative of the play's bitter theme.

Mommy and Daddy, two of the characters from *The American Dream,* sit on the stage-right chairs for most of the play with their backs symbolically turned away from Grandma, as they prepare for their night's vigil. Mommy is described as an imposing figure, while Daddy is pictured as thin and small. Their obvious physical differences underscore their relationship throughout the play, which amounts to complete domination of Daddy by Mommy. Their kinship is more than slightly reminiscent of Philip Wylie's now famous essay on "Momism" in his *Generation of Vipers.* He says:

> I give you mom. I give you the destroying mother. . . . I give you the angel—and point to the sword in her hand. . . . I give you the woman in pants, and the new religion: she-popery. I give you Pandora. I give you Proserpine, the Queen of Hell. The five-and-ten-cent store Lilith, the mother of Cain, the black widow who is poisonous and eats her mate, and I designate at the bottom of your program the grand finale of all the soap operas: the mother of America's Cinderella.[3]

Albee's prototype is congruent with Wylie's model. Both men are out to criticize the tyrant-ogre who imposingly goes about squelching any and all who come into intimate contact with her. She is the boss in the American household, to the detriment of her weak-willed husband and consequently confused children. Mom is Albee's target and he is about to attack her with his avenging caustic humor—both in this play and certainly in its continuation, *The American Dream.*

Albee describes Mommy and Daddy as presenile, while Grandma, who is eighty-six, wizened though she is, has kept hold of all her faculties. She is actually much saner than her children. To Albee, Grandma represents the vitality and honesty of the pioneer stock in our country. She is the vestigial

remains of a bygone era, no longer functional, having outlived her usefulness.

There are two other characters in this concise piece: a good-
looking young man who the author tells us is the Angel of
Death, and a musician of no particular description. Albee
doesn't want us to become involved with the musician as it
will take our focus away from the family unit. It is the family
unit that now comes under his personal scrutiny as the social
critic begins to penetrate further into the life of his times.
The musician is only there to help insinuate mood changes,
much as a fiddler in the wings helped suggest mood changes
in *The Glass Menagerie*. Similarly, there is an allegorical
character (the Angel of Death) with whom we mustn't become too involved either, because we'll stop watching
Grandma. Albee's stage directions, however, have the young
angel continuously performing his calisthenics, using only his
arms to suggest the flutter of wings. While the symbolism is
justifiable, in performance this physical action would appear
to take away much of the focus from Grandma since he is
standing near her all the time she is on the stage.

Before we proceed to the play proper, a word or two ought
to be said about Albee's use of a child's sandbox in a play
where no child appears. (An interesting note is that no child
ever appears in any of Albee's plays—a theme that will be
discussed in more detail in *Who's Afraid of Virginia Woolf?*)
The sandbox is described as having in it a toy shovel and
pail. What did Albee have in mind when he listed these infant playthings? As the play proceeds, we see Grandma being
carried and dumped by Mommy and Daddy into the sandbox; it is her place in the play. Consequently, certain conclusions can be reached. First, there is a strong connection,
for Albee, between the very old and the infant; both are
unable to care for themselves; both require an inordinate
amount of patience from whoever is responsible. Obviously
Mommy, who was once Grandma's infant, has no sense of

responsibility, since it was she who convinced Daddy to bring Grandma to the beach to die.

Institutions and old-age homes all across this country are filled with mothers and fathers whose children find it either impossible or undesirable to care for them. We are not much different from the primitive Eskimos who used to place their parents on some remote patch of ice, leaving them there to die as soon as it was apparent to the community they could no longer function as contributing members. Elder citizens, put in homes and isolated from the family, disintegrate rapidly. It is interesting that Albee has, in both *The Sandox* and *The Zoo Story,* taken sides with the castoffs of our society, graphically displaying the injustice of their plight to his audience. We neatly pack them away in a socially approved manner, rationalizing that they'll get better care in an institution than at home. This particular theme is further developed by Albee in *The American Dream,* and will be discussed again in the chapter devoted to that play.

The second most obvious symbolic meaning is that the sandbox, which is square and full of sand, is made to keep in whoever is placed there—much like an oversized coffin. It is, in fact, just that. For Grandma is destined to cover herself up (dig her own grave) and remain there until the Angel of Death takes over. Grandma, too old to walk, has to be placed in the sandbox. Yet she's not ready to die—not with those bright eyes. Mommy and Daddy have forced the issue. They have decided Grandma has lived long enough and so they dump her into the sandbox-coffin to await her death:

DADDY: (*Pause*) What do we do now?
MOMMY: (*As if remembering*) We . . . wait . . . We sit here . . . and we wait . . . that's what we do.

It is very intriguing that Albee has chosen to portray Death in the guise of a rather sexually aware young man. This strange pleasantry reminds me of Jean Cocteau's film *Orphée* in which Death arrived as a beautiful woman. Cocteau's reasoning, spoken through the mouth of this female apparition, was that Death takes on many forms—all of them enticing. Death's sensual guise attracts us and we naively follow with mistaken expectations.

Mommy, who has picked out the exact spot for Grandma's forthcoming demise, proudly surveys the grave site. "This will do perfectly . . . don't you think so, Daddy? There's sand here . . . and the water beyond . . ." Daddy doesn't much care what spot Mommy picks for Grandma's expiration; he has long since given up any original thoughts in order to prevent the horrid possibility of a family argument. He has sold his individuality and happiness down the proverbial river just to keep peace in the house; he does whatever Mommy wants. Vaguely he responds to her question with "whatever you say, Mommy." Daddy also shrugs off responsibility for the old woman's death with "she's *your* mother not mine," hoping that Mommy will accept the job of extermination enabling him to relinquish his part in it. Either he is squeamish or feeling very guilty. Mommy promptly jumps to her duty and signals the musician to begin playing, which marks the beginning of their vigil.

Mommy and Daddy quickly exit, returning in a moment, as described in the stage direction, carrying GRANDMA. She is borne in by their hands under her armpits; she is quite rigid; her legs are drawn up; her feet do not touch the ground; the expression on her ancient face is that of puzzlement and fear." Grandma's somewhat rigid fetal position reminds us of the toddler who is usually carried from one section of his environment to another under the armpits. It is the quickest, most expedient way of transporting one too young to walk fast enough on his own, but old enough to know where he doesn't want to go. Albee again has shown the similarity between the very old and the very young. Grandma's rigidness might also imply that the first

stages of death have already begun. Albee continues the description of Grandma's entrance: "Together they carry
GRANDMA over to the sandbox and more or less dump her
in." The first physical action Mommy and Daddy do to
Grandma is to dump her, as they would some cast off gar-
ment, into the nearest garbage pail. They decide to wait there
until Granny dies. Daddy can't think of anything new to say
while they wait, and Mommy in her constant effort to emasculate him, snorts, "Of course not." The husband and wife,
having nothing to say to one another, prepare for a night of
silent vigil as they stare fixedly out into the audience. At this
point Albee's style changes as Grandma props herself up in
the sandbox to talk directly to the audience. This shift to a
more presentational form seems to bring the audience into
more intimate contact with Grandma, but it is not jarring.
The change comes as a natural development of the play's
overall structure, and it allows Grandma to voice her major
complaint, which is that no one respects her.

Grandma's dilemma is more prevalent throughout the
United States than she imagines. Her problem, as a matter
of fact, is the norm according to David Reisman, who has
said about American grandmothers that "as authorities they
are almost as obsolete as governessess . . . grandparents stand
as emblems of how little one can learn from one's elders about
the things that matter."[4] No one pays any attention to her.
Ironically it is only the young man, or Angel of Death, with
whom Grandma is able to communicate during this play.
She continues to talk about life at home, letting us know
that Daddy is very rich. He and Mommy have taken Grandma from her farm and placed her, with her own dish, under
the family stove. She has been reduced to family pet, but
has now outgrown even that pitiful role, to be pushed out of
the house altogether. Mommy is busy instructing the musician to keep the music "nice and soft" when suddenly an
off-stage rumble is heard, signifying the approach of Grand-

ma's death. Mommy, directly responsible for pushing Grandma out of the house, now hypocritically begins crying. Apparently the actuality of Grandma's impending doom is too
much even for Mommy to bear, and she weeps tears of guilt.
Granny nobly tries to reassure her daughter saying, "I'm
fine! I'm all right! It hasn't happened yet!"

Grandma knows precisely why she has been carted off and
placed in the sand. In fact, she helps things along by half-
burying herself with sand. While it is comic to watch Grandma, using a toy shovel, busily covering herself with sand, it
becomes clear, with just a little further thought, that what she
really is doing is digging her own grave. The joke then becomes an ugly one. There is nothing left for Grandma to do.
Her family doesn't want her, and at the age of eighty-six the
possibility of old friends still alive is quite remote.

As the lights come up signaling both Grandma's death and
the approach of a new day, Mommy, with amazingly little
difficulty, manages to shake off her tears of mourning and
greet the new day feeling better than ever. She and Daddy
walk to the sandbox to take a last look at Grandma's supposed
cadaver: "GRANDMA plays dead." She has only half-buried
herself, signifying that she is only half-way gone, but Mommy
and Daddy are convinced of her death, commenting on how
happy she looks. They compliment each other on their mutual bravery and exit. We are very glad to see them go. Albee
has made Mr. and Mrs. America totally despicable in their
crass handling of what we euphemistically refer to as our senior citizens.

For a brief moment after Mommy and Daddy exit, Grandma thinks she has outwitted them. She isn't dead, nor does
she show any intention of dying—at least not yet. But Grandma is quickly shocked into reality when she realizes that
she cannot move her legs. The young man finally stops his
calisthenics and asks Granny to be quiet. Then he kisses her
gently on the forehead (the kiss of death) and explains his

mission. Grandma listens, graciously complimenting him on his delivery of the lines, which, according to the author, should be said very amateurishly. The young man then puts his hands (or wings) on top of Grandma's hands and she, finally resigned to her fate, nobly acquiesces by closing her eyes. The musician continues to play throughout this final tableau as the curtain comes down slowly. The final scene is quite moving and not at all comic.

As a last comment to this surrealistic departure from the realism of *The Zoo Story*, it should be remembered that nowhere in the play's dialogue is there any mention of children. Mommy and Daddy have no children, suggesting the possibility that one of them is sterile. This particular theme will continue into *The American Dream* as an integral part of the play's action, returning with even more ferocity as a major component in *Who's Afraid of Virginia Woolf?* The vacuous couple have, in ridding themselves of Grandma, also destroyed the only symbol of life in a household more dead than alive.

In spite of this sterile outlook for Mommy and Daddy, the fact remains that they are alive and Grandma is not, reminiscent of Philip Wylie's famous comment concerning the future outlook for our American Mommy:

> Mom still commands. Mom's more than ever in charge. Hardly five Americans in a hundred know today that Mom and her bogus authority have ever been questioned—by me, or by anybody else. The nation can no longer say it contains many great, free dreaming men. We are deep in the predicted nightmare now and mom sits on its decaying throne. . . .[5]

CHAPTER 3

FAM AND YAM

PERHAPS the least known of Edward Albee's plays is a short comic sketch entitled *Fam and Yam,* which the author describes as "an imaginary interview." In barely fourteen pages of very funny dialogue, he surveys the entire theatrical scene on Broadway, lampooning the establishment of playwrights, directors, theatre owners, agents, critics, and even the audience, until only the actors and new playwrights are left to revitalize the art without shame of sham. In fact this little playlet, when produced on August 27, 1960, at the White Barn Theatre in Westport, Connecticut, could easily have been called *Yam, Fam and Sham.*

The character FAM actually means Famous American Playwright, described by Albee as "a no-longer thin gentleman." He goes on:

> What does he look like most? . . . a slightly rumpled account executive? . . . a faintly foppish Professor of History? Either will do.

Protected and cut off from the world in his glass-enclosed penthouse with a panoramic view, he is no longer in touch with city life below.

> YAM: The view!
> FAM: (*Defensive*) What . . . what about it?
> YAM: Joan Crawford, Susan Hayward . . . everybody . . . !
> FAM: (*Frightened*) What?
> YAM: (*Laughs*) Oh, you know, all those movies they made . . . and they all had apartments over there, and they always had a view . . . just like this.

Mr. Fam is still living in the past. He's pre-war vintage and quite sour in the 1960's. In fact all through the play he drinks sherry, emphasizing his artistry which, like the wine, is a bit genteel.

The only other character in this skit is YAM, otherwise known as Young American Playwright. He is described as:

> . . . an intense, bony young man, whose crew cut is in need of a trim; sweat socks, an over-long scarf, an old issue of *Evergreen Review* under one arm.

This portrait, which sounds very much like the young Mr. Albee, tells us that Yam hasn't enough money to keep his hair neatly trimmed and his stomach properly filled and at the same time purchase a back issue of *Evergreen Review*.

The dialogue continues with Yam apologizing to the established Fam for being too early. Then, after making an appreciatory comment about Fam's original paintings, he thanks Fam for taking the time to see him. Yam next compliments Fam on his productive ability.

> YAM: I think it's the continuum, really, that's so important.
> FAM: The . . . uh . . .?
> YAM: The way you keep writing them . . . one after the other.

The supposition, of course, is that Mr. Fam is a hack, banging plays out a bit too frequently.

The talk continues and Yam admits he is going to write an article on the present state of affairs in the theatre. Mr. Fam, however, is not impressed and remains polite and evasive. But when Yam reveals that the article is really speculative and not commissioned, Fam interprets this as an attempt on Yam's part to write something safely vague, an idea that appeals to the prissy playwright. Doubtless, he is familiar with the approach.

FAM: Ah, an indefinite article . . . (*Chuckles*).

YAM: And . . . uh, what? Oh! Yes . . . very good, very good, indeed.

FAM: (*Still chuckling*) Words; words . . . they're such a pleasure.

Fam, now convinced he is facing a continuer of the tradition, compliments the young playwright on his first produced Off-Broadway play even though he hasn't seen it in the four months it's been open. The play is called *Dilemma, Dereliction and Death,* a curious title that fits the events of *The Zoo Story* rather well. Encouraged by Fam's compliment, Yam's pride gets the better of him and he boasts that the play has been running four months. Unfortunately, Fam is not able to share Yam's exuberance. In fact, the play's success creates an adverse effect in Fam, and we see the first tinge of fear for his position creep over him.

FAM: (*Shooting his cuffs, aggressively cheerful*) The new generation's knocking at the door. Gelber, Richardson, Kopit . . . (*Shrugs*) Albee . . . you . . . (*Mock woe*) You youngsters are going to push us out of the way . . .

YAM: (*An unintentionally teeth-bearing smile*) Well, maybe there'll be room for all of us.

FAM: (*Rocking back*) Uh . . . well . . . yes! (*Suspiciously*) Let's hope so!

Albee is quite clear in his attack on the unwillingness of the theatrical establishment to help the next generation of artists. Albee, of course, never let himself succumb to the paranoia of the firmly entrenched, realizing that it is the youth who will determine how and where the theatre is going. Albee, though still a young man himself, has constantly kept in touch with the younger generation of playwrights through the formation of the Playwrights Unit in 1961, which is run by Albee and his two producers, Richard Barr and Clinton Wilder. The purpose of the unit, Albee says, "is to allow young playwrights to develop their talents before they have to face Broadway."[1] The Playwrights Unit provides the fledgling playwrights with a theatre, professional acting and directing talents, and an atmosphere that removes the pressure of paid attendance and critical reviews. Barbara La Fontaine, writing in the *New York Times Magazine* section, summed up Albee's involvement with new playwrights quite succinctly:

> Edward Albee who, for a man supposedly striding around thinking, "I am America's finest playwright," is putting an awful lot of his time and money into the search for his successor.[2]

Fam, of course, would like to get rid of his successor, but Yam quickly announces his reason for seeing the famous playwright. He wants to write a scathing exposé of the crass opportunistic commercialism of the establishment theatre. Yam would like Fam to help out by talking openly about his own experiences. Refusing to admit there is anything wrong with the New York theatre, Fam escapes into another glass of sherry, his fifth in ten pages. Fam keeps backing away until Yam, cornering him, produces a list of theatre "villains." He gives it to Fam for his perusal and frank comment. Yam then explains his article a bit more specifically:

> YAM: You get the idea?
>
> FAM: (*Pouring himself another sherry. He is pacing, now, the decanter in one hand, the glass in the other*) Yes . . . yes, I do. That's . . . that's really laying it on the line. (*Chuckles*)
>
> YAM: And I thought it would be good to say that most of our playwrights are nothing better than business-men themselves . . . you know . . . out for the loot . . . just as cynically as anyone else. . . .
>
> FAM: (*A little tipsy by now*) Oh, ho ho ho ho!

YAM: . . . and that our directors are slick, sleight-of-hand artists . . . talking all noble and uncompromising *until* they get into rehearsal . . . and *then* . . .

FAM: (*Doubled over with mirth*) Yes . . . yes! Ha ha ha ha!

YAM: . . . and about the critics . . . how they've set themselves up as sociological arbiters . . . misusing their function . . . and . . .

FAM: (*Wildly amused . . . encouraging*) Yes . . . yes . . . go on . . . go on!

YAM: . . . and then tacking into the agencies . . . call them assembly lines or something. . . .

FAM: Ha ha ha ha!

YAM: . . . and then the pin-heads. . . .

FAM: (*Beside himself*) The pin-heads! Hee hee hee . . . who are they?

YAM: (*Modestly*) Oh, the theatre parties . . .

FAM: The theatre parties. (*Laughs uncontrollably . . . knocks over an occasional table*) Boy! Give it to 'em, eh? . . . Lay it right on the line! Ha ha ha ha . . . mow 'em down!

Fam, now good and potted, is laughing uncontrollably. Hysterically he eggs Yam on, no longer frightened of the young man. Just as soon as that article is published with its blistering denunciations, where names are named, Yam will be blacklisted by the establishment and Yam's first article will be his last. The mental picture of Yam's early demise keeps Fam laughing after the young playwright has left the apartment. Then the phone rings in the playwright's cushy duplex. He picks it up, still trying to control the urge to laugh. The final minute of dialogue builds to the skit's punch-line.

FAM: . . . The pin-heads! Ha, ha, ha! (*Roams around the room, giggling, laughing. The telephone rings. He moves to it.*) Heh, heh heh. Hello . . . ?

YAM'S VOICE: (*Loud—over a speaker*) Uh . . . hello there . . . it's me again.

FAM: Oh . . . you . . . C'mon back up an' have a drink.

YAM'S VOICE: Oh no . . . no . . . I just wanted to thank you again. I'm just downstairs . . . and I wanted to thank you again.

FAM: Don't mention it, my boy! Thank *you*. Ha ha ha ha!

YAM'S VOICE: Thank you very much for the interview. Thank you sir.

FAM: You're welcome . . . you're welcome . . . heh heh heh. (*He hangs up . . . strolls*) You're welcome . . . you're welcome. (*Suddenly stops*) THE INTERVIEW!!! THE INTERVIEW!!! (*His face turns ashen . . . his mouth drops open. One of the Modiglianis frowns . . . the Braque peels . . . the Kline tilts . . . and the Motherwell crashes to the floor*).

CURTAIN

It seems our young playwright is not so stupid as one would suppose. The joke is on our punctilious senior playwright when it becomes unmistakably clear that the supposed article has become an interview. The worm has turned, and in turning, has cracked, peeled, and split open Mr. Fam's comfortable, insulated interior. Total collapse is imminent as the changing air rushes through the newly opened fissures, threatening a devastating implosion.

Albee's brief playlet, uniformly ignored by the critics as too trivial for their consideration (not one article, review, or chapter on Albee mentions the script though it has been in print for nine years), turns out to be poetically prophetic. The winds of revolution in this country and throughout the world against the establishment have already penetrated our theatre. Today, the new generation of playwrights can find anti-establishment publishers willing to publish their scripts before they have received the stamp of a successful Broadway or Off-Broadway production. New, mixed forms of presentation have so completely disposed of the old theatre that Mr. Albee's latest play, reflecting that trend, is devoid of a traditional story line, and presents instead, a contrapuntal score for alternating voices. Perhaps Julian Beck, founder of the recent theatrical revolution in this country, is right when he says:

> The revolution is coming. The forces are gathering, and the power is located among those who will not accept the burdensome and unfulfilling life offered by the society of our time. . . . When the revolution comes the theater of Broadway will disappear. . . .[3]

CHAPTER 4

THE AMERICAN DREAM

IN HIS PREFACE to *The American Dream,* Albee says:

> The play is an examination of the American Scene, an
> attack on the substitution of artificial for real values in
> our society, a condemnation of complacency, cruelty,
> emasculation and vacuity; it is a stand against the fiction
> that everything in this slipping land of ours is peachy-
> keen.

Albee's sardonic examination of American life both delighted and offended the critics. Walter Kerr wrote that
"Mr. Albee has taken a good nasty look at most of our
success images and found them marvelously empty."[1] In a
somewhat more general statement, Richard Watts raved that
the play "is packed with untamed imagination, wild humor,
gleefully sardonic satirical implications, and overtones of
strangely touching sadness, and I thought it was entirely de-
lightful . . ."[2] Many critics, however, felt as did *Variety,* that
the tone of the play was "shallow and negative."[3] The moral
content of the play bothered enough of the critics for Mr.
Albee to include the following statement in his preface:

> May I submit that when a critic sets himself up as an
> arbiter of morality, a judge of the matter and not the
> manner of a work, he is no longer a critic; he is a censor.

Nevertheless the majority response to the play was positive,
and once again Albee became the most discussed playwright
of the season.

Perhaps a closer examination of the play may reveal what
it was that angered one critic so deeply that he is reported to
have refused to review Mr. Albee's next play.[4] The play is an
enlargement of his shorter playlet, *The Sandbox,* in which
the characters of Mommy, Daddy, Grandma, and to some
degree, the Young Man, are seen, but in a slightly altered
setting. While the situation in *The Sandbox* is acted out on
a sandy ocean beach, the bizarre happenings of *The Amer-*

ican Dream are contained within what Albee calls a "stuffy apartment." The scene is described very briefly as a "living room . . . two armchairs, one toward either side of the stage, facing each other diagonally out toward the audience. Against the rear wall, a sofa. A door, leading out from the the apartment in the rear wall, far stage-right, the archway, leading to other rooms, in the side wall, stage-left." In comparing the stage directions with those of *The Sandbox*, we notice that Mommy and Daddy are not seated next to one another as they were in the shorter version, which points up their emotional and physical separation even further. The play opens with Mommy and Daddy seated in their respective chairs, awaiting the arrival of an indefinite guest or guests called "them":

> MOMMY: I don't know what can be keeping them.
> DADDY: They're late, naturally.
> MOMMY: Of course, they're late; it never fails.
> DADDY: That's the way things are today, and there's
> nothing you can do about it.

This kind of purposefully bland, uncommunicative dialogue, stereotyped characters, and ludicrous incidents—all vaguely similar to the world of Ionesco's Mr. and Mrs. Smith—have led to the mistaken identification of Albee as a "brilliant first example of an American contribution to the Theatre of the Absurd."[5] Let us examine what the Theatre of the Absurd is and why it is a mistake to connect Albee with this movement. According to Martin Esslin, those plays which deal primarily with the "sense of metaphysical anguish at the absurdity of the human condition,"[6] should be called absurdist plays. Esslin, as do most other critics, gives credit to the formation of the absurdist concept in drama to Albert Camus, who wrote, in his treatise, *The Myth of Sisyphus*:

> A world that can be explained by reasoning, however faulty, is a familiar world. But in a universe that is sud-

denly deprived of illusions and of light, man feels a stranger. His is an irremediable exile, because he is deprived of memories of a lost homeland as much as he lacks the hope of a promised land to come. This divorce between man and his life, the actor and his setting, truly constitutes the feeling of Absurdity.[7]

The Theatre of the Absurd, then, is a theatre whose disciples believe in a chaotic world where man is caught and helpless as he tries to struggle against Fate, which toys indifferently with his vulnerable life. But Albee is not concerned with Fate's caprices. His interest is in reflecting the inequities and hypocrisies of man-made ills. His concern is not with man's metaphysical condition as much as it is with what man has done to himself. "Man's inhumanity to man" is what Albee is desperately involved with, not man's relationship to an absurd universe. The *Catholic World*, reviewing *The American Dream*, quite properly made this same point, saying: "Albee and the generation of new American dramatists who are just beginning to appear, understand themselves as . . . society's critics and its foes. They have not made the world they live in; they disapprove of its phony mores and demands. Unlike some of his European colleagues, Albee's outlook has nothing in it of despair. His argument is less with life than with society. . . ."[8]

Albee is primarily a social critic, eclectic in his style, sometimes borrowing from the surrealism of the absurdist, at other times using more realistic forms. Only in *Tiny Alice* is he concerned with matters beyond social injustice.

As we return to the play at hand we notice, amid the general air of familial frustration, that everywhere in the house things are breaking down. The refrigerator, the doorbell, and the bathroom need repair, and the repairman is very late in coming. Evidently Albee has decided to begin his exposé of the American scene at its roots: the family unit. And according to Albee it is breaking down, in need of immediate repair.

The author has chosen the obvious, rather crude symbols of life's most basic needs as his starting point. The refrigerator represents our hunger drive, which is at the moment not being taken care of adequately. The broken-down bathroom suggests that waste is pilling up in this comically grotesque household. The broken doorbell symbolizes the family's isolation. If someone were to try to announce his arrival, no one would hear the bell. Mommy and Daddy are completely removed from their immediate surroundings. We hear Mommy talking to Daddy. She is irritated and outraged that life has not given her satisfaction. People are out only to exploit poor Mommy, and she relates an unbelievably prosaic anecdote, expecting her little dilemma to take on world-shattering significance, to prove her paranoiac point.

Mommy had bought a new beige hat yesterday and was completely satisfied with it until she chanced upon the chairman of her local woman's club who immediately asked her where she obtained that wheat-colored hat. Convinced that there was an appreciable difference between the color of wheat and that of beige, she returned to the store demanding satisfaction for having been victimized by the salesman. The fact that she liked the color was not important; she was concerned only that in her friend's eyes she had been taken advantage of. Albee has taken our compulsive need to be admired by our friends and reduced it to its logical and absurd conclusion.

Mommy, of course, returned to the store boasting that it was she and not her friend whose careful scrutiny had uncovered this deception. She screeched at the clerk, saying, "the minute I got outside I could tell that it wasn't a beige hat at all; it was a wheat hat." In the end, however, Mommy let herself be sold the same hat again; but she feels better now because the salesman had to apologize to her for making a mistake. Daddy joins in the conversation:

DADDY: (*Clearing his throat*) I would imagine that it was the same hat they tried to sell you before.

MOMMY: (*With a little laugh*) Well, of course it was!

DADDY: That's the way things are today; you just can't get satisfaction; you just try.

MOMMY: Well, I got satisfaction.

Mommy is quite proud of the "terrible scene" she caused in the hat store. She is proud because she thinks she has received satisfaction—satisfaction at any price, just to stave off, temporarily, her daily failures.

Mommy soon begins questioning her hubby to be sure that she has his undivided attention as she spouts her trivia:

MOMMY: . . . What did I say? What did I just say?

DADDY: You didn't like any of them, not one bit.

MOMMY: That's right; you just keep paying attention.

Daddy, naturally, will pay strict attention because he fears his wife and, ironically, needs her support, though it is she who has dismembered him psychologically. It is with this kind of emotional cripple that Mommy can best operate and maneuver in order to control her environment. She wants no interference from any one—especially a man. Every now and then she will listen to a woman if the woman has status such as her chairman friend. She is terribly impressed with Mrs. Barker because she is chairman and above all because she has "an absolutely adorable husband who sits in a wheel chair all the time." Mrs. Barker has gone one step beyond Mommy, for Daddy can still manage to hobble around, while Mr. Barker is completely immobilized. Albee carries the American Mom's need to be boss to its logical and ridiculously grotesque conclusion.

As the conversation continues, Mommy tells Daddy that she has the right to live off him because, "I married you, and because I used to let you get on top of me and bump your uglies. . . ." Philip Wylie, writing a sociological attack on life in America, came to much the same conclusion:

> It long ago became . . . the notion that the bearing of children was such an unnatural and hideous ordeal that the mere act entitled women to respite from all other physical and social responsibility. Woman, indeed, has capitalized heavily on that theory. . . .[9]

Sexual rejection leads us into a slightly tangential but related major theme permeating much of Albee's work. The theme is sterility. To begin with, we find out that Daddy has recently had an operation and since then has lost his desire for Mommy. It is Mommy, unashamed, who gives us this information when she says, "Daddy doesn't want to sleep with anyone. Daddy's been sick." In fact Daddy is so unhappy in his wife's tyrannical grip that he would really prefer not living at home, but he is too cowardly to leave, and he consoles himself by hoping for it all to end soon:

DADDY: I've been sick. I don't even want to sleep in the apartment.
MOMMY: You see? I told you.
DADDY: I just want to get everything over with.

Further evidence of the couple's sterility is expressed by Grandma when she confesses to Mrs. Barker that twenty years ago Mommy and Daddy adopted a "bumble" (baby) because Mommy couldn't have one. So it seems that originally the sterility was Mommy's, and during the ensuing twenty years she has made it her business to equalize things by slowly emasculating Daddy. Daddy has difficulty making decisions now, so Mommy uses his impotency to convince him that it's virile to decide to answer the knock at the door:

MOMMY: Open the door.

DADDY: Was I firm about it?

MOMMY: Oh, so firm, so firm.

DADDY: And was I decisive?

MOMMY: So decisive. Oh, I shivered.

DADDY: And masculine: Was I really masculine?

MOMMY: Oh, Daddy, you were so masculine; I shivered and fainted.

Finally, and not to belabor the point, Grandma admits that the only reason Mommy wanted her around was so Mommy could sleep in her room when Daddy got fresh. Their sterility, which was originally due to an organic condition, has now become a way of life, with the complete consent of both parties.

Actually Grandma is the only sympathetic character on stage. She represents "those who can still faintly remember the great ideals and potential of the American people."[10] She is truthful, intelligent, and hardworking. Mommy would love to get rid of her, but she can't bring herself to give up the free maid service. Grandma does the cooking and housework, polishes the silver, and moves the furniture while Mommy supervises. Henry Goodman, writing for *Drama Survey*, rightly feels that "Grandma stands for vitality, the lost vitality of a sturdier age, the pioneer stock, which had real values."[11] Nevertheless, Granny is determined to get out of this stifling existence. Our first inkling of her true feelings comes when Grandma grandly makes her first entrance carrying an arm full of wrapped boxes, the contents of which remain undisclosed.

MOMMY: Daddy! Look at Grandma; look at all the boxes she's carrying!

DADDY: My goodness, Grandma; look at all those boxes.

GRANDMA: Where'll I put them?

MOMMY: Heavens! I don't know. Whatever are they for?

GRANDMA: That's nobody's damn business.

MOMMY: Well, in that case, put them down next to Daddy; there.

Assuredly the perfect place to deposit anything of a private nature is at Daddy's feet, because Daddy is supposed to keep himself out of household activities. The American Daddy is not to be concerned with what goes on in his own household; emancipated Mommy has become completely capable. Daddy's job is to mind his own business, and bring home the money. Mommy will run the house. Commenting on this sad state of affairs, Philip Wylie says that ". . . the mealy look of men today is the result of momism. . . ."[12] Daddy again complains that the bathroom should be fixed because he can't stand Grandma whimpering about it. It seems that she can't get out of the house to relieve herself, while Daddy still has his club and Mommy her shopping. Grandma is hurt by Daddy's attitude, and he apologizes, which pleases Grandma because "people being sorry, makes you feel better; gives you a sense of dignity, and that's important." Mommy admonishes Grandma for her philosophy, accusing her of reading her book-club selections again. Mommy mustn't allow anyone in the house to read anything that might enlighten them intellectually because the act is threatening to Mommy's dictatorship.

There follows another Mommy anecdote, this time concerning her childhood. When Mommy was a little girl, Grandma was poor, and being poor, would give up her own supper and put it into Mommy's school lunch box the next day. Smart Mommy never opened her lunch box during the lunch hour, making the other children think "my lunch box was empty, and that's why I wouldn't open it. They thought I suffered from the sin of pride, and since that made them better than me, they were very generous." Mommy's moral then becomes: be deceitful and you can have anything you want. It never occurs to her that the point of the anecdote is that Grandma went without suppers so her little daughter could have lunches.

Grandma's next complaint has to do with her need for an allowance. Mommy and Daddy are not interested, nor do they care to remember, that Granny once struggled to bring up Mommy. They do not see the need for old people to have any money. Actually, Mommy wants everyone to be completely dependent on her; it keeps her in power. If Grandma has her own money, she can gain independence and be free of her shrike-like daughter. The only reply Grandma receives to her monetary complaints is that she ought to go to bed even though it is early in the afternoon. Grandma would rather remain up and wait for whoever they're expecting. Mommy agrees, provided Granny keeps her mouth shut; Granny promises but has no intention of keeping the promise. The short episode vividly shows how our senior citizens are forced to accept a life in which they are continually treated as children with very few adult privileges. David Reisman has pointed out the same problem in American life when he writes that grandmothers can't "any more than the children themselves, find a useful economic role."[13]

Family problems are momentarily put aside when Mrs. Barker (big mouth) makes her entrance. Mrs. Baker is the local do-gooder. She works for various ladies' auxiliary organizations and volunteers her services for the Bye-Bye Adoption Service. She is Albee's personification of what Philip Wylie has called the "organization-minded women." Wylie says of women like Mommy and Mrs. Barker:

> Organizations, she has happily discovered, are intimidating to all men, not just to mere men. They frighten politicians to sniveling servility and they pulverize school boards. Mom has many such organizations, the

real purpose of which is to compel an abject compliance of her environs to her personal desires. . . . As an interesting sidelight, clubs afford mom an infinite opportunity for nosing into other people's business. Nosing is not a mere psychological ornament of her; it is a basic necessity. Only by nosing can she uncover all incipient revolutions against her dominion and so warn and assemble her co-cannibals.

Knowing nothing about medicine, art, science, religion, law, sanitation, civics, hygiene, psychology, morals, history, geography, poetry, literature, or any other topic except the all-consuming one of momism, she seldom has any especial interest in *what,* exactly, she is doing as a member of any of these endless organizations, so long as it is *something.*[14]

A propos Wylie's final statement, Mrs. Barker announces that because she is so busy with various committees she really has no idea why she has come. She knows she is here for something, but can't seem to remember what it is. In spite of her temporary amnesia she still has enough presence of mind to pride herself in saying what she feels and immediately compliments Mommy on her unattractive house. Mrs. Barker represents the truly emancipated women, the free thinker. She has broken away from the "feminine mystique."[15] She no longer feels inhibited because she has broken her household bonds:

MOMMY: . . . are you sure you're comfortable? Won't you take off your dress?
MRS. BARKER: I don't mind if I do. (*She removes her dress*)

Albee reduces her emancipation to its ridiculous conclusion.

Grandma intervenes, breaking her promise only to listen, by asking if anyone would be interested to know why there are so many boxes in the living room. Mommy snaps back at her with "nobody is interested." Grandma doesn't give up, and periodically tries to gain Mrs. Barker's attention by quoting ridiculous statistics concerning the longevity of this country's old people. Mommy is now exasperated and orders Daddy to break Grandma's television set--the last remaining link with the outside world. Daddy exits to do his duty, and Mommy follows him to get a glass of water for Mrs. Barker, who doesn't seem to be bearing up under the strain of this macabre household. Grandma and Mrs. Barker are alone now and Mrs. Barker, eager to find out why she has been asked to come to this house, beseeches Grandma to help her out. Grandma, happy to feel needed again, tries to assist her by relating a true story which is to have bearing on Mommy and Daddy's mysterious invitation. It so happens that twenty years ago Mommy and Daddy came to her at the Bye-Bye Adoption Service, looking for an orphaned child:

GRANDMA: . . . The woman, who was very much like Mommy, said that she and the man who was very much like Daddy had never been blessed with anything very much like a bumble of joy.
MRS. BARKER: A what?
GRANDMA: A bumble; a bumble of joy.
MRS. BARKER: Oh, like bundle.
GRANDMA: Well, yes; very much like it. . . .

Granny's sardonic word reference to the bumble of bumblebee, that annoying, stinging little insect, is actually appropriate because the new baby turns out to be more of a pain to Mommy and Daddy than a joy. Grandma explains to Mrs. Barker exactly what happened:

GRANDMA: Weeeeellll . . . in the first place, it turned out the bumble didn't look like either one of its parents. That was enough of a blow, but things got worse. One night, it cried its heart out, if you can imagine such a thing.

MRS. BARKER: Cried its heart out! Well!

GRANDMA: But that was only the beginning. Then it turned out it only had eyes for its Daddy.

MRS. BARKER: For its Daddy! Why, any self-respecting woman would have gouged those eyes right out of its head.

GRANDMA: Well, she did. That's exactly what she did. But then, it kept its nose up in the air.

MRS. BARKER: Ufggh! How disgusting!

GRANDMA: That's what they thought. But *then*, it began to develop an interest in its you-know-what.

MRS. BARKER: In its you-know-what! Well! I hope they cut its hands off at the wrists!

GRANDMA: Well, yes, they did that eventually. But first, they cut off its you-know-what.

MRS. BARKER: A much better idea.

GRANDMA: That's what they thought. But after they cut off its you-know-what, it *still* put its hands under the covers, *looking* for its you-know-what. So, finally, they *had* to cut off its hands at the wrists.

This gem of grotesque comedy was aptly noted by Whitney Balliett, reviewing for *The New Yorker,* to be similar to the technique of the Greek classicists when they were writing an account of death or dismemberment. He says: "The play's horror is only reported or implied, and it is further pointed up by being juxtaposed with an unfailing and wholly original comic inventiveness that is by turns, ridiculous, satiric, sardonic, and sensibly surrealistic. No sooner has a Sophoclean dismemberment been mentioned than it is illuminated by a comic sense that matches . . . Gertrude Stein, Lewis Carroll, and Jacques Tati."[16] Balliett is correct when he realizes that Albee's savage social attack on his society is always tempered by an excruciatingly funny sense of humor. Nevertheless, Mommy and Daddy's blinding, castration, and even-

tual dismemberment of their child, serves as a stinging surrealistic accusation thrust at American parenthood. No
wonder the play was offensive to those who saw it. But as
Walter Kerr has said, ". . . thus the genus Americanus, 1961.
. . . The image is cruel and funny and hollow and eerily
familiar, and I'm pretty sure it serves us right."[17]

We find out through Grandma that Mommy and Daddy
have sent for Mrs. Barker to gain satisfaction after being terribly disappointed with their first selection, obtained at the
Bye-Bye Adoption Agency. Mrs. Barker, not quite able to
understand the full meaning of Grandma's story, decides to
go after a glass of water, leaving Grandma alone with her
boxes.

Suddenly the broken doorbell rings, and in steps what
Albee has called the personification of the American Dream.
Actually, he is an unemployed Hollywood hopeful looking for
any job that will pay money. He is well-built and very good-
looking. Grandma, having answered the doorbell, says:

> GRANDMA: Oh, that's nice. And will you look at
> that face!
>
> YOUNG MAN: Yes, it's quite good, isn't it? Clean-
> cut, midwest farm boy type, almost insultingly good-
> looking in a typically American way. Good profile,
> straight nose, honest eyes, wonderful smile . . .
>
> GRANDMA: Yup. Boy, you know what you are, don't
> you? You're the American Dream, that what you are. . . .

Unfortunately, our young man has nothing else to offer. His
only interest is in making money, and he tells Granny that
he will do anything to obtain some. Granny says she will help
him if he first helps her take her boxes out to the street. The
young man agrees, confessing to her that because of his basic
inadequacies, he is forced to take on whatever job is thrown
his way. Grandma doesn't see any inadequacies in this handsome boy and asks him to explain his problem to her. There

follows a brutal disclosure linking him with Mommy's first baby. It seems that the young man was an orphan and a twin. He and his brother were separated at birth, and during the following years, as he grew to manhood, he suffered an unexplainable loss of innocence, punctuated by periodic twinges of pain that might have occurred as sympathetic reactions to pain being suffered by his lost twin. Albee wants us to believe that this young man's lost twin is the little orphan Mommy and Daddy got rid of. The young man's pain and inability to love stem from the periodic removal of whatever part of his twin happened to irritate Mommy and Daddy's sensitivities, which he felt sympathetically and simultaneously *a la* the "Corsican brothers." He continues this revelation expressing his present feelings:

> . . . And since that time I have been unable to see anything, anything, with pity, with affection . . . with anything but . . . cool disinterest. And my groin . . . even there . . . since one time . . . one specific agony . . . since then I have not been able to *love* anyone with my body. And even my hands . . . I cannot touch another person and feel love. And there is more . . . there are more losses, but it all comes down to this: I no longer have the capacity to feel anything. I have no emotions. I have been drained, torn asunder . . . disemboweled. I have, now, only my person . . . my body, my face. I use what I have . . . I let people love me . . . I accept the syntax around me, for while I know I cannot relate . . . I know I must be related to. I let people love me . . . I let people touch me . . . I let them draw pleasure from my groin . . . from my presence . . . from the fact of me . . . but, that is all it comes to. As I told you, I am incomplete . . . I can feel nothing. I can feel nothing.

There is one other possible interpretation that ought to be discussed. Whether or not the young man is the twin to Mommy's and Daddy's child, he is the living result of the kind of upbringing their baby would have received had it survived. In other words, this young man might be the vacant shell of what remains after all individuality and sensitivity have been removed by ignorant, prejudiced parents.

The young man begins carrying out Grandma's boxes. While he is busy at work Grandma gets a brilliant idea that will solve Mommy and Daddy's need for satisfaction. As Mrs. Barker returns to the living room, having been unable to find either Mommy or Daddy, Granny calls her and whispers the idea into Mrs. Barker's ear. Mrs. Barker is delighted with it and runs off again in search of Mommy and Daddy so that she can tell them about it. Granny leaves with her boxes, but the decision is a difficult and frightening one. She says, "1 didn't really like wrapping them; it hurt my fingers, and it frightened me. But it had to be done." With that she leaves the house, carrying her wrapped possessions, never to return.

At last, Mrs. Barker, Mommy, and Daddy all find each other and return to the living room. The couple, realizing that Granny is gone, dissolve into tears until Mrs. Barker reminds them of their new surprise. The young man re-enters and Mommy and Daddy are presented with a new orphan, all grown up and beautiful, to take the place of the "bumble" with which they were so unhappy. Mommy is ecstatic; she has gotten satisfaction. Mrs. Barker introduces the young man to his newly acquired family, and all celebrate the occasion with a bottle of sauterne. The play ends with Mommy feeling that there is something familiar about her reborn child.

As the play ends, Granny enters, unseen by Mommy and Daddy, and stands at the side of the stage to deliver her last speech to the audience. Alan Schneider, when questioned about the sudden change in style from representational to presentational in the play's last minutes, said that Albee was trying to break down the barriers between audience and the play.[18] Grandma's last speech reminds us that the play is a comedy, and that everybody has got what "they think they want." She then wishes the audience a good night and departs. I asked Albee to explain what happens to Grandma at the end of this grotesque comedy and he replied that she dies, as in *The Sandbox*. However, he qualified his statement by saying her death is really a departure "from a form of life that is a great deal more dead than anything else. I guess I meant her specifically to die, but not in the sense that we understand die; to move out of the death within life situation that everybody else in that play was in."[19]

Most of the critics got the message as Albee, bitterly but theatrically, commented on his own time, reflecting back at us the hypocrisy of much of modern American life. Probably the most succinct summary of the social outlook of *The American Dream* comes from Henry Hewes, writing for the *Saturday Review*. Mr. Hewes said bluntly: "The women want to castrate the men, the men want to return to the cozy comfort of the womb, and the whole society is preoccupied with money, status, convenience, and conformity."[20] As far as grandmothers are concerned, according to David Reisman, "there is no room for them in the modern apartment. . . ."[21]

CHAPTER 5

THE DEATH
OF BESSIE
SMITH

The Death of Bessie Smith is Albee's second play, although it was produced in this country after *The Sandbox* as a belated companion piece to *The American Dream*. *The Death of Bessie Smith* was fitted into the evening's program at the York Playhouse on March 1, 1961, five weeks after *The American Dream* had begun its successful run. The play seeks to interpret the somewhat hazy details of blues singer Bessie Smith's fatal car accident on September 26, 1937, in the state of Tennessee. Albee's characters comprise three Negroes (Bessie is never seen) and four whites, meshed in a fervent denunciation of Southern bigotry, sometimes reminiscent in theme to the social drama of the thirties.

While the general approach to the characters is realistic, Albee's use of the setting is impressionistic. This one-act play whips through eight scene changes in about one hour's playing time, using only the barest amount of scenery needed to effect a change in locale. The basic structure is a unit set, and lighting is used as the main source of environmental change. Each successive scene is played in front of an open sky effect much like the arrangement in *The Sandbox*. It might be worthwhile to note that Albee's first play, *The Zoo Story*, made no attempt to reflect the play's constant mood changes through effects of lighting thrown on an open sky, though the play did take place out-of-doors where this technique would have been possible. *Bessie Smith* is the first of Albee's plays to show his awareness and concern with the problem of mood variances within a production, and he has written very definite stage directions to see that his idea is realized. A description of the stage setting follows:

> . . . the central and front area of the stage reserved for the admissions room of a hospital, for this is where the major portion of the action of the play takes place. The admissions desk and chair stage-center, facing the audience. A door, leading outside, stage-right; a door, lead-

ing to further areas of the hospital, stage-left. Very little more: a bench, perhaps; a chair or two. Running
along the rear of the stage, and perhaps a bit on the
sides, there should be a raised platform, on which, at
various locations, against just the most minimal suggestions of sets, the other scenes of the play are performed.
All of this very open, for the whole back wall of the
stage is full of sky, which will vary from scene to scene;
a hot blue; a sunset; a great, red-orange-yellow sunset.
Sometimes full, sometimes but a hint.

At the curtain, let the entire stage be dark against the
sky, which is hot blue. *Music* against this, for a moment
or so, fading to under as the lights come up. . . .

Though Albee mentions music in his stage directions, its
use here is more peripheral than in *The Sandbox*. Albee had
the same opportunity to integrate the music in this play but
didn't take advantage of it. The obvious choice of using
Bessie Smith records within the action was discarded in favor
of original blues music composed especially for this play by
William Flanagan. I asked Albee why he hadn't taken advantage of Bessie's records, incorporating them into the play's
action. The opportunity certainly presented itself as these
characters are periodically shown listening to the radio or
phonograph:

FATHER: Turn it off! Turn that goddam music off!
NURSE: Honestly, Father . . .
FATHER: Turn it off!
(*The* NURSE *turns wearily, goes back inside. Music
stops*)
Goddam nigger records. . . .

Albee's answer to my question went like this:

The reason I did it may have been the wrong reason,
but I didn't want to capitalize on the sensational aspects.
It seemed to me that it would have been cheating. That
it would have been getting an audience emotional re-

sponse by cheap methods . . . that it wouldn't have allowed the play to stand on its own feet as much as I wanted it to.[1]

The play, however, didn't stand up too well, and if the New York production had thought of using the records as did the Los Angeles production, I think the critics would have given it more recognition than they did. James Baldwin was right when he wrote of Albee's play that it doesn't hold together because there is nothing in it that will "illuminate the contrast between the wonderfully reckless life and terrible death of Bessie Smith and the white sepulchre in which the nurse is writhing."[2] Bessie's voice reverberating throughout the theatre might have been the illumination Baldwin was looking for. As it happened, the play was not particularly well received. Judith Crist called it a "heavy-handed diatribe on race relations . . . this is scarcely art. Nothing is individualized, nothing left to the imagination. There are no suggestions, only screams."[3] Miss Crist concluded her review by saying that the production overused William Flanagan's music. Perhaps if the music had been Bessie's, Miss Crist would not have objected. It is interesting to note that for the play's Broadway revival seven years after its premiere, Albee reversed himself and allowed the production to start with a large projection of Bessie Smith while a recording of her singing was played.

Albee has structured his play so that Bessie never comes on stage, presumably because her particular death isn't the issue with which he is concerned. Her death is only a symbol for the whole problem of Southern white supremacy, which Albee has chosen to view through the eyes of a white Southern nurse and her intern boyfriend. Bessie's death becomes a springboard from which he will launch his feelings about prejudice and bigotry. Once again, Albee has chosen the victims of our society's wretchedness and tried to side with them in an attack on the corruption that caused it. Howard Taub-man wrote: "He is not concerned only with Bessie's tragedy; he uses it to reveal the tragedy of an environment that allows such things to occur."[4]

If Albee's original intention was to write the kind of play that Taubman says it is, he has not succeeded for a variety of reasons. First of all, Albee has not really sided with anyone as he has in his other plays. He draws a repulsive picture of everyone we meet, including the Negro victims of oppression. Hitherto we were able to feel compassion for Jerry in *The Zoo Story* or Grandma in *The Sandbox* and *American Dream*, but in *The Death of Bessie Smith* we are shown only neurotic white bigots or frenzied Negro ineffectuals. The one person whose greatness we could have been drawn to, does not appear except in the title. The idea of making Bessie an absent symbol, representing the wanton destruction of a great human being because of race hatred, is a good one. Albee, however, should have reminded his audience of her greatness throughout the early portions of his play, instead of showing only an oblique glimpse of her last debilitation. If he had done this, the utter waste and stupidity of her death would have outraged his audience. Instead, Albee's technique has been sketchy, giving us a quick superficial look at a few uninteresting people caught in the grip of stupid racial bias.

The only character who is even mildly sympathetic is the young Intern, and his one strong action in the play turns out to be as ineffectual as his whole life has been. He voices his dissatisfaction, realizing he has wasted much of his young life:

> INTERN: (*Quietly; intensely*) . . . My dissatisfac-tions . . . you call them that . . . my dissatisfactions have nothing to do with loyalties . . . I am not concerned with politics . . . but I have a sense of urgency . . . a dislike of waste . . . stagnation . . . I am *stranded* . . . here . . . my talents are not large . . . but the emergencies of the

emergency ward of this second-rate hospital in this second-rate state . . . No! . . . it isn't enough. Oh, you listen
to me. If I could . . . If I could bandage the arm of one
person . . . if I could be over there right this minute . . .
you could take the city of Memphis . . . you could take
the whole state . . . and don't you forget I was born here
. . . you could take the whole goddam state. . . .

Unhappy and guilt-ridden, he champions the need for revolution but never takes the necessary steps toward a commitment. Albee allows us to become involved with the Intern
and his personal problems. Yet, the more we become involved with the hospital staff and their individual anxieties,
the less we are concerned with Bessie Smith's tragic death.
Bessie Smith died almost thirty-one years ago. Most likely the
present generation is unfamiliar with her recordings. Yet
Albee expects his audience to share his personal enthusiasm
for her so that her great loss can be symbolic. If the tragic
death of this particularly great Negro woman is not important
to the point, then why didn't Albee write about the pathetic
end of any unknown black person? Obviously her magnifi-
cence, destroyed by a prejudiced group of Southerners, was
his original motivation for writing this play. Albee, in
addition to using her records, might have incorporated the
Brechtian use of slides showing Bessie singing—anything to
keep her greatness apparent and in juxtaposition to the
mediocrity of the hospital staff. The play is didactic in nature,
and this technique would have given those sparsely connected
scenes a strong thread to tie them together.

Albee, too, has admitted some dissatisfaction with the play
when he wrote, in the foreword to his play:

> . . . while the incident, itself was brawling at me, and
> while the characters I had elected to carry the tale were
> wrestling it from me, I discovered I was, in fact, writing
> about something at the same time slightly removed from
> and more pertinent to what I had imagined. . . .

It seems to me that when Albee began moving away from his original concern, the play began to slip away from him. Perhaps a closer look at the play's structural development might show where the play's weaknesses occur.

Scene one, a bare three pages of dull dialogue (which was rightfully cut for the Theatre 1969 presentation), takes place in a barroom. We are introduced to two characters, one of whom is never seen again. They are both black and presumably old friends. This scanty scene, played over beer at one of the barroom tables, displays little depth of character. We learn only two things: first, that the weather is hot, and second, that one of the two men is involved in an undisclosed scheme which he is planning to incorporate into a trip to New York. The main problem in this scene is that Albee leads his audience to believe that Jack, one of the two men, is the protagonist, and that the story will center about him. Consequently, when scene two suddenly shifts to the back porch of a white Southern household, with no sign of Jack, the audience becomes uncomfortable. They are now asked to forget him and become involved with two new characters — one of whom may also turn out to be the play's protagonist. These two, found in the midst of an argument, are a hypochondriacal white father and his daughter, a nurse at a nearby hospital. This scene, very similar in its dialogue to the early Odets plays, never really progresses past a petty quarrel over the daughter's boyfriend. The father is unhappy with his daughter's present suitor because she refuses to bring him home, preferring to bestow her affections on the boy in his car, which he parks indiscreetly near the house. This domestic squabble degenerates even further from Bessie's tragic death when the two begin arguing over who is going to drive the family car. The Nurse wins the dispute, and the Father's subsequent emasculation is graphically described in the stage directions:

NURSE: (*very quietly*) I said, you make me sick, Father.

FATHER: Yeah? Yeah? (*He takes his cane, raps it against the floor several times. This gesture, beginning in anger, alters, as it becomes weaker, to a helpless and pathetic flailing; eventually it subsides; the* NURSE *watches it all quietly*)

The great problem of social injustice in this country has suddenly taken on the quality of soap opera, as this prosaic scene comes to an end. Albee, I imagine, was trying to trace the source of this girl's prejudices to a bitterly frustrated homelife; otherwise, the scene is completely irrelevant. George Wellwarth, in his book *The Theater of Protest and Paradox,* discusses this very point:

> The main character . . . is the admissions nurse at one of the hospitals that refused to treat Miss Smith because she was a Negro. Through her, Albee tries to probe the mentality of a typical Southern white woman. He tries to show that the viciousness of such a person's resentment against the Negro is the result of a series of constant frustrations.[5]

Unfortunately the more we get to know the underlying motivations of the Nurse, the less we care about Bessie. Albee has begun to concern himself with the Nurse, and Bessie now becomes a peripheral problem, related to, but not directly concerned with, what is presently the play's central issue: Will the Nurse, her boyfriend, and the hypochondriacal father ever get together?

Scene three attempts to bring Bessie back into focus with a three-page monologue spoken by Jack, which reminds us of O'Neill's one-acter, *Before Breakfast.* Albee, however, has already decided that his play will be about the Nurse caught in the web of her own prejudices; hence scene three, instead of bringing us back to the core of his play, is an intrusion on this new theme. We are informed that Jack's big plan is to exploit Bessie's dwindling abilities by sobering her up just enough to keep a recording date in New York with a New York impressario. Jack is more interested in getting "exclusive rights" then in helping Bessie out of her debilitated condition.

As the scene progresses we notice that the play's style abruptly changes, adding still another confusing element to the production. Up to now each scene has used a bare minimum of suggested scenery and properties, but scene three eliminates even these and calls for pantomimed activity similar to the technigue of *Our Town*. The stage directions read that scene three be played in "a bare area. Jack enters, addresses his remarks off stage and to an invisible mirror on an invisible dresser." It is late afternoon and Jack is busily dressing and talking to Bessie who is in the next room off stage. Her absolute silence throughout Jack's monologue means that she is either completely indifferent to her future or, more likely, still in too drunken a stupor to react. Whichever the case, her silence is demeaning to her image.

The audience's first encounter with the great Bessie brings the realization that she is fat, down-and-out, and "sleeping off last night." The image is truthful. Bessie was a drunkard. But her pitiful condition can only rip through our emotions if we know from what heights she has fallen. Albee shows us only Bessie's final moments, which is unfair to her greatness and subsequent tragedy. The scene ends, and Albee notes that the sunset on his open sky is predominant, suggesting, I suppose, that Bessie's last day has come to an end. During the scene fade, only the sky remains lit as we hear Jack's voice and the slam of a car door, followed by the sound of an automobile driving off into the sunset, recalling the technique used in the last act of *Death of a Salesman*. The scene is then ended, and the play creeps into its fourth segment.

Scene four takes place in a hospital admissions room. The

style switches back again to real desk, telephone, and general hospital paraphernalia. We find Albee's antagonistic heroine busily displacing her private frustrations onto a Negro orderly who, frightened for his bedpan job, meekly and politely permits her abusive attack against his color. The conversation revolves around the fact that the mayor is flat on his belly in the hospital with a case of hemorrhoids. The Nurse then explains to the Negro orderly that the mayor's condition receives first call no matter who else may be in need of emergency treatment: "Now it's true that the poor man lying up there with his guts coming out could be a nigger for all the attention he'd get if His Honor should start shouting for something . . . he could be on the operating table . . . and they'd drop his insides right on the floor and come running if the mayor should want his cigar lit. . . ." Obviously in this town people are not equal.

The Nurse, not satisfied with giving the orderly the facts of life in Tennessee, continues to berate him for his desire to better himself: "Tell me, boy . . . is it true that you have Uncle Tom'd yourself right out of the bosom of your family . . . right out of your circle of acquaintances?" The orderly's answer to her malicious question is pitiful and sniveling in his desire not to offend her: "You . . . you shouldn't do that. I . . . work hard . . . I try to advance myself . . . I give nobody trouble." Albee has introduced us to three blacks in this social-protest play, and all display revolting personalities. Only Jack, originally out to exploit Bessie for his own benefit, redeems himself by a final show of moral strength when he brings Bessie to the second hospital knowing she is already dead. Jack tries in his own inarticulate way to tell us what hell it is being black in the United States. He also is determined not to let Bessie die like a worm. Unfortunately, his action is ineffectual. Nevertheless his cry for respect is heard; the Intern does go to her aid even if it is in vain. And it is with the Intern that our hopes lie, because of all the Southern whites in the play, he is the only one who is deeply touched by this tragedy. Perhaps this tragic event will awaken his conscience sufficiently to propel him into a real commitment instead of lip service to social justice.

Alan Lewis, however, thinks the play's ending is negative and that nothing has been learned from this encounter with death. He says, "the play does not hammer away at Race Relations but implies that when prejudice is the order of the day, all who live by it are trapped. . . . It is a drama of helpless and hopeless lives."[6] The play's inherent weakness, however, does not depend on whether the ending is nihilistic or not. As mentioned earlier, the problem centers about Albee's particular choices as he develops the play's structure—not his ending.

In scene five he focuses on two sections of the stage simultaneously. They are the admissions rooms of two different hospitals in the same general locale. The downstage area represents the hospital shown in the previous scene, while the second is on a portion of the upstage platform. The admission nurses are talking to each other by phone, engrossed in the latest hospital gossip which happens to concern the mayor's hemorrhoids. As the telephone conversation continues, the lights in the two areas dim, leaving the two figures in silent silhouette. At the same time, over the theatre's loudspeaker or public address system, we hear Jack's voice rising above the sound of his automobile. Suddenly he shouts "watch out," and we hear the sound of his car crashing. Jack calls to Bessie, his voice fading, as the lights in the two hospitals areas come up bright again.

The juxtaposition of Bessie's fatal crash with the nurses' chit-chat should be terribly sardonic, but the effect doesn't work. The dramatic possibilities of this fatal event are never realized because it happens off stage. Everyone in the theatre knows that no car has crashed in the stage wings. Suspension of disbelief works as long as the playwright doesn't place a recorded smashup next to the live stage actor, expecting it to have the same impact on his audience as live action. I think a series of slide projections showing the horrible results of an auto accident would produce the shock Albee was after. As it is, Albee's technique remains a feeble attempt at recreating the horror and pain of an accident that virtually tears off Bessie's arm, allowing her to bleed to death.

The next scene, while interesting in its own right, has little to do with the original action of the play. Almost all remembrance of Bessie's fatality is pushed aside in favor of exploring the flirtations, advances, and subsequent rejections of the Intern and his girlfriend-nurse. If Albee had made Bessie's accident really shocking and kept, say, a constant series of changing slides depicting that collision flashed on the upstage wall overshadowing these repulsive two, their adolescent, sexually-charged repartee might have become more than a tasteless display of vulgarity. One example of the scene's dialogue should suffice. The Intern confesses that ". . . at night the sheets of my bed are like a tent, poled center-upward in my love for you. . . ." He yearns; she rejects. The characters wrench themselves from Albee's social-protest play and begin taking on the traits of the Mommy and Daddy of his earlier plays—namely, sterility and emasculation in the male-female relationship. The early glib humor eventually gives way to vituperation, foreshadowing George and Martha in *Who's Afraid of Virginia Woolf?*:

> NURSE: (*Flicks her still-lit cigarette at him, hard; hits him with it*) You are disgusting!
> INTERN: Damn you, bitch!
> NURSE: Disgusting!

The dialogue continues along its searing path until the Intern forthrightly insinuates that his girlfriend is really a whore, and the Nurse, in retaliation, vows to destroy him.

The scene ends, having served no dramaturgical purpose

other than to awaken Albee to the possibilities of extending it into three acts—which he promptly did in *Virginia Woolf.* Robert Hatch, writing for *Horizon,* noted that the play had wandered far away from its original idea when he wrote: "Bessie Smith never appears in the play that bears her name, nor is her death its subject. The subject is mutilation as a substitution for love."[7] A similar comment is made by Henry Goodman in his article in *Drama Survey.* Mr. Goodman believes that the play is a "fierce 'battle of the sexes' outwardly resembling a play of social protest."[8]

Scene seven, barely one page long, serves to let us know that Jack will get no emergency treatment because he has entered a white hospital. This pathetic scene, important because Bessie is still alive, should have been extended long enough for the inhumanity of it to sink deeply into the audience. Jack is in and out before anyone has realized the implications of what has happened.

The action quickly shifts back to the forestage area, returning once more to the admissions room of the main hospital for the last scene of the play. The Nurse, in a tirade against her environment, brings the play back into focus as a play of social protest:

> NURSE: . . . I am *sick.* I am sick of everything in this hot, stupid, fly-ridden *world.* I am sick of the disparity between things as they are, and as they should be! I am sick of this desk . . . this uniform . . . it scratches . . . I am sick of the sight of you . . . the *thought* of you makes me . . . itch . . . I am sick of him (*Soft now: a chant*) I am sick of talking to people on the phone in this damn stupid hospital . . . I am sick of the smell of Lysol . . . I could die of it . . . I am sick of going to bed and I am sick of waking up . . . I am tired . . . I am tired of the truth . . . and I am tired of lying about the truth . . . I am tired of my skin . . . I WANT OUT!

This self-loathing denunciation is interrupted by Jack as he
enters in a fit of drunken hysteria, begging for help. He is
immediately told to find assistance elsewhere, as this hospital,
too, is for whites only. But for one brief moment both the
Nurse, representing the Southern oppressors, and Jack, symbol of the oppressed, are joined together by the personal
anguish each suffers. The Nurse, despite her momentary display of truth, soon regains her composure, and together with
the Negro orderly, orders Jack out of the hospital:

> ORDERLY: (*Backing off*) You can't come in here
> like this . . . banging your way in here . . . don't you
> know any better?
>
> NURSE: You drunk?
>
> JACK: (*Taken aback by the irrevelance*) I've been
> drinking . . . yes all right . . . I'm drunk (*Intense*) I got
> someone outside : . .
>
> NURSE: You stop that yelling. This is a white hospi-
> tal, you.
>
> ORDERLY: (*Nearer the* NURSE) That's right. She's
> right. This is a private hospital . . . a semiprivate hospi-
> tal. If you go on . . . into the city . . .

Jack defiantly refuses to leave as the Nurse's boyfriend returns. Despite the Nurse's blaring threats to have him fired
if he treats the colored woman, the Intern decides to admin-
ister aid to Bessie, who is outside in the automobile. The
young doctor leaves, followed somewhat reluctantly by the
Orderly. Jack, left alone with the Nurse, drifts off into a
stream-of-consciousness reliving the events of his accident.
The Nurse's reaction to the tragic episode is unbelievably
apathetic: "I know who she is . . . I heard her sing." She is
much more interested in calling the police so that Jack can be
punished for leaving the scene of an accident. She has also
found a way to destroy her Intern.

When the Intern returns with the news that Bessie is

already dead, we see the remains of her blood on his white uniform. Symbolically, the ending may mean that the Intern will carry the memory of Bessie's blood with him wherever he goes, much like Peter in *The Zoo Story,* or it might represent his own destruction, now that he has broken the hospital rules. The Nurse glories in her opportunity to destroy his future.

> Great . . . white . . . doctor . . . Where are you going to go now . . . great white . . . doctor? You are finished. You have had your last patient here . . . Off you go, boy! You have had your last patient . . . a nigger . . . a dead nigger lady . . . WHO SINGS. Well . . . I sing, too, boy . . . I sing real good. You want to hear me sing? HUNH?

The final moment is a sad commentary on the Southern black. The Orderly, representative of his race, unwilling to allow thoughts of social injustice to anguish his little world of bed-pans and Lysol, is sickeningly pathetic in his refusal to face the day's ordeal. He says, "I never heard of such a thing . . . bringing a dead woman here like that . . . I don't know what people can be thinking of sometimes. . . ."

Today the majority of his Afro-American brothers can no longer bear a life of suppression and are actively engaged in putting an end to it. Unfortunately the reaction of many white racists to equality for all Americans has made Bessie's bloody death sadly prophetic. Although Albee has written a play whose subject matter is of great importance to modern America, is still remains fragmentary, diffuse, and poorly constructed.

CHAPTER 6

WHO'S AFRAID OF VIRGINIA WOOLF ?

THROUGHOUT all of his earlier plays, Edward Albee has stood apart from his society as an outraged social critic, siding with the victimized and the oppressed, protesting against social injustice in a nation whose very beginnings were founded on equality and justice for all. In his first major work he has shifted his vantage point, leaving this country's outcasts, to focus instead on those who have won the esteem of their countrymen. Albee turns his social microscope on the very essence of our civilization, revealing immorality, opportunism, cruelty, hypocrisy, and sterility in the private lives of those whose job it is to shape and guide the tastes and morals of this country's next generation.

Who's Afraid of Virginia Woolf?, Albee's most successful play, takes place in the living room of a professor's house on the campus of a small New England college. There are four characters in this play: George, a history professor, his wife Martha, Nick, a biology instructor, and his wife Honey. The play begins slightly after two in the morning as George and Martha return home from a faculty party. Just before the stage lights come up, and the two chief characters have made their entrance, we hear the opening lines:

> MARTHA: Jesus . . .
> GEORGE: . . . Shhhhhh . . .
> MARTHA: . . . H. Christ . . .

This blasphemous entrance is only a mild indication of the depravity and cruelty about to be unleashed in a saga of matrimonial strife reminiscent of Strindberg's *The Father.* The action begins slowly as Martha lets George know what a "dumb cluck" he is for suggesting that she keep her voice down because of the late hour. Not satisfied with calling him a stupid man, she strikes again, remarking that they live in a "dump." She then asks George to tell her what movie the line "what a dump" comes from. George suggests *Chicago,*

95

but she quickly slaps him down verbally with, "Good grief! Don't you know anything? *Chicago* was a thirties musical, starring little Miss Alice Faye. Don't you know *anything?*" George is not to be put down again, and suggests that the picture was probably before his time, indicating that Martha in somewhat older than he—a sore spot for his wife which he will pick at during the course of the evening. We are presented with a typical Albeean situation; that is, an obdurate "Mommy" intent on emasculating "Daddy." This time, however, Daddy doesn't meekly accept his fate; he fights back, protecting his masculinity as best he can. John Gassner has called the play the "most harrowing sex-duel on the stage since Strindberg's *The Dance of Death.*"[1]

The battle continues as Martha criticizes George for not mixing at faculty functions. George prefers to end the conversation and go to bed, but Martha admits she has invited a young couple from the party to join them this night for a few more drinks. She describes the young instructor as blond, thirty, and good-looking, reminding us that he is a descendant of Albee's disemboweled young man in *The American Dream,* willing to do anything to get ahead. George angrily insinuates that Martha's sudden interest in this young couple is more than social. It appears that Martha, at the age of fifty-two, has a liking for young men. Martha's reaction becomes more vicious. She retorts, "You make me puke!" George returns the attack by again reminding her of her age, as Martha shouts, "I swear . . . if you existed I'd divorce you . . ." George retaliates by asking her to control herself when the other couple arrives and adds, ". . . and try to keep your clothes on, too. There aren't many more sickening sights than you with a couple of drinks in you and your skirt up over your head, you know. . . ."

This kind of constant verbal flagellation has made *Who's Afraid of Virginia Woolf?* the most controversial play of the decade. Some critics have said that "there is nothing more in this than a dissection of an extremely ambiguously sick marriage."[2] The now defunct *New York Mirror* said that it:

> . . . is a sick play about sick people. They are neurotic, cruel and nasty. They really belong in a sanitarium for the mentally ill rather than on a stage. This sordid and cynical dip into depravity is in three lengthy and repetitious acts. . . . We loathed it. But we do not enjoy watching the wings being torn from human flies."[3]

Yet, Richard Watts, in the *New York Post,* called it "the most shattering drama I have seen since O'Neill's 'Long Day's Journey Into Night.' "[4] The play was also nominated for the Pulitzer Prize by John Gassner and John Mason Brown. When the advisory board rejected the recommendation, both Mr. Gassner and Mr. Brown resigned their positions as members of the Pulitzer jury.[5] Is the play only an insight into what many have called domestic butchery, or does it have some broader social significance? L. E. Chabrowe, in the *Kenyon Review,* believes the play has a wide social scope. He says: "The main characters of Martha and George are meant to suggest Mr. and Mrs. America. . . . The play is political out-and-out, remaining on the level of social criticism from beginning to end."[6] Asked whether George and Martha stood for George and Martha Washington, and the play an allegory on American life, Mr. Albee has commented that:

> This country hasn't lived up to its beginnings. But the naming of George and Martha was supposed to be a small irony, not a large truth. . . . It all starts out terribly private. Then somewhere along the line you realize you're talking about general matters. If it stays private,it's no good. . . .[7]

Whether the play does transcend the private agonies of two desperately sick marriages and make a substantial social comment on life in America as well as Western civilization in general, will be the major concern of this chapter.

George and Martha temporarily call a halt to their private

vilifications as the doorbell announces the arrival of their guests. George warns Martha not to mention the "kid," but Martha threatens to do whatever she wants. George "fake-spits" at Martha and, as he opens the door to receive their guests, she gets in the last words yelling, "SCREW YOU." George manages to open the door at exactly the instant of his wife's' last utterance, so that her obscenity is the first thing that greets the late-night callers. The moment is overlooked, however, and the young couple enter the house as the four-some exchange salutations.

Nick's wife, who is described as a rather plain, petite blonde, giggles as she enters, and George, amused at her slight intoxication, mimics her. Martha does not appreciate her husband's mimicries, and the previously private family quarrel becomes more public as she refers to him, in front of their visitors, as "muck-mouth." The party gets under way as each is offered a fresh drink. Martha, we learn, is the daughter of the college president. She boasts that some men would give their right arm for the chance to be married to the president's daughter. George quietly explains that "in reality it works out that the sacrifice is usually of a somewhat more private portion of the anatomy."

With George's remark, Albee offers the first of the many themes permeating this work: emotional castration of the male by the female in our society. According to recognized books in the field of psychiatry, "the continued existence of *penis envy* in girls through adult life is by no means uncommon . . . the woman . . . gradually gives up her father as a love object and proceeds to identify herself with her mother in the hope of growing up to be able to marry a man like her father."[8]

Martha's character fits this psychological description well. Throughout the play she complains that George has not measured up to her father. She says of her husband, rather indiscreetly, that "he was going to be groomed. He'd take

over some day . . . first, he'd take over the History Department, and when Daddy retired, he'd take over the college . . .
you know? That's the way it was supposed to be." Later she
makes her position more explicit. "He didn't have any . . .
personality, you know what I mean? Which was disappoint-
ing to Daddy, as you can imagine. So, here I am, stuck with
this flop. . . ." Martha is so vehement on this one point that it
becomes a major motivation for her actions in the play. The
Catholic Transcript noted the imbalance in her motivational
make-up when it wrote that the only reason for Martha's verbal lacerations and humiliations, in addition to her allegedly
frequent promiscuities, is that "George has been content
with a subordinate position at the college."[9] Because Albee's
text is so rich in verbal texture, no other critic noticed that
Martha's character, as written, seems too one-dimensional. I
would tend to agree with the *Transcript* that her frustrations
do not go beyond the fact that George does not have a public-
relations personality.

The conversation ends with Honey asking where the
bathroom is. Martha accompanies her, leaving the two
men alone. Nick, sensing the friction between George and
Martha, suggests that he and Honey leave as soon as she
returns. George reassures Nick that what looked like a family
argument was only their way of exercising their wits. Not
wanting to offend George, Nick tries to explain his sudden
decision to leave:

> NICK: It's just that I don't like to . . . become in-
> volved . . . (*an after-thought*) ah . . . in other people's
> affairs.
> GEORGE: (*Comforting a child*) Well, you'll get over
> that . . . small college and all. Musical beds is the faculty
> sport around here.

George's admission leads the audience to reconsider its
image of the puritanical New England college. The image, it

appears, is a sham—at least in this particular house of learning. It is apparent that Albee is out to prove that the most sexually provincial society in the world is in reality not at all as prudish as its citizens would have one believe. Promiscuity is the practice at New Carthage.

It might be well at this point to raise the question as to whether Albee, in his denunciation of faculty life, really expects to be taken literally. I don't think so. The campus setting is only symbolic. It represents a place dedicated to the pursuit of truth but headed for complete annihilation instead. It is not a coincidence that this college is named after the ancient city of Carthage, founded by the Phoenicians and eventually destroyed by the Romans. The name insinuates inevitable doom for whatever place this campus really represents.

I asked Mr. Albee whether he had Nikita Khrushchev in mind when he named the biology instructor Nick. He said he had.[10] Since he has already admitted parables in the names George and Martha, it does not seem too far-fetched to suggest that what we have here is a symbolic confrontation of world leaders and their wives in the guise of an intimate faculty party. Henry Hewes, in the *Saturday Review,* explained that Nick "was related to Nikita Khrushchev and was therefore an exponent of a totalitarian society."[11] *Theatre Arts* in its review of the play referred to both men as types. The review forwarded the idea that the play is a meeting of "the biologist who looks ahead to man as a uniformly produced conformist cipher versus the historian who looks backward and knows that conformity is the bane of man's creativity."[12] Alan Lewis calls Nick the "scientist . . . in charge of reordering the world toward a mechanized dehumanization of the future." He says that George "is a historian sensitive to world forces and the decline of civilization."[13] The theme of Western decline was also alluded to by Walter Kerr, who called the play a "decline-of-the-Western,"[14] and by Henry Hewes who wrote that "the playwright suggests, a mass progress towards impotence and depersonalization by the declining Western World. . . ."[15]

Impotence, as a matter of fact, is the very next subject of conversation between Nick and George:

> GEORGE: . . . You have any kids?
> NICK: Uh . . . no . . . not yet (*Pause*) You?
> GEORGE: (*A kind of challenge*) That"s for me to know and you to find out.

This peculiar answer stems from George's inability to tell Nick the truth: that since he and Martha are sterile, they have created a make-believe son which both have vowed never to discuss with outsiders. It is their secret. This fact, not exposed until the third act, has raised more critical eyebrows than any other aspect of the play except, perhaps, Martha's pervasive obscenities which the *Catholic Transcript* has compared to "a sewer overflowing."[16] The sudden revelation that the couple have an imaginary son has caused the critics to argue over the validity of the play's denouement. Howard Taubman remarked in his review:

> Mr. Albee would have us believe that for twenty-one years this older couple have nurtured a fiction that they have a son, that his imaginary existence is a secret that violently binds and sunders them. . . . This part of the story does not ring true, and its falsity impairs the credibility of his central characters. . . .[17]

Time magazine echoed Mr. Taubman's sentiments, reporting that "after two acts of cascading turbulence, this plot resolution is woefully inadequate and incongruous, rather like tracing the source of Niagara to a water pistol."[18] Critic Robert Brustein has come up with what is probably the most imaginative analysis of the child's critical unacceptability:

> Everyone seems to have boggled at this fictional child. . . . But the difficulty is not that the author introduces a

101 |

spurious element into an otherwise truthful play. It is rather, that he suddenly confronts us with a moment of truth after an evening of stage illusions . . . mainly incongruous juxtapositions . . . George aims a shotgun . . . it shoots not bullets but a Japanese parasol . . . alienating the spectator from the action the very moment he begins to accept it. George launches a blistering attack on the evils of modern science . . . undercuts it with a ludicrous non-sequitur: "I will not give up Berlin" . . . George responds to Martha's infidelity by nonchalantly offering her flowers . . . and when asked about the telegram announcing his son's death, he claims to have eaten it . . . after three and a half hours of prestidigitation, we become reluctant to accept one of these magical tricks as the real thing.[19]

Brustein's argument looks very logical on the surface, although if we go just a bit deeper into his analysis, flaws soon appear. To begin with, Albee is a master comedian. Taubman has called Martha and George "wildly and humanly hilarious."[20] And as a master of comedy Albee knows, as Henri Bergson has pointed out, that one element of the comic is incongruity. The technique Brustein has been referring to is Albee's method of getting the audience to accept an alienating subject: the self-destructiveness of man. The play is not filled with trickery; on the contrary, it is so filled with bitter truths that the author must present them coated with comic relief. When seen in the light of an allegory on the Western world, the "Berlin" line is not so ridiculous. Finally when George enters with flowers, hideously chanting "Flores; flores para los muertos. Flores, . . ." it is a vicious announcement that George is about to kill their son, in addition to reminding us of the flower woman in *Streetcar Named Desire*.

Albee has answered the critics' refusal to accept the play's outcome by stating that "it should be very easy for an audience . . . to accept the highly intelligent, imaginative people who have the brains to invent and maintain this child which they need for their battles, together, stretched out for nearly twenty-one years. . . ."[21] In other words, Albee feels that they have created this child both as a support to their divergent viewpoints and as a weapon to use against each other, because periodically in their illusion-filled world the imaginary child will side with one or the other. I agree with him.

Not all the critics dismissed the idea of an imaginary child as unbelievable. John Gassner has felt that "the child represents a common illusion; an illusion that binds two people together—that is used to solace these people in their loneliness."[22] I asked Mr. Albee if he thought that the child might have been created out of a need to ease their barren loneliness. He conceded that it was so, but on an "unconscious level."[23] Conversely, Alfred Chester, writing for *Commentary* has complained that the child:

> . . . is neither the product nor the means of self-deception, for Martha and George are perfectly conscious of the fact that their son is a fiction. I can't, whether Albee wants me to or not, accept that human beings may be sustained by illusions they know to be such. What might possibly sustain them is the anguish . . . that comes when a man pretends to believe in what he wishes were true but knows it is not. And this . . . is an acknowledgment of reality, a facing of reality.[24]

Probably the most perceptive comment concerning the child comes from another article written by John Gassner for the *Educational Theatre Journal*. Professor Gassner suggests that "the childlessness of the couple revealed at the end is hardly a cause or an explanation of their real plight, which is their lostness. Their state of being."[25] That is, the worth of the play does not stand on whether the creation of the child is psychologically valid or not. The entire question is beside the point. The couple's motivations can not always be specifically delineated because Albee writes on more than one level, shifting his characters dramatically back and forth between realistic behavior and allegorical illusions. The only approach to an understanding of the child's place in the drama is to accept it as an effect and not a cause of the couple's predicament.

Honey re-enters, interrupting the conversation by congratulating George on his son's twenty-first birthday—to be celebrated tomorrow. Martha has broken their vow. George is hurt, but he manages to conceal his feelings, waiting for the right moment to strike back at Martha. He doesn't wait long, however, for Martha prances into the room wearing an outfit which the author suggests should make her appear voluptuous. The change is obviously for Nick's benefit. The scene develops into a visible flirtation as Martha tries to prove she is still attractive to young men.

If we consider, for a moment, the multi-billion dollar cosmetic industry in this country entirely geared to making women look younger than they really are, or notice the television commercials proudly showing how difficult it is to tell mother from daughter, we can realize that Martha is a product of her time, caught up in her society's need to worship youth. She is determined to hold on to her lost youth, even if it makes her repugnant to her husband. In retaliation against Martha's tasteless coquetry, but mainly because she has broken her vow and spoken of the child, George picks up a shotgun and seems on the verge of killing his wife:

(George takes from behind his back a short-barreled shotgun, and calmly aims it at the back of MARTHA'S head. HONEY screams . . . rises. NICK rises, and, simultaneously, MARTHA turns her head to face GEORGE. GEORGE pulls the trigger)

GEORGE: POW!!

(Pop, From the barrel of the gun blossoms a large red and yellow Chinese parasol. HONEY screams again, this time less, and mostly from relief and confusion)

You're dead! Pow! You're dead!

This attempt is symbolic. George does wish his wife dead. It is also prophetic, foreshadowing his decision to kill the child at the end of third act. George's sudden display of armed hostility is mistaken for a show of masculinity which excites Martha sexually.

> MARTHA: Yeah . . . that was pretty good. (*Softer*) C'mon . . . give me a kiss.
> GEORGE: (*Indicating* NICK *and* HONEY) Later, sweetie.
> (*But* MARTHA *will not be dissuaded. They kiss,* GEORGE *standing, leaning over* MARTHA's *chair. She takes his hand, places it on her stage-side breast. He breaks away*) Oh-ho! That's what you're after, is it? What are we going to have . . . blue games for the guests? Hunh? Hunh?
> MARTHA: (*Angry-hurt*) You . . . prick!

Martha's sexual needs have been mocked by George, who rejects her advances because he knows it is the surest way to hurt her. The act builds up to an hysterical climax as Martha, in a rage, screams out what a flop her husband is. In the midst of the emotional chaos that ensues, Honey announces she is going to vomit, and the curtain comes down on the appropriate note of regurgitation.

The second act opens with the two men alone on stage. Nick asks George why he must subject outsiders to his flagellant relationship with his wife. George's only answer is that Nick's question is self-righteous and smug. The question, however, seems fair enough, yet is never answered in the play. Perhaps it is George and Martha's misguided sense of pride that doesn't allow either to be put down by the other in public without some sort of retaliatory action. Neither must ever show defeat in public.

The conversation quickly changes course as Nick unexpectedly confesses that he married Honey because he thought her pregnant. Alfred Chester, in his article for *Commentary,* feels that Nick's confession is a sign of inconsistency in his character and therefore poor writing on Albee's part.[26] I must admit that I tend to side with Chester and with Richard Watts who has also mentioned that Nick's character is "somewhat underdeveloped."[27] When asked about this Albee has admitted that the major concentration was on George and Martha, but that in a power situation like this one, where Nick has to be careful of what he says, he "isn't going to be terribly loquacious."[28] It would seem that by Mr. Albee's own admission, Nick's reticence would not permit him to disclose intimacies about his own marriage. Nevertheless, Nick does divulge the information and the play continues. It seems that after his marriage to Honey, her assumed pregnancy turned out to be hysterical. The practice, though, of trapping a prospective eligible male through pregnancy is much more widespread than might be expected. A recent sociological study discusses this very approach, showing that many college girls were willing to admit rather proudly that premarital pregnancy is a most agreeable and expedient way of marrying the man they want.[29] Albee reflects the immorality of his time, perhaps more accurately than he has been given credit for. Ironically, Honey, now that she is married, wants nothing to do with babies. Critic R. H. Gardner calls her "an empty-headed, brandy-tippling 'mouse' who hasn't got the guts . . . to have a baby."[30] Nick's young marriage, we find out, is as sterile as George and Martha's.

Sterility is a major theme permeating the play. Allan Lewis has said that "Albee's obsession with sterility has Martha destroy George's novel by ridicule, so that it is unborn; then provokes him to kill their imaginary child. . . ."[31] Lewis then concludes that what Albee is trying to show is that "the cam-

pus, too, is directionless and impotent. . . ."[32] *Time* magazine's critic said: "It's theme is sterility—actually in marriage,
symbolically in modern United States life."[33] In trying to
understand the motivations underlying George and Martha's
abusiveness, Alfred Chester declared, "Sterility is our enlightenment. . . . Everytime the little bugger is mentioned, we
hear 'barrenness' instead. And Martha and George become
less horrible."[34] And so, as John Gassner mentioned when
reviewing the Columbia Record Album: "The recognition
and the implicit criticism of a sterile way of life in our society are firmly established."[35]

The sadness of a childless marriage moves George to tell
Nick of a parentless boy—a college chum of George's—who,
by the time he had reached his sixteenth year, had accidentally killed both his parents. The boy, as a result of the acci-
dents, went into a state of catatonic psychosis from which he
has never recovered. George continues saying that the boy
is still in an asylum, and "for these thirty years he has . . .
not . . . uttered . . . one . . . sound."

George has managed to soften Nick enough to get him to
admit that he allowed Honey to deceive him for her money,
suggesting that our younger up-and-coming generation is no
longer as concerned with love as with the prospective mate's
bankbook. The idea that love has disappeared in favor of
what is most expedient is a theme running through all of
Albee's plays. It is part of man's predicament. How does one
succeed in the most highly specialized, competitive, society
the world has ever known? Albee's answer is that man has
forsaken the idea of love for a more practical approach to the
success syndrome. The recent increase in college cribbing
throughout the country reflects this condition. The end
justifies the means.

The *Catholic World* related George and Martha's trouble
to an "opportunistic marriage between an ineffectual college
professor and his college president's daughter."[36] The confes-

sional continues as each refreshes his drink. Nick comments
on the amount of liquor consumed at New Carthage:

NICK: Everybody drinks a lot here in the East.
(*Thinks about it*) Everybody drinks a lot in the Middle
West, too.
GEORGE: We drink a great deal in this country, and
I suspect we'll be drinking a great deal more, too . . . if
we survive. . . .

George is talking about man's predicament and one of the
ways he has found of handling it. The world is threatened
with impending doom, and man would rather lose himself in
a whiskey bottle, escaping the issue, than find some method
of dealing with the thought of complete devastation. The
frightening fact that drug addiction has increased at an
alarming rate is really just another example of society's inability to cope with the pressures of modern life.[37]

Nick continues his drunken avowal with a plan for advanc-
ing himself that will overcome campus politics: ". . . You
know . . . Take over a few courses from the older men, start
some special groups for myself . . . plow a few pertinent
wives. . . ." George sardonically agrees that Nick has the right
approach toward bettering himself. George informs him that
he should do well, as the faculty wives are exceedingly ap-
proachable. Nick joins in, suggesting that Martha is probably
the most indiscriminate of the bunch. Suddenly, in a moment
of paternalism brought on by the realization that he is in
some way responsible for Nick's immorality, George advises
him to get out while he can—change his attitude before he
gets dragged into the slime and quicksand of a world reeking
from the stench of corruption:

GEORGE: There's quicksand here, and you'll be
dragged down, just as . . .
NICK: Oh boy . . .!

GEORGE: . . . before you know it . . . sucked down . . .
(NICK *laughs derisively*)
You disgust me on principle, and you're a smug son of
a bitch personally, but I'm trying to give you a survival
kit. DO YOU HEAR ME?
NICK: (*Still laughing*) I hear you. You come in loud.

George pursues the issue but all he receives for his pains is
Nick's vehement "UP YOURS." Nick's remark ends George's
appeal. Philosophically, almost stoically, he comments on the
irony of this supposedly sophisticated civilization:

GEORGE: You take the trouble to construct a civilization . . . to . . . to build a society, based on the principles of . . . of principle . . . you endeavor to make com-
municable sense out of natural order, morality out of
the unnatural disorder of man's mind . . . you make government and art, and realize that they are, must be, both
the same . . . you bring things to the saddest of all points
. . . to the point where there *is* something to lose . . . then
all at once, through all the music, through all the sen-
sible sounds of men building, attempting, comes the
Dies Irae. And what is it? What does the trumpet sound?
Up yours. I suppose there's justice to it, after all the
years . . . Up yours.

What then is Albee saying about man and his reaction to
the modern predicament? Bluntly, that expediency, escap-
ism, and opportunism are accepted, taught, and sought-after
methods of survival in a world at the brink of nuclear annihilation. Albee was more direct than critics gave him credit
for when he explained that the play was "probably about the
ways we get through life."[38]
As the play resumes we see the girls re-enter, Martha leading Honey from the bathroom back into the living room. No
sooner has Honey apologized for vomiting at the end of the

first act than George, anxious to begin whipping Martha again, reports to all that their son used to become nauseous because of Martha's uncontrollable incestuous advances. Martha flies into a rage, braying that she never "cornered the son-of-bitch in my life." Suddenly, Honey, now very drunk, decides she would like to dance. Nick and Martha dance together slowly and sensuously as a prelude to Nick's later seduction, as George vulgarly asks Honey, "you want to dance with me, angel-tits?" Honey decides against dancing after all, and both sit it out watching their spouses undulate to the music. During the dance, Martha resumes her husband's defilement as she returns to his earlier attempt at writing a novel about a boy who killed his mother and father in an accident. Martha's father thought that the subject matter was not the proper material for an upstanding conservative New England college instructor to write and called it "crap." The novel, it turns out, was not a novel at all, but actually an autobiography. The unfortunate boy was George — not a childhood friend as he had told Nick. Martha's exposé turns George volcanic with fury, and he tries to strangle his wife to quiet her. He is stopped by Nick and profoundly humiliated by his wife. The discarded novel represented George's one chance at creativity, or perhaps individuality, which he relinquished for fear of losing his monthly paycheck. His reference to the long silence retained by the psychotic boy in the asylum is in reality an allegory of his own silence as a writer, for which he has had to suffer a marital life of insanity.

George regains his composure, quickly admitting that while the name of their last game was called "Humiliate the Host," his new game, "Hump the Hostess," is about to begin. The game has a preamble to it called "Get the Guests'" in which Nick is revealed as an opportunist and Honey as a deceitful trickster. Honey, realizing that Nick has confided their private secret, runs out of the room ready to vomit again. Nick threatens George, telling him he will regret what he has done. As he leaves to attend to his wife, Martha rips into George for his savage and willful attempt at destroying Nick and Honey's already dubious marriage. She defends Nick and attacks her husband's viciousness. The motivation is now set up for Martha and Nick to commit adultery in the next room as the second act comes to a close. George prophetically reads aloud from one of his history books: "And the west, encumbered by crippling alliances, and burdened with a morality too rigid to accommodate itself to the swing of events, must . . . eventually . . . fall." The final moments of the second act are concerned with George's supreme retaliation for his wife's blatant adultery; he will kill their imaginary child. This ultimate act is contemplated while the audience is allowed a ten-minute respite.

In the early moments of the third act, Martha is seen putting Nick down for his poor sexual performance. (Ironically enough Martha admits that George had been the only man to sexually satisfy her.) Albee, sardonically, injects the idea of impotence as a form of poetic justice for a world turned proudly immoral. George returns with flowers heralding the imminent destruction of their illusional child. The game is called "Bringing Up Baby." George has Nick fetch his wife and makes him stay to view the last game of the evening by threatening to cause a scandal if he should decide to leave. Nick, afraid for his newly acquired position, agrees to stay until the end. George begins to slap Martha, goading her to talk about their son publicly. The style of presentation suddenly swerves into an hysterical public confessional, presenting the imagined baby's life so vividly that Honey, caught up in the mood, screams that she wants a baby. Martha continues to affirm the child's existence as the scene becomes a liturgy with George reciting correctly from the Catholic Mass for the dead. The chant ends with George's announcement that the child has died in an auto accident. He himself received the news by telegram as Martha was busy copulating in the next room. Martha, outraged and frantic, screams out that George has no right to kill their son. But Martha has broken their vow and so, pathetically, moanfully, she slumps to the floor, accepting the rules of the game. George announces that the party is over and sends Nick and Honey away. The child is already gone—exorcized by George.

The death of the fantasy child has brought forth as much critical commentary as its original creation. The controversy is over what the child's death symbolizes. One possible interpretation forwarded to me by Benjamin Fulghum, chairman of the English Department at Central Connecticut State College, is that the child might be a symbolic Christ child. George then would be the personification of the Protestant Church and Martha the Catholic Church, making their family quarrel allegorical. George mentions in the play that he is about six centuries younger than Martha. The subsequent exorcism is to be taken as a sign that religion is no longer needed to fill our lives with illusion. Nick, incidentally, says: "Jesus Christ I think I understand this," twice, directly after the exorcism. Albee has said: "I begin to suspect that I put an awful lot more Christian symbolism into my plays than I was consciously aware of."[39] Yet contrary to Albee's admitted Christian symbolism, he has stated the illusional child is not a Christ image. I asked him whether any allegory could be drawn from the role of the child, and he answered that it could. According to Albee, the child stands for the "revolutionary principles of this country that we haven't lived up to yet."[40] It is the birth of an idea, but the idea remains only an illusion.

The most realistic interpretation, and the one generally accepted by the critics, is that the child represents the illusions we create to make life bearable and that "people who cherish false illusions for all kinds of reasons . . . are better off without them."[41] This particular idea brings Albee very close to O'Neill. Walter Kerr, as well as many other critics, has compared the two playwrights:

> O'Neill shows us men surviving on lies. He shows us the deflation and the despair and the impotence that follow from the exposure or even the questioning of the lie. Then gives the lie back . . . he blesses them with fresh forgetfulness, with the unholy water of a renewed illusion. He lets the poor bastards live . . . he does not hate his characters for being dishonest with themselves, he simply supposes they cannot help it . . . self-deception is better than death . . . the newer attitude of dramatists [Albee] . . . say, in effect, that no fraud is worth perpetuating. Self-deception is a vice *even* if it seems to make someone happier . . . Only truth, the whole truth . . . can satisfy men's minds. . . .[42]

When George and Martha destroy that child they destroy whatever illusions they have created in reaction to a reality that has been responsible for the loneliness they feel. And the reality they try to keep away, by conjuring up a fantasy child, is actually the reality of man's predicament. That is, man—in this very complex and bureaucratic world whose sheer organization is dehumanizing—feels an overwhelming sense of aloneness and separation. His inability to deal effectively with this predicament has left him filled with despair and boredom, for he no longer has the joy of individual creativity —only dependency on an outside power. And when he can no longer create, he begins to destroy, because either activity lifts him out of his insignificance.[43] George and Martha feel this dislocation, almost abandonment, brought on by our modern world—only more so because their marriage is sterile. Consequently, in order to overcome their predicament, they have resorted to the illusion that they are not alone; they have a child who loves them. But, according to Albee's existential philosophy, life cannot be lived through illusion, no matter how comforting. Man must learn to face his world in all its hostility and accept his isolation and insignificance in it. As Albert Camus has said: "He can . . . decide to accept such a universe and draw from it his strength, his refusal to hope, and the unyielding evidence of a life without consolation. . . ."[44]

Only George and Martha are left on stage. They are totally alone. All illusion has been stripped away or vomited up. There are no more games to play. Shame and hypocrisy have been destroyed by truth. Exhausted, they lie in each others arms seeking kindness, perhaps love. For the first time in the play Martha refuses a drink. As Henry Hewes has clearly realized, they "are left together in a state of peace following the violent but gratifying games that seem to have served them as a sex-substitute. . . . And like his play *The Zoo Story* it accepts the necessity for violence as the ultimate means of human contact. . . ."[45] Tired and spent, Martha simply and honestly expresses her fear of facing whatever is ahead for them with nothing but the truth that they are alone. George tenderly tries to comfort her:

> GEORGE: (*Long silence*) It will be better.
> MARTHA: (*Long silence*) I don't . . . know.
> GEORGE: It will be . . . maybe.
> MARTHA: I'm . . . not . . . sure.
> GEORGE. No.
> MARTHA: Just . . . us?
> GEORGE: Yes.
> MARTHA: I don't supose, maybe, we could . . .
> GEORGE: No, Martha.

George softly sings "Who's Afraid of Virginia Woolf?" which, as Albee has revealed, means ". . . 'Who's Afraid of the Big, Bad Wolf?' means 'Who's afraid of living life without illusions?' "[46] Martha finally admits "I . . . am . . . George . . . I . . . am . . .," as the curtain slowly falls.

It is not easy to like this play. It is extremely painful to watch. But as Albee has said: "I don't write reassuring plays,

not opiates . . . I'm not interested in the kind of problems
that can be tied in a bundle at the end of the third-act curtain. You walk out of that sort of play, and all you think
about it where you parked your car. . . ."[47] Those who have
seen this play realize that it is a cruel play. Perhaps the best
answer to those who cannot stomach cruelty and pain in the
theatre is to quote from a letter written by Julian Beck,
founder of the Living Theatre:

> The Theater of Cruelty. The only prediction I venture:
> More and more will be seen and heard of and about this
> kind of theatre . . . Artaud, who envisaged a theater
> which did not numb us with ideas for the intellect, but
> stirred us to feeling by stirring up pain. We are a feel-
> ingless people (consider all the suffering we permit in
> this world as we go about our business) ; and if we could
> at least feel pain, we might turn towards becoming men
> again instead of turning more and more into callous
> automata.[48]

There is still an inclination among those who know the
script to dismiss it as an ill-founded exaggeration of matrimonial strife in this country. Yet in a recent article by psychiatrist Vincent Mazzanti, he affirms that *"Who's Afraid of Virginia Woolf?* is in closer touch with reality than most
films."[49] John Gassner has acknowledged that the play can
easily create resentment, but he reacts to it affirmatively "because of the fighting spirit of the principals whose behavior
breathes the fire of protest along with the stench of corruption."[50]

CHAPTER 7

TINY ALICE

THE OVERPOWERING feeling of abandonment experienced by modern man is, I think, the motivation behind, and the key to understanding, Edward Albee's enigmatic play *Tiny Alice*. Albee senses that contemporary man feels alone and insignificant within his infinite universe. Is it because he has been forsaken by his fellow man? Is it because he has been abandoned by his God? Perhaps there is no God. Perhaps man has lost his Faith. Albee explores this awareness of dislocation in what is his most ambitious play, though I imagine —from what the critics have said—that this is a minority opinion.

Opening night proved to be the most controversial evening since *Who's Afraid of Virginia Woolf?* opened two years earlier at the same theater. The storm of controversy concerning *Tiny Alice* centered around whether Mr. Albee had not in fact perpetrated ". . . a huge joke on the American culture industry. . . ."[1] Critical reactions to the play went from "a clutter of confused thought,"[2] to "far and away the most significant play on Broadway this year."[3] George Oppenheimer, reviewing for *Newsday*, said:

> There may be some, including the producers, the five actors and, I presume, that fine director Alan Schneider, who have been let in on Mr. Albee's secret, but I regret to tell you that I am not one of them. In the ten years that I have been reviewing, I have not encountered so completely baffling a play. . . . It has moments of beauty and drama as is to be expected from one of our finest playwrights but unhappily they are largely obscured in a fog that settles and seldom lifts.[4]

Harold Clurman was even less tolerant when he wrote: "The play struck me as the sort of thing a highly endowed college student might write by way of offering us a Faustian drama."[5] One could go on and on quoting choice sections of the critics' reactions to this play, but Richard Watts probably included most of the reviewers' opinions when he confessed: "I am not even certain I can describe adequately enough of the surface plot to provide some idea of what takes place."[6] On the positive side of this critical clash was Norman Nadel writing for the *New York World-Telegram and Sun*: "*Tiny Alice* is massive theater. Edward Albee has written an allegory in conventional dramatic form, which transcends conventional dramas in almost every dimension . . . only by looking closely and carefully at *Tiny Alice* do you begin to grasp its magnitude."[7] Albee himself has said, "It is indecent to fault a work for being difficult. Are we to assume that audiences can grasp nothing more complex than simple addition or subscription?"[8]

Tiny Alice is a metaphysical dream play concerning the relationship of man to his God. The play's plot concerns the desire of the world's-richest woman to grant the Church one hundred million dollars for a period of twenty years, provided certain requirements are met. There is a curious similarity between the premise of *Tiny Alice* and the much more bitter play, *The Visit*. This similarity, plus the multi-level plot of *Tiny Alice,* is what has led the critics astray in their interpretations of Albee's metaphysical mystery. Briefly, let us compare Durrenmatt's play with Albee's *Tiny Alice*. In both plays the premise is that the world's richest woman is willing to grant a huge sum of money provided those who receive the money agree to carry out her one request. In *The Visit,* the woman wants the death of a childhood boyfriend who perjured himself in court in order to be relieved of the responsibilities of a secret misalliance which left her pregnant. Now, many years later, fabulously rich, she has returned to her home town to extract "justice." She is willing to pay for his murder and give the town enough money to overcome its present desolate economic condition, enabling its inhabitants to live in comparative luxury. The first reaction to her morbid proposal is indignant refusal—but not for long. One by one the townspeople begin to believe that this man's guilt is so great that the only true justice is for him to die. Even the church officials are persuaded that a new bell is needed for the church steeple. Finally, the man's wife and children turn against him—all for the love of money. He is deserted by everyone, and in a mock town trial found guilty and strangled by one of the villagers. The medical report reads "heart attack." The woman is vindicated; the town becomes wealthy, and she, having gotten away with murder, leaves with her former lover's body in a coffin. Because *Tiny Alice* uses a similar plot device, and because both men appear to be the victims of some organized plot to destroy them for money, Albee's play has been misunderstood and misinterpreted.

The play opens in a Cardinal's garden. We quickly learn that a lawyer, who is an old schoolmate of the Cardinal and is now in the employ of a Miss Alice, has come to the Cardinal offering a huge grant to the Church in the name of his employer. We also learn that these two men have loathed each other since their youthful days at school and only tolerate their meeting because of the immensity of Miss Alice's offer. The Cardinal sarcastically refers to the lawyer as a solicitor which is the British term for an attorney but carries with it connotations of prostitution in this country. The lawyer is also referred to as "Satan" by the Cardinal at one point during the scene. Combining the idea of soliciting for money and the somewhat Mephistophelean demeanor of the character, Albee's lawyer appeared evil, which suggested that his employer was not much different. Consequently, the audience began to think of the Lawyer as the legal representative of some evil power. Even his school background fitted the picture. The Cardinal, remembering his schoolmate, says, "You *were* a swine at school. . . . A cheat in your examinations, a liar in all things of any matter, vile in your personal habits—unwashed and indecent, a bully to those you could intimidate and a sycophant to everyone else." The Lawyer's character became more dubious with each minute. Nor was the Cardinal some deeply pious, humble servant of the Lord. He appeared to be an arrogant, smug, overly pompous opportunist, who had not incorporated much of Christ's humility.

When the final act revealed the characters to be allegorical, the first scene took on a symbolic meaning, but the critics confused the symbolism. The Cardinal became the surrogate for the Church, and the Lawyer became the representative of some equally powerful evil Deity, personified by Miss Alice. They all appeared to be bound together in a conspiracy to destroy Julian's soul by leading him to carnal temptation while at Miss Alice's mansion. In this way the Church would benefit, as the townspeople did in *The Visit,* by sacrificing not the man, but his soul. It appears that both plays present a world so corrupt that not only will an entire village commit murder for cash, but the Church will sacrifice one soul as expendable in order to receive an enormous amount of money. Harold Clurman saw precisely this interpretation when he wrote about *Tiny Alice:*

> . . . but the play's intention is clear enough. It tells us that the pure person in our world is betrayed by all parties. The Church is venal, the 'capitalist' heartlessly base, the 'proletarian' cynical and, for all the good he may do, powerless and subservient. There remains Women: enticing mother image and never-perfectly-to-be-possessed mate . . . those who rule us—Church, the Economic Forces and Woman—bid him accept the world as it is. Being pure he cannot do so. Isolated and bereft of every hope, he must die—murdered.[9]

Even the perceptive Walter Kerr thought the play unnecessarily nihilistic. In the *Herald Tribune* he said that the conspirators were against Julian and out to destroy his faith in God, in human union, and in any possibility that life had meaning. One might conclude that because of certain artistic choices in the Broadway production, the idea that Evil triumphs over Good could be interpreted as the plays theme. But that was not Albee's intention. He is concerned mainly with exploring his generation's sense of abandonment. He is not attempting to prove that Evil can triumph over Good.

There is symbolism in the seemingly realistic first scene, tying it more closely with the end of the play than might be realized on first viewing. When the Lawyer, in the Broadway production, told the Cardinal his robes were "the color of your mother's vice," the line was said viciously, implying that his mother was a whore. Yet, when we look at Albee's script, his notation indicates that the line should be said, "softly; sadly." The Lawyer's remark is symbolic, meaning the Church was born out of vice and immorality. In fact, among its first followers, it boasted Rome's most incorrigible sinners. Edward Gibbon, in his *Decline and Fall of the Roman Empire,* writes: "The friends of Christianity may acknowledge without a blush that many of the most eminent saints had been before their baptism the most abandoned sinners."[10] It is correct to interpret this scene as a meeting of two surrogates, each representing a Deity. What those Deities are we shall eventually discover. The Lawyer's employer wants to give one hundred million to the Church. She asks only that the final details of the grant be worked out at her estate by the Cardinal's secretary, a lay brother named Julian. The scene ends with the Cardinal agreeing to send his secretary to Miss Alice's manor house.

Scene two begins in the library of an immensely large and cavernous castle. In the library there is a miniature replica of the castle which is designed after Chambord, the palatial sixteenth century hunting lodge that was built by Francis I.[11] The enormity and power of this woman's domain is awesome. Julian is introduced to Butler, who is the butler. We find out that at one time Butler was Miss Alice's lover, but now he only serves her. Actually, his intimacy with Miss Alice is symbolic, similar to what Julian will go through, and will be better understood once it is decided who Miss Alice really is. The Lawyer is her present lover, and that too is symbolic, foreshadowing Julian's eventual relationship with Alice.

Julian awaits his first interview with the woman, and while he waits he is introduced to the replica. The model rests majestically center stage and is reported by Butler to be an exact duplicate of the huge castle, down to tiny miniature representations of each room, complete with tiny furniture and accessories. The replica's library also has a little model of the model. The question then posed by the Butler (but never answered until the very end of the play) is: does the replica within the replica have a replica and so on into infinity? Conversely, could there be still a larger castle than the one they are living in, and if so, are they then merely tiny replicas of a larger Deity within an unending universe? The metaphysical question is not as irrelevant to the play's action as it may seem. Consider that one of the themes Albee is concerned with is whether man creates a giant God in his own image, or does God create us as smaller versions of Himself? The conversation changes and Julian is asked to account for a six-year period that is not represented in his dossier. It seems Miss Alice has a complete dossier on this lay brother, and the choice that he complete the financial arrangements was deliberate on her part. At first Julian refuses to discuss the past, but as the second scene comes to a close he confesses to Butler that during those six years he lost his faith in God because he was not able to reconcile himself to the idea that "men create a false God in their own image." With the past revealed, he is allowed to have his first interview with Miss Alice, who awaits him upstairs.

Scene three takes place in Miss Alice's sitting room. The audience, however, was not clear as to where it took place because scene changes were not listed in the play's program. The audience was told only that there would be two intermissions. The locale was therefore left to the viewer's own imagination. Yet every setting (and there are three) was handled with a great deal of realistic detail, so that the omission of an act breakdown seemed either an oversight or a deliberate abstraction which, when not carried out by the style of the settings, proved confusing. In the printed script the play is broken down into scenes with each place briefly described. According to the printed version of the play, scene three takes place in "an upstairs sitting room of the castle." It is small, containing only a throne-like chair and an upholstered bench. In the chair, Alice's deified position within her glorious mansion is reinforced. The scene begins with the throne-chair facing away from the audience, its royal occupant hidden from view. She is presumably looking out the window surveying her estate which, judging by the complexity of the model in the library, is vast. As she rises from her throne and turns to face Julian and an equally curious audience, she appears to be a wizened old woman, hard of hearing, supporting herself with the help of two canes. Within a few minutes, however, the old woman turns out to have been a masquerade, as she removes a false wig and rubber face, exposing a rather attractive woman.

Howard Taubman wrote that the masquerade does not work because Albee "has not worked it out." I find that the symbolism of the masquerade is quite clear. Albee wanted Alice to represent a Deity. She should, therefore, be quite old—as old as the history of man's search for God. For Miss Alice to be an aged lady is preposterous once the stipulation to her bargain with the Church is revealed. The masquerade has to be considered as symbolic. Our first impression is one of great age, and we retain the image long after the accoutrements have been removed. Alice's masquerade also foreshadows a revelation in the third act in which Julian is told that Miss Alice is only a surrogate masquerading for a powerful Deity. Miss Alice is not the manipulator she appears to be.

Alice, exposed, the interview begins. Julian learns that because Alice has so much wealth and property, it has become impossible for her to enjoy it in all its splendor. She therefore loves her throne-chair because it is a symbol through which her vast fortune can be comprehended and absorbed. She cannot enjoy the vastness of her wealth unless there is a symbolic replica of it wherever she goes. Hence, each room has a special chair or piece which stands for all her wealth. She needs the symbol; the reality is not sufficient. She needs to experience the magnitude of her castle by using the replica as a substitute, because the contemplation of the actual castle in its entirety is too much for her to grasp. She must reduce it in size in order to keep its total image in her mind:

> MISS ALICE: . . . in the drawing rooms, or the li-
> brary, or whatever room you wish to mention, I have a
> chair that I consider my possession.
> JULIAN: But you possess the entire . . . (*Thinks of a
> word*) establishment.
> MISS ALICE: Of course, but it is such a large . . . es-
> tablishment that one needs the feel of specific possession
> in every . . . area.

Miss Alice then questions Julian about the six years not accounted for in his dossier. He confesses that "there is no mystery to it, my faith in God left me, and I committed myself to an asylum." He, unlike Alice, has always fought against accepting the symbol. He has never been able to re-duce God to a palpable form in order to understand His omnipresence. Julian does not feel that man is incapable of attaining union with the abstraction; consequently, he has fought all his life to establish this personal relationship with the infinity of God's presence, rather than pray to a man-made image or substitution for Him. He tells Alice that after six years he was released from the asylum, having learned only that his nature was perhaps overly sensitive. His feeling of spiritual dislocation remains with him because even though he has not yet experienced a union with the abstraction, he will not pray to any substitute.

Miss Alice then asks if he has ever broken his vow of chastity. Julian relates that he might have during one of his hallucinatory moments in the asylum, but he is not sure. He describes the orgasmic hallucination to Miss Alice, revealing a suppressed desire for sexual intercourse that he is not really aware of, having channeled it into the appearance of religious ecstasy. With the confession made, Alice ends the interview, asking Julian to stay on at the castle in order to execute more easily the arrangements she has made with the Church. He agrees and leaves. The scene ends in a disturbingly conspiratorial tone which defeats Albee's intention in the play because it leads the audience to believe that Alice and her Lawyer are plotting against Julian:

> MISS ALICE: . . . do you really think we're wise?
> LAWYER: Wise? Well, we'll see. If we prove not, I can't think of anything standing in the way that can't be destroyed. (*Pause*) Can you?
> MISS ALICE: (*Rather sadly*) No. Nothing.

CURTAIN

Act two begins in the library. What takes place resembles a prosaic domestic quarrel between lover and mistress. At first glance the Lawyer seems to be jealous of the amount of attention Julian has been receiving from Alice. He accuses her of avoiding him and becoming personally involved with Julian. There are suggestions in the scene that Alice's purpose is to seduce Julian, but without becoming emotionally involved—otherwise she will pay the consequences. Julian enters, and the argument is controlled. Suddenly a fire breaks out in the chapel room of the model, indicating that a larger fire has started in the very room Julian has come from. The

Lawyer and the Butler rush to put out the blaze in the chapel with Julian, confused, but not far behind them. Only Alice remains in the library. She kneels and prays. To whom she prays is not particularly clear, but there are suggestions that whatever the force is, she is an incarnation of it, tiny in proportion to its magnitude and power. She prays that the fire will not consume them. This symbolic scene can be difficult to understand because there are two distinctly antithetical interpretations easily read into its action. The first, and the interpretation I think Albee had in mind, is that the fire represents the possibility that Julian will be destroyed as an outcome of whatever bargain Alice and her Lawyer have made with the Church. Julian's possible destruction is prevented, however, when all involved—including Julian—put out the fire.

There is, I must admit, another way to view this scene. Since Julian now resides in the castle, his fiery religious devotion has started a blaze that has the potential to destroy those who plan to conspire against him. When the fire is put out with the help of Julian, it is a sign that his religious beliefs are not powerful enough to consume the conspirators (if they are conspirators), giving them the strength to destroy Julian through his own weakness. This scene is absolutely crucial, because whichever interpretation is followed, directly determines the outcome of the play.

Theatrically speaking, seeing a fire on stage, even if it is only a tiny one representing something bigger, is dramatically more effective than hearing about it from the proverbial messenger. The fire provides an unnerving and mystical connection between the castle and its tiny replica.

One fact is certain: the fire has been extinguished along with its miniature counterpart in the replica. Julian is the only one who is concerned that the replica burned exactly as the real chapel did. Everyone else accepts the phenomenon. He cannot believe that this reduced model has mystical powers; there must be a logical explanation. Nevertheless, he is caught up in the middle of this strange household where Lawyer and Butler call each other "dearest and darling," suggesting a homosexual relationship between them, so that his mind is temporarily diverted from the unexplainable fire in the replica. There is another hint of homosexuality as a subsidiary theme in the very first scene of the play. The Lawyer insinuates that the Cardinal is homosexual. I don't believe homosexuality is a theme inherent in this play, but Albee's slight references do cause critics to write that "he toys with you, suggesting a homosexual relationship between the lay brother and the Cardinal."[12] Albee should be more selective, otherwise his audience will pick up a small reference and weave it into a major theme, as did Philip Roth in his very controversial review. I believe great credit should go not to Roth but to the play, because its grandeur can absorb Roth's interpretation. Here is the essence of his review:

> The movement of the play is not towards a confronta-
> tion of ideas: it is finally concerned with evoking a sin-
> gle emotion—pity for poor Julian. In the end the play-
> wright likens him to Jesus Christ—and all because he
> has had to suffer the martyrdom of heterosexual love.
> *Tiny Alice* is a homosexual daydream in which the celi-
> bate male is tempted and seduced by the overpowering
> female, only to be betrayed by the male lover and mur-
> dered by the cruel law, or in this instance, cruel lawyer.
> It has as much to do with Christ's Passion as a little
> girl's dreaming about being a princess locked in a tower
> has to do with the fate of Mary Stuart. . . . How long
> before a play is produced on Broadway in which the
> homosexual hero is presented as a homosexual, and not
> disguised as an angst-ridden priest, or an angry Negro,
> or an aging actress; or worst of all, Everyman?[13]

Scene two in the second act serves to tell us exactly what the household wants from Julian. Butler and Lawyer are talking about the best way to make Miss Alice's bargain

understandable to the Cardinal because, while he is a man of
God, he "worships the symbol and not the substance." They
are determined that he will agree to the arrangements because it is really what Julian has wanted all along. Finally,
through much verbal play, the audience realizes that Miss
Alice's condition is this: In order for the Church to receive
one hundred million dollars for twenty years, the Cardinal
must condone Julian's marriage to Alice. In fact, they would
like him to officiate at the wedding ceremony. On the surface
the bargaining point of the grant seems to be the demise of
Julian's soul. Sacrifice Julian and receive enough money to
benefit the entire world. Because no information is given to
the audience about who is behind this plot, the audience is
convinced that Albee is writing another Durrenmatt play
with Julian as the sacrificial lamb. This is not quite the case.

The next scene gives us the first substantial clue to this
metaphysical mystery. The scene takes place in Miss Alice's
sitting room. It is here that Julian admits his life-long wish:
to be of service to the Church and then be forgotten. But
Alice questions this seemingly humble wish, forcing Julian
to confess that his true wish is to die as a martyr, bathed in
the blood of sacrifice:

MISS ALICE: (*Moving on him again*) You are *being*
used, my little Julian. I am being used . . . my little
Julian. You want to be . . . employed, do you not?

JULIAN: I have . . . there are no secrets from you,
Miss Alice . . . I have . . . dreamed of sacrifice.

She beseeches him to tell her of his dreams, which he does
in an outpour of religious ecstasy and sexual hysteria:

JULIAN: . . . Oh, martyrdom. To be that. To be able
. . . to be that.

MISS ALICE: (*Softly, into his ear; he does not hear
it*) Marry me, Julian.

JULIAN: The . . . death of the saints . . . was always
the beginning of their lives. To go bloodstained and

worthy . . . upward. I could feel the blood on my robes, as intense as paint . . . and warm . . . and painless.

MISS ALICE: Marry me.

JULIAN: "Here I have come. You see my robes? They're red, are they not? Warm? And are not the folds caught together . . . as the blood coagulates? The . . . fingers of my left hand—of both are . . . are hard to move apart, as the blood holds finger to finger. And there is a wound in me, the warm dark flow . . . runs down my belly . . . to . . . bathing my groin. You see? I have come . . . bloodstained and worthy."

MISS ALICE: Marry me.

JULIAN: (*Still self-tranced*) Bathed . . . my groin. And as the thumbs of the gladiator pressed . . . against . . . my neck . . . I . . . as the lion's belly pressed on my chest, I . . . as the . . . I . . . or as the woman sank . . . on the mossy hillock by the roses, and the roar is the crunching growl is the moan is the sweat-breathing is the . . .

MISS ALICE: (*Behind him, her arms around his neck, on his chest*) . . . sweat-breathing on the mossy hillock and the white mist in the perfumes. . . .

JULIAN: . . . fumes . . . lying . . . on the moss hill in the white filmy gladiator's belly pressing on the chest fanged and the soft hard tongue and the blood . . . ENTERS . . . [sic].

During his hysteria Alice convinces him to fulfill his craving by sacrificing himself to God through her. The scene ends as Julian, unable to control his repressed libido, drops to his knees facing her and is enveloped in her robes.

Whether Alice is out to destroy Julian through carnal pleasures or whether she really wants to give him the opportunity to fulfill a life's desire is answered in the third act. Albee touches upon the subject of orgasmic pleasure during heightened religious rapture.

From this section of the play until the end there are strong indications that Julian is a Christ figure. To begin with, he dies in the posture of crucifixion. Butler kisses him, reminding us of Judas. Alice holds him in the position of the Pieta, as he lies dying. Finally, he shouts "MY GOD, WHY HAST THOU FORSAKEN ME?" Undoubtedly these are elements of the Christ story, but I don't think Mr. Albee was out only to retell the Christ Passion in modern dress. He has raised too many questions about reality and illusion, God and His relationship to man, martyrdom, the necessity for symbols, and finally, man's sense of abandonment, to have decided on limiting his play to the Passion story.

At the beginning of the third act we find that Julian has indeed given up his vows as a lay brother and married Miss Alice. The ceremony has just ended, performed, as was planned, by the Cardinal. Julian, of course, does not know that his wish for martyrdom is about to be fulfilled. He is too busy trying to find his new bride, who seems to have disappeared. Julian leaves the library in search of her. During his absence the Cardinal and the Lawyer discuss the transaction. Julian will soon receive what he has always wanted, a chance to serve God in a way that will benefit mankind. The Church has agreed to sacrifice him. Within a few minutes all five gather in the library for the final confrontation. Julian must now be told the truth about his marriage. There is a toast, the loud pop of the cork foreshadowing the gun shot that will kill Julian, and all drink in celebration of Julian's marriage. Then suddenly the marriage guests prepare to leave— including Alice. Julian, bewildered, is told that only he must remain because he has really married Tiny Alice, a Deity, through Miss Alice, her surrogate. Julian does not believe them. Nor does he believe that Tiny Alice lives in the replica because he cannot see her—though he cannot see his own God either. He is asked to accept what is happening to him as an act of Faith. He refuses, thinking that a mockery has been made of his beliefs. They tell him that he can now have a union with the abstraction rather than a man-made image of God if he will only believe and accept Tiny Alice as that Deity. Julian, at the brink of sanity, threatens to return to the asylum because he has been betrayed, abandoned, and mocked.

He is then shot so that the original bargain with the Church can be consummated. The Cardinal, somewhat un-nerved by witnessing Julian's sacrificial murder, runs from the castle, but not before picking up the first payment of the grant. Butler begins covering the furniture, and all make hasty last-minute preparations to leave, ignoring Julian who lies dying on the floor. They finally leave, sealing up the tomb-like structure as they depart, presumably to strike the bargain somewhere else. Julian crawls nearer the replica as the life and blood pour out of him. He is utterly alone now, except for the skull-like bust supporting the discarded hag's wig that Alice wore earlier, which Butler has placed near Julian before leaving the castle. The small "phrenological head" reinforces the symbolism of Christ's death at Golgotha, which can be translated as place of the skull, and Alice's wig reminds us that she represents an ancient Deity.

Julian then lapses into an almost hallucinatory state, re-membering disconnected childhood events, finally realizing that in all his dreams he has never thought of martyrdom as abandonment and betrayal. He says, "It is what I have wanted, have insisted on, have nagged . . . for (*Looking about the room, raging*) IS THIS MY PRIESTHOOD, THEN? THIS WORLD? THEN COME AND SHOW THYSELF BRIDE? GOD?" As soon as he utters the words he begins to sense the power of an encroaching force. He can hear its giant heartbeat and breathing as it comes closer and closer, completely engulfing him. He screams out at the deaf-ening sounds, "I accept thee, Alice, for thou art come to me. God, Alice . . . I accept thy will." At that moment he slumps into the position of the crucifixion, then falls over dead. The curtain comes down, the thumping sounds cease, and darkness covers everything.

The ending presents two possibilties. First, if Tiny Alice is not really God but only Julians' hallucination and in the last moment of his life he has deluded himself by swearing allegiance to a false God, he has betrayed his own God and in so doing has destroyed his own soul. Ironically his destruction will still benefit the Church and possibly mankind because of the millions granted through Julian's marriage. Second, if Julian accepts Tiny Alice as God and his sacrifice as God's will, the abstraction, which up to now he has not been able to see, now becomes real and apparent to him. Whether there is a God or not is unimportant. If we believe in Him "on faith" he becomes real. Ironically, Julian, who has fought all his life against turning the abstraction into some man-made image to pray to, does not until the very end believe in the reality of an abstract God. That is, Julian, in his final moment of life, has been able to accomplish what he always believed was possible: communion with an abstraction; and if this abstraction called Tiny Alice is really his God taking a form he has never conceived of and not an evil Deity, then what happens at the end of the play is the transfiguration and union of a Christian martyr with his God.

Perhaps the best way to conclude this chapter is to quote Abraham N. Franzblau, a noted psychiatrist:

> Albee tries to pluck the masks from life and death, sex, love and marriage, God, faith, and organized religion, money-greed wealth, charity and even celibacy. Part of our puzzlement undoubtedly comes from believing that some of these do not wear any mask, but are solid and authentic, at least in our personal value system. But no one comes out of the theater with all of his own psychological blinders and colored glasses still in place. . . . Albee penetrates the superficial layers of our conscious personality and, using the mysterious escalators of the unconscious, reaches the citadels of our private certainties and shoots them full of question marks.[14]

CHAPTER 8

A DELICATE
BALANCE

Notwithstanding the fact that Edward Albee received the Pulitzer Prize for *A Delicate Balance*, it still remains, aside from *Tiny Alice*, his most underrated play. Premiered on September 12, 1966, at the Martin Beck Theatre, its generally mild reception generated immediate controversy over Albee's continuing talent as a first-rate playwright. Martin Gottfried, reviewing for *Women's Wear Daily*, called the play "two hours of self-indulgence by a self-conscious and self-overrating writer."[1] Robert Brustein, now Dean of the revitalized Yale School of Drama, said the writing was "as far from modern speech as the whistles of a dolphin."[2] Conversely, John Chapman called it "a beautiful play—easily Albee's best and most mature."[3] And Harold Clurman considered it "superior to the more sensational *Virginia Woolf*."[4]

While the critics could not agree on the play's merits, they seemed to be in general agreement on its theme, which they stated in various ways as man's responsibility to man. Albee had hinted at the theme before the play's opening (he wasn't going to be misunderstood again) when he revealed that the new work was about "the nature of responsibility, that of family and friends—about responsibility as against selfishness, self-protectiveness, as against Christian responsibility."[5] In their reviews the critics simply paraphrased what Albee had said about the responsibilities of friendship since a major plot episode concerns the protagonists' best friends.

Norman Nadel claimed that the "delicate balance" was between "the right of privacy and the obligations of friendship."[6] *Vogue's* reviewer echoed the other critics when he remarked that it is "when our friends make demands on us that we fail them."[7] Leonard Probst, reviewing for NBC-TV, said in his one minute critique that "the delicate balance is the balance between responsibility to friends (when they're in trouble) . . . and the conflict with our own reasonable desires."[8] John Gassner, in analyzing the play's structure, concluded that it was most concerned with saying "if we do not want to betray a friendship, we do not really want to carry it very far."[9] With this general agreement on its theme, the critics turned out an onslaught of reasons why the new play was not well written.

Norman Nadel, referring to the neighboring couple who decide out of a private fear to stay on indefinitely, commented that their personal problem split the play into two parts which "do not relate as they should."[10] John Gassner, writing for the *Educational Theatre Journal,* concluded that Albee had brought too many other elements into the play to simply resolve the friendship theme.[11] Perhaps the most outspoken criticism of the play's structure came from the *Village Voice.* Michael Smith wrote that the play's crisis had "not been resolved but uncreated . . . [because] . . . Harry and Edna, quite on their own, simply go away. . . . Balance has been restored not by the called for heroic leap, but by removal . . . this play is a cop-out."[12]

Each critic's evaluation was based on the premise that Albee had not carefully thought out the play's events as it related to the problem of friendship and its ensuing responsibilities. Professor Gassner, concentrating on what he considered Albee's intention, went so far as to say that certain major characters should not have been included in the play —specifically, that the alcoholic sister's appearance seemed somewhat arbitrary and the daughter's sudden homecoming uncalled for.[13] Walter Kerr complained that "there are no events—nothing follows necessarily from what has gone before, no two things fit, no present posture has a tangible past."[14] The critic for *Newsweek* summed up all the adverse criticism when he said there was a division between theme and procedure.[15]

But the play examines more levels of our existence than the need for truer friendship among men. Once properly understood, the play's events are perfectly sequential (though I am not categorically against a plotless play as we shall see in the chapter on *Box-Mao-Box*), revealing an analysis of the modern scene that goes deeper than the reviews imply. One of the elements not discussed in any of the reviews is a continuation, and I believe culmination, of a major Albee theme.

From the very first Albee drama, through this play, two characters continually make their appearance: that domineering, man-eating, she-ogre of the American family—Mom—and her playmate, that weak-willed, spineless, castrated, avoider of arguments—Dad. Together these two have woven their way through every single play of Albee's with the exception of *Tiny Alice*—although some critics have made an incorrect case for the existence of this sado-masochistic pair there also. Mom and Pop first showed up obliquely in *The Zoo Story* when Jerry began explaining his orphaned status to Peter. They next appeared as characters in both *The Sandbox* and *The American Dream,* its extention, playing out their roles of emasculator and emasculated, with Mom doing her part with such zest and relish that it made her male audience cringe with empathic pain. Even *Bessie Smith,* Albee's supposed civil rights play, got out of hand when his obsession with the battle of the sexes allowed the play's original theme to get away from him. It did, however, plant the seed of Daddy's fight for survival which came to fruition in the highly successful *Virginia Woolf.* The play's huge success is directly attributable to both the rich verbal texture and the fact that for the first time Albee gave Mom a formidable antagonist. This time Daddy would fight to the death before acquiescing to Mom's husband-destroying intentions.

Many critics have been quick to insist that Albee was really writing about his own foster parents and not about a typically American condition. A look into the many sociological texts on American life would negate that analysis. One such treatise, examining Dad's position in the American home, bluntly asserts that "in few societies is the role of the father more vestigial than in the United States."[16] This same text vividly points out that the success of such comics as *Blondie* (now seen on television) or its home-screen predecessors, *The Honeymooners* and *The Flintstones,* is that the American public is convinced that the American father is a blunderer and has given up authority, because with him at the head "the family would constantly risk disintegration and disaster."[17] One further example, this time analyzing Mom, should suffice as a preamble to the conflicts set forth in *A Delicate Balance.* The following condensed statement on Mom can be found in a standard sociology textbook sold in most college bookstores across the country:

> 'Mom' is the unquestioned authority in matters of mores and morals in her home. . . . She stands for the superior values of tradition, yet she herself does not want to become 'old.' In fact, she is mortally afraid of that status which in the past was the fruit of a rich life, namely, the status of the grandmother. . . . Mom—is not happy: she does not like herself; she is ridden by the anxiety that her life was a waste.[18]

A Delicate Balance is a continuation of the Mom and Pop relationship as they enter the age of retirement. Through a rather bizarre event, Albee has forced the famous couple to re-examine the sum total of their lives with conclusions startlingly similar to the ones reached by the above sociological analysis. Albee wrote this play on boat trips to Europe.[19] The relaxed slow pace of the ship's journey fit the needs of the playwright as he began to write his most introspective play. This particular style, not common to the American stage since it isn't filled with obvious physical action, was alien to many of the critics. Walter Kerr, in particular, reacted traditionally when he claimed that the play was "speculative rather than theatrical, an essay and an exercise when it might have been an experience."[20] In spite of Kerr's criticism, Albee went on to develop the introspective technique further until he completely broke from theatrical narrative in *Box-Mao-Box.*

Mom and Pop begin *A Delicate Balance* in "the living room of a large and well-appointed suburban house." The couple, it will be remembered, started their careers as typically middle-class, later moved on to the university as intellectuals, and have now become well-to-do as they prepare for retirement. Placing Mom and Pop in the privileged class at the end of their lives is quite correct, because it is the symbolic end—the fitting reward for the dedicated American life. The American dream has come true; Mom and Pop have enough money now to isolate themselves from people and avoid any commitment to society. At one point in the play, Mom (Agnes) remarks, "I have reached an age, Tobias, when I wish we were always alone, you and I, without . . . hangers-on . . . or anyone." We find the two, self-isolated at the beginning of the play, as Agnes speaks to her husband, having quietly contemplated the possibility of going mad:

AGNES: . . . that it is not beyond . . . happening; some gentle loosening of the moorings sending the balloon adrift.

There is a death wish in her thought of insanity. Not verbalized yet, it's subliminally in her very description of madness. A recent movie, *Charlie Bubbles,* commenting on our society today, used the same imagery to suggest the death or suicide of its hero. At the end of the film, Charlie, totally alienated from his society and unable to live alone, performs the ultimate retreat from life as he steps into a balloon and sails out of this world.

Death is not a new concern in Albee's writing. *The Zoo Story* states that only at the supreme moment of death is there any human contact. *The Sandbox* and *The American*

Dream are noticeably concerned with the death and removal of grandma from the American home. The title of *The Death of Bessie Smith* speaks for itself. *Virginia Woolf* builds to the death of the imaginary child which symbolizes the demise of all illusions. Finally, *Tiny Alice* examines the death and subsequent martyrdom of a lay brother. This ever-present concern with death is continued in *A Delicate Balance* and is instrumental to the deepest meanings of the play.

Agnes is reassured by Tobias (Pop) that "there is no saner woman on earth," but unwilling to reciprocate her husband's support, she replies in her typically emasculating way that she "could never do it—go—adrift—for what would become of you?" Once again, as in all the past plays, Pop is reminded of his ineffectualness and total reliance on Mom. Presumably his life would disintegrate should Mom suddenly expire. Agnes continues her preoccupation with insanity, admitting now that thoughts of old age motivate her:

> AGNES: Yes; Agnes Sit-by-the-fire, her mouth full of ribbons, her mind aloft, adrift, nothing to do with the poor old thing but put her in a bin somewhere, sell the house, move to Tucson, say, and pine in the good sun, and live to be a hundred and four.

Ironically, in an earlier version of Mom, notably *The Sandbox,* she put her mother in a bin to die—which grandma promptly did. Agnes now wonders when it will be her turn to inherit the fate of our senior citizens. Tobias, too, is aware of his coming old age for he says a moment later, "I'm not as young as either of us once was." Agnes, still unnerved over her future, asks Tobias to tell her what he'd do if she really did go insane:

> TOBIAS: (*Shrugs*) Put you in a bin somewhere, sell the house and move to Tucson. Pine in the hot sun and live forever.

AGNES: (*Ponders it*) Hmmmm, I bet you would.
TOBIAS: (*Friendly*) Hurry, though.

Tobias is presumably joking, but under the friendly kidding is the same hatred that made George pull out a phony rifle in *Virginia Woolf* and shoot Martha. Agnes, somewhat taken aback by Tobias's admission that her senility and eventual death would not disturb him in the least, retaliates by assuring him that the perpetual blandness of her emotions would never lead to the psychological disintegration of insanity. She says, "I can't even raise my voice except in the most calamitous of events." Actually she makes the case for eventual psychosis even stronger by admitting that her personality doesn't allow her to respond normally to most events that circumscribe her life. She begins to consider various chemical ways to induce psychosis, and there is a hint that she would like to try LSD or its narcotic equivalent to induce the excitement needed to bring about a drastic change in her day-to-day boredom. She quickly gives up this idea of chemical madness when she realizes it isn't permanent:

AGNES: Ah, but those are temporary; even addiction is a repeated temporary . . . stilling. I am concerned with peace . . . not mere relief.

Here, Agnes unconsciously wishes for death, the permanent peace, because it has begun now "to mean freedom from the acquired load and burden of the irrational."[21] Still unable to rid her mind of its chronological inheritance, she resumes describing the dreary picture of their remaining years:

AGNES: You have hope, of growing even older than you are in the company of your steady wife, your alcoholic sister-in-law and occasional visits . . . from our melancholy Julia. (*A little sad*) That is what you have, my dear Tobias. Will it do?
TOBIAS: (*A little sad, too, but warmth*) It will do.

143

Ted Hoffman, reviewing for New York radio station WINS, was completely correct when he realized that so much of *A Delicate Balance* "deals with the loneliness and corrosion of growing old."[22] This theme, introduced early in the play, propels the play's action and is directly related to its resolution.

This first section of the play ends as Claire, Agnes's alcoholic sister, enters and apologizes for her somewhat inebriated condition. She nevertheless accuses her sister of mistreating her because she is a drunk. Agnes defends herself in a way that Albee's heroine has never done, foreshadowing the change that will take place in her by the time the play ends:

> AGNES: . . . If I scold, it is because I wish I needn"t. If I am sharp, it is because I am neither less nor more than human. . . .

Only in this play does Mom apologize for her unpleasantness. This gnawing self-awareness later becomes a factor in her surprising decision to step down, at the end of the play, and relinquish her long-held role as head of the family. She leaves Claire and Tobias together in order to call her daughter Julia who is far enough away from her mother to effect a time differential of three hours. No sooner has Agnes left the living room than Claire asks Tobias why he doesn't kill Agnes. Tobias replies "Oh, no, I couldn't do that," intimating that he doesn't have the guts for an act of bloody passion.

Albee uses Claire periodically as a quasi-narrator, sardonically commenting on the action. I find this practice unnecessary and her peripheral position alienating and at odds with the otherwise tight entanglement of his characters. One illustration of this annoying practice should be sufficient. When, in the midst of family crises, father, mother, daughter, and audience became deeply involved with the situation at hand, Albee breaks this involvement and, using Claire, gets cute:

CLAIRE: (*To* TOBIAS, *laughing*) Crisis sure brings out the best in us, don't it, Tobe? The family circle? Julia standing there . . . *asserting*; perpetual brat, and maybe ready to pull a Claire. *And* poor Claire! Not much help there either, is there? And lookit Agnes, talky Agnes, ruler of the roost, and Maitre d', *and* licensed wife—silent. All cozy, coffee, thinking of the menu for the week, *planning*. Poor Tobe.

Ostensibly, Claire's monologue is supposed to alienate the audience, in the Brechtian sense, by describing the moment while it's happening. Claire, in giving us information that is not necessary to the plot, serves no purpose other than to hold up the action while the viewer is jolted out of his empathy. Albee has used the aside as far back as *The Sandbox,* where Grandma talked to the audience and commented on the action. He used it again to less advantage in *Everything in the Garden,* but in these examples the aside was presentational in that the characters talked directly to the audience. It is clear now that Albee's periodic experiments with presentational speeches was a long-time predisposition, which eventually found its form in the later *Box-Mao-Box.* However, *A Delicate Balance* is structured representationally and periodic comments on the action from the sidelines does not work well in a post-Ibsen play.

Claire does serve another purpose, and it is here that her presence is effective. Claire tells the truth. She sees (clairvoyant) and tells it like it is. Perhaps this is why she drinks. She cannot cope with what she perceives and rather than kill herself or go insane, she drinks. When she isn't commenting sarcastically on the action, her propensity for the truth prods the characters on toward the play's resolution. The first truth emerges when Claire forces Tobias, now retired, to examine the genuineness and durability of his past business friendships.

145 |

CLAIRE: . . . With your business friends, your indistinguishable if not necessarily similar friends . . . what did you have in common with them?

TOBIAS: Well, uh . . . well, everything. (*Maybe slightly on the defensive, but more vague*) Our business; we all mixed well, were friends away from the office, too . . . clubs, our . . . an, an environment, I guess.

CLAIRE: Unh-huh. But what did you have in common with them?

Claire asks the question twice more, but all Tobias can answer is "please, Claire." Claire's insistence serves two purposes: first, it reveals the relative superficiality of most friendships because Tobias cannot think of one thing he has had in common with his friends except proximity. An eminent sociologist came to the same conclusion when he noted that "Americans change both residence and job with the greatest of ease; and with each change of either, friends are changed, too."[23] Second, this brief revelation foreshadows and prepares the audience for the final tragic event concerning Tobias's closest friends.

Claire has made her point and is soon on to a new subject. She asks Tobias why he's switching from anisette to brandy. Tobias replies that the effects of anisette don't last as long. We realize that quiet, well-mannered Tobias looks to escape his surroundings by dulling his mind and memory for as long as possible. It is interesting to note that while Claire is said to be the alcoholic, Tobias drinks as often and as much as she does. Tobias is not off the hook though, because Claire will not let him forget. Reminding him of the time he was unfaithful to Agnes, she builds more evidence to dispel the image of tranquil, thoughtful Tobias, happily spending the final years of his life as the devoted, loving husband.

Claire then lies on the floor, arms outstretched in what Albee calls "a casual invitation." Tobias only moves away;

he is not interested. Later we find out that he's not sexually interested in his wife either. Years of constant emasculation have debilitated his sex drive until he is now like George in *Virginia Woolf:* impotent.

Impotency in Dad is a recurring theme in Albee's plays. We first hear of it in *The American Dream* (though Mommy and Daddy have no children in *The Sandbox*) when Mommy refers to Daddy's impotency as a result of a recent operation. The theme again appears in *Virginia Woolf* if we consider the inability of George and Martha to have a child. Impotency suggests loss of manliness as well as depletion of physical strength—both characteristic of the American daddy, according to Albee. It also implies sterility or the inability to produce a new generation. We do not create anything new; we only perpetuate the old. At one point in the play Agnes corroborates this indictment. Talking about her only daughter she admits: "We see ourselves repeated by those we bring into it all. . . ." At another moment Claire makes the same observation when she says: "We can't have changes—throws the balance off."

Claire's remark also clarifies the title of the play, which is meant to mean the delicate balance of the *status quo,* whether it be in reference to an existing relationship within the family, a friendship outside, or the general state of affairs within the country or, for that matter, the world. Each and every relationship hangs in the balance of time, doggedly resistant to change. This difficulty of change within our lives is dramatically depicted as the play progresses, developing into the major theme of its denouement.

Unwilling to recognize Claire's open invitation to have sex with her, Tobias changes the subject, confessing that he can't remember the last time he saw his wife cry, "no matter what," indicating she is as dried up emotionally as he is sexually. Tobias asks Claire why Alcoholics Anonymous never helped her. She replies, in a rather descriptive monologue, that she could not accept a belief in God—the first tenet of the organization. Besides, she doesn't admit to being an alcoholic. Agnes re-enters and stuns Tobias with the news that their daughter, Julia, is coming home after the dissolution of her fourth marriage. Apparently everyone has been aware that the breakup was coming, except Tobias. He offers to talk to his son-in-law in an effort to save the marriage, which seems, from Agnes's reaction, to be a new role for her husband:

> AGNES: (*As if the opposite were expected from her*) I wish you would! If you had talked to Tom, or Charlie, yes! even Charlie, or . . . uh. . . .
> CLAIRE: Phil?
> AGNES: (*No recognition of* CLAIRE *helping her*) . . . Phil, it might have done some good. If you've decided to assert yourself, finally, too late, I imagine. . . .

This sudden turnabout for Tobias is structurally important because it represents the first manifestation of an inner crisis that will grow during the course of the play, finally forcing Tobias to act contrary to his nature, in a last-ditch attempt to hold together his fast disintegrating ego. Agnes's remark, "too late, I imagine," foreshadows the tragic failure of his attempt.

Claire breaks in and alters the mood temporarily by singing a little ditty about Julia's ex-husbands, which is Albee's way of reintroducing the death theme. This time it is to inform us of the death of four marriages, the stigma of which, Julia carries with her:

> CLAIRE: (*A mocking sing-song*)
>   Philip loved to gamble.
>   Charlie loved the boys.
>   Tom went after women,
>   Douglas. . . .

It seems that Julia has a knack for picking marriage partners who must fail her. Unconsciously she doesn't want these marriages to work because she needs a reason to return home to the protection of her parents and to resume the old parent-child relationship. Whatever happened over the years, we can only know that Julia feels deprived of something in that relationship and keeps coming back to get it. Agnes reinforces Julia's neurosis by taking her back into the house and allowing her to resume the mother-daughter premarital kinship because it gives her the illusion she is still young enough to have an unmarried daughter.

Cued by Julia's homecoming, Tobias obliquely gives us the needed information about Julia's years at home. He does this by confessing to a rather pathetic and apparently unrelated incident in his past. It seems that for many years before his marriage to Agnes, he and a pet cat enjoyed a mutual affection. One day Tobias realized that his pet cat no longer liked him; it would not come to him when called, and retreated whenever he approached. The cat's unexplainable rejection made Tobias all the more anxious to win back his pet's love. Finally, after many overtures, in desperation and utter frustration, he shook the cat violently yelling, "Damn you, you like me; God damn it, you stop this! I haven't *done* anything to you." Frightened at the outburst, the cat bit him, and Tobias, in retaliation, viciously smacked it. Tobias describes the outcome:

> TOBIAS: . . . She and I had lived together and been, well, you know, friends, and . . . there was no *reason*. And I hated her, well, I suppose because I was being accused of something, of . . . failing. But I hadn't been cruel by design; if I'd been neglectful well, my life was . . . I resented it. I resented having a . . . being judged. Being betrayed.
>
> CLAIRE: What did you do?
>
> TOBIAS: I had *lived* with her; I had done . . . *every-*

149 |

thing. And . . . and if there was a, any responsibility I'd failed in . . . well . . . there was nothing I could do. And, and I was being accused

CLAIRE: Yes; what did you do?

TOBIAS: (*Defiance and self-loathing*) I had her killed.

Almost every critic referred to the "cat story." It is obviously Albee at his best. The critics likened it to the dog monologue in *The Zoo Story,* maintaining that the telling of it meant more than the unfortunate experience of one man and an animal. Henry Hewes thought it meant that Albee was trying to puncture the myth that "people who are sufficiently happy together and are enough in love to get married will forever remain in love."[24] Other reviewers thought the account was a lesson on friendship and tied the monologue to what they thought was the major point of the play. This is not at all the case. What Albee wanted, in having Tobias relate the tale, was to have the audience realize Tobias's sense of failure as a father. The thought is so unbearable that he is unable to confess it directly. The narrative implies that like the cat, Julia once loved and related to her father and that despite his attempt to provide a home for his daughter, she inexplicably withdrew from him until they now no longer communicate. The last thing Tobias says before he begins the cat story concerns his failure to relate to her. Filled with anxiety, he reneges on his earlier offer to talk to his daughter about reconsidering the dissolution of her marriage:

TOBIAS: (*Not rising from his chair, talks more or less to himself*) If I saw some point to it, I might—if I saw some reason, chance. If I thought I might . . . break through to her, and say, "Julia . . .," but then what would I say? "Julia . . .," then nothing.

Tobias blames himself for his failing relationship with his daughter and her resulting inability to develop a satisfactory and durable relationship with a man. The results of his ineffectualness are all around him. Guilt ridden because of his failure as husband and father, he privately yearns for change.

Unexpectedly, the scene is interrupted by the arrival of Harry and Edna, their closest friends. At first the call seems nothing more than the routine visit of lifetime friends, but after ignoring a question put to them four times, the family begins to sense that something is terribly wrong. Finally, after a little prodding from Claire, Harry and Edna tell their story:

> HARRY: (*Looks at* EDNA) I . . . I don't know quite what happened then; we . . . we were . . . it was all very quiet, and we were all alone. (EDNA *begins to weep, quietly;* AGNES *notices, the others do not,* AGNES *does nothing*) . . . and then . . . nothing happened, but . . .
>
> EDNA: (*Open weeping; loud*) WE GOT FRIGHTENED. (*Open sobbing; no one moves*)
>
> HARRY: (*Quiet wonder, confusion*) We got scared.
>
> EDNA: (*Through her sobbing*) WE WERE . . . FRIGHTENED.
>
> HARRY: There was nothing . . . but we were scared.
>
> AGNES: (*Comforts* EDNA, *who is in free sobbing anguish,* CLAIRE *lies slowly back on the floor*)
>
> EDNA: We . . . were . . . terrified.
>
> HARRY: We were scared. (*Silence;* AGNES *comforting* EDNA. HARRY *stock still. Quiet innocent, almost childlike*) It was like being lost; very young again, with the dark, and lost. There was no . . . thing . . . to be . . . frightened of, but . . .
>
> EDNA: (*Tears, quiet hysteria*) WE WERE FRIGHTENED . . . AND THERE WAS NOTHING. (*Silence in the room*)

Harry and Edna then ask if they may lie down in one of the bedrooms because they are too fearful to return home. Agnes admits them to Julia's room as Claire, in her clairvoyant role, predicts that something ominous is about to happen. Not until the next day, after Julia has come home, do Harry and Edna reveal just what it is they are up to. They have decided (without consulting Agnes or Tobias but in the name of friendship) to move into the house and live in Julia's bedroom; the thought of living alone another day is too terrifying for them. Julia hysterically screams that they have no right and demands that they leave. Harry and Edna refuse, and Julia looks to her parents to throw them out.

Much has been written about Harry and Edna and much has been suggested. In fact most of the adverse criticism has centered around who and what these people represent. Perhaps the most misguided interpretation of the intruders was that they are a questionable plot device to initiate conflict between Mom, Dad, and their daughter. The reviewer felt that the play concerned "the difficulty rich, emotionally immobilized parents faced with a daughter who at 36 is still an adolescent."[25] It is, of course, true that Agnes and Tobias are affluent and emotionally alien to the events in their lives, and that Julia is immature, but this situation is only a result and not the core of a much larger issue still to be resolved.

While most critics did not try to explain what it was the couple feared or why this fear had come about—even though the death imagery is quite clear in Harry's description of being "very young again, with the dark, and lost"—they did complain that the fear was not transferred to the audience. Walter Kerr, in an article printed after his review of the play, explained that Albee only talked about fear; he never showed it. He then went on to cite Harold Pinter as an example of a playwright who can frighten his audience without using the word fear.[26] Kerr, however, has missed the point concerning the frightened couple. It was not Albee's intention to put his audience into moral trepidation. All he wanted to do by introducing Harry and Edna was to exhibit two people traumatized by the sudden realization that death was not only a certainty, but close by. Psychologists would agree that fear of being lost in the dark is a symbolic death fear and that this "belief in one's death is an acquired and usually a late belief."[27] With the realization that most of their life is over (Edna specifically mentions it), it is natural that their thoughts should turn to wondering how much time there is left and whether they have wasted what time has already been given them. Relating the story of their sudden and inexplicable fright leads Harry to sum up his life with Edna:

> HARRY: (*Subdued, almost apologetic*) Edna and I . . . there's so . . . much . . . over the dam, so many . . . disappointments, evasions, I guess, lies maybe . . . so much we remember we wanted, once . . . so little that we've settled for . . . we talk, sometimes, but mostly . . . no . . .

Harry looks into his memory and finds little, almost nothing, to comfort them in their mature years, underscoring the fact that both continually mention that "nothing" was there when they became frightened. Clurman described Harry and Edna's state very well when he wrote that there is "no past to sustain them or future to which they aspire. . . . It is as if they were survivors of some devastation of the moral order. . . . They hardly know to what universe or society they belong, the old having been so decimated that their memory apart from ache and disgust has become fragmentary, leaving them without sufficient energy to reconstruct anything new."[28] Clurman's vivid description points up rather clearly how completely alienated Harry and Edna are. They have no past, no forseeable future, and almost nothing in their present to hang on to except friendship with Agnes and Tobias.

It is precisely this sense of "nothingness" that terrifies them. Erich Fromm recently wrote that "the alienated person . . . is lacking in a sense of self. This lack of self creates deep anxiety. The anxiety engendered by confronting him with the abyss of *nothingness,* [italics mine] is more terrifying than even the tortures of hell."[29] Fromm also mentions the way friendships are created in this country: "It is only another aspect of the alienated kind of interpersonal relationship that friendships are not formed on the basis of individual liking or attraction, but that they are determined by the location of one's own house or apartment in relation to the others."[30]

Harry and Edna, in the throes of personal anguish, try in the only way they know to refute their sense of nothingness, of alienation. They demand that Tobias and Agnes become more than superficial in their friendship to them. They try, in their demand for sanctuary, to refute the neutralness of the relationship by forcing it to take on more meaning than it has. Fromm again underscores Harry and Edna's feelings when he writes "there is not much love or hate to be found in human relationships of our day. There is, rather, a superficial friendliness and a more than superficial fairness, but behind that surface is distance and indifference."[31]

Albee's concern with modern man's sense of isolation and abandonment led him first to examine the possible truth of the Nietzschean "God is Dead" theory in *Tiny Alice.* Now, in *A Delicate Balance* he has dropped the metaphysical probings and returned to a more sociological explanation, which seems to assert that it is the death of friendship that produces these feelings of alienation. Evidence of this theme grows as it becomes clear that the weekend's episode has wrecked what superficial relationship the two couples had:

EDNA: I'm going into town on Thursday, Agnes. Would you like to come? (*A longer pause than neces-*

sary, CLAIRE *and* JULIA *look at* AGNES)

AGNES: (*Just a trifle awkward*) Well . . . no, I don't think so, Edna; I've . . . I've so much to do.

EDNA: (*Cooler; sad*) Oh. Well . . . perhaps another week.

AGNES: Oh, yes; we'll do it.

Edna tries pitifully to hold on to the severed friendship, but it's dead. The image of death, which has permeated this play from its first act until its conclusion, is reflected again in the final destruction of the forty-year friendship.

Perhaps the most devastating criticism of Harry and Edna concerned the diffusion of focus the interlopers caused. Evidently the strangeness of the couple's undisclosed fear and their apparent vulnerability to it, plus the outright daring of their demand to the right to disrupt another's privacy in the name of friendship, created a most impelling effect on the critics. Many felt that instead of remaining peripheral characters designed to upset the delicate balance of "the family armed truce,"[32] they took hold and pushed the protagonists right out of focus. Harry and Edna suddenly became the characters to write about, and the critics began tactfully suggesting that Albee rewrite his play because "those two people who are afraid of their own house are worth a play."[33] Norman Nadel was the most articulate in his analysis of the intruders:

> And this becomes the element of the play we **want** to know most about. We all have known the nameless fears, the terrors without shape or identity, that unexpectedly invade our lives. Yet only obliquely does Albee return to that theme. Fear is never even the tangible presence in the play that it should be. . . . The drama's insights impinge on this element of fear, without ever quite penetrating it. . . . And therein lies its weakness.[34]

Nadel's analysis presupposes that Albee was most concerned with writing a play that explored the nature of fear.

If this were the case, there would be justification to his critique. Albee, however, uses fear as a by-product of other
issues. As we have seen, he is most concerned with the rami-
fications of growing old in an alienated world. Agnes and
Tobias should easily keep the audience's interest because
their friends' demands have created enough of a turmoil
within the household to jolt these two out of their emotional
cocoons. The family crisis that takes place should be com-
pelling enough to keep even Harry and Edna in their place
as catalysts.

Tobias believes Harry and Edna are right when they say
he must allow them to remain or admit that a forty-year
friendship is meaningless and symbolic of his entire life. Yet
Tobias is not used to making decisions; he has always de-
ferred to Agnes. But this time Agnes will not accommodate
him. Why she suddenly abandons her role as "ruler of the
roost" is not at first clear. Perhaps she has finally seen a
glimpse, a reflection, of her aliented life with Tobias as she
watches her friends attempting to fill the "nothingness" in
their lives. Edna does say to her, "Our lives are . . . the
same." As she realizes that her marriage is much the same as
her friends, it is conceivable that she will try to change it by
forcing Tobias to assume a role he long ago abdicated. If she
can get him to commit himself to accepting his traditional
place as head of the household, this reaffirmation of the
historical role might alter the present course of their lives
and close the chasm that has isolated one from the other. She
attempts the change:

> AGNES: (*Quiet, calm and almost smug*) We follow.
> We let our . . . men decide the moral issues.
> TOBIAS: (*Quite angry*) Never! You've never done
> that in your life!
> AGNES: Always, my darling. Whatever you decide . . .
> I'll make it work; I'll run it for you so you'll never know
> there's' been a change in anything.

Tobias does not feel that it's necessary for him to make the decision. He tries again to resume the old relationship, maintaining it is Agnes's place to admit Harry and Edna. He asks her again to make the choice:

> TOBIAS: (*Quiet, rhetorical*) What are we going to do?
> AGNES: What did you decide?
> TOBIAS: (*Pause; they smile*) Nothing.
> AGNES: Well, you must. Your house is not in order, sir. It's full to bursting.
> TOBIAS: Yes. You've got to help me.
> AGNES: No. I don't *think* so.

Tobias is upset now; he wants an explanation for his wife's contrary behavior. Agnes tries to explain. In the ensuing dialogue her reasons for stepping down become clearer. We find out that she is convinced the marriage is a failure. Apparently she spent the night reviewing her life, for she approaches the subject by first telling Tobias that what she has to tell him stems from having "revisited our life, the years and years."

This is an important moment for Agnes and Tobias. In the early plays Mom was perfectly content to be king of the mountain. As a matter of fact she wouldn't have it any other way. She did all she could to insure her continued domination of the household—even if it meant the destruction of Dad's identity. In *Virginia Woolf*, Mom is still content to let everybody who'll listen know that Daddy is a "bog" incapable of accomplishing anything worthwhile. Only at the end does she submit to him at all, but we wonder if it occurs simply out of sheer exhaustion. This is an historic moment for Mom, because only in *A Delicate Balance* does she actively attempt to return the family unit to what it originally was —and only after a total re-examination of her history with Dad. It has taken Albee seven plays and two adaptations to allow Mom to come to the conclusion that her life with Dad is empty. Unfortunately, as we shall see, the decision to change has come too late for Mom. For the moment though, Agnes is unaware that her historic change of heart will be in vain. She again attempts the reversal of roles by a recapitulation of their lives, starting first with remembrances of Julia:

AGNES: Each time that Julia comes, each clockwork time . . . do you send her back? Do you tell her, "Julia, go home to your husband, try again?" Do you? No, you let it . . . slip. It's your decision, sir.

TOBIAS: It is not! I . . .

AGNES: . . . and I must live with it, resign myself one marriage more, and wait, and hope that Julia's motherhood will come . . . one day, one marriage (*Tiny laugh*) I am almost too old to be a grandmother as I'd hoped . . . too young to be one. Oh, I had wanted that: the *youngest* older woman in the block, *Julia* is almost too old to have a child properly, *will* be if she ever does . . . if she marries again. *You* could have pushed her back . . . if you'd wanted to.

It is here that Agnes tries to show Tobias that the emptiness of their lives is symbolized in the discontinuance of the family line. She tries to explain that Tobias never wanted to see himself perpetuated in his grandchildren—that he is the one who all these years has chosen isolation and sterility as the symbols of their life together. Tobias's refusal to accept the blame forces Agnes to turn to a more brutal example of his wish to kill any chances of living on through a son. The death motif that hovers over this play emerges once again:

AGNES: (*Remorseless*) When Teddy died? (*Pause*) We *could* have had another son; we could have tried. But . . . No . . . those months—or was it a year—?

TOBIAS: No more of this!

AGNES: . . . I think it was a year, when you spilled on my belly, sir? "Please? Please, Tobias?" No, you wouldn"t even say it out: I don't want another child, another loss. "Please; Please, Tobias?" And guiding you, *trying* to hold you in?

TOBIAS: (*Tortured*) Oh, Agnes! Please!

AGNES: Don"t leave me then, like that. Not again, Tobias. Please? I can take care of it; we *won't* have another child, but please don't . . . leave me like that. . . . Such . . . silent . . . sad, disgusted . . . love.

It is clear now that it was Tobias who first removed himself from the intimacies of marriage. Tobias may have felt he could not bring himself to risk another loss, but it may be more realistic to assume that his self-evaluation would not allow his seed to be continued into the next generation. Tobias on his own accord withdrew from the responsibilities of a father and husband, content to let Agnes take his place. Agnes pleads for him to return to her as she plays out her part in the evolution of the American family unit. One glimpse at a standard source book in sociology corroborates her predicament:

> American mothers stepped into the role of the grand-fathers [sic] as the fathers abdicated their dominant place in the family, in the field of education, and in cultural life. The post-revolutionary descendants of the Founding Fathers forced their women to be mothers *and* fathers, while they continued to cultivate the role of freeborn sons.[35]

Unquestionably, it is the first time in an Albee play that the blame for whatever mess the American family is in, is placed with the father. Mom is not the usurper she was in the early plays; she has simply responded all these years out of a sense of duty, filling a position that has been vacated. Agnes even says to her husband, when she tries to define the woman's job in the home, that she "assumes whatever duties are demanded—if she is in love, or loves; and plans." And since she has always thought of herself as the "fulcrum" within the family, she will continuously adjust to wherever the new balance places her. Agnes continues her exposition, linking their present alienation to past sexual problems, implying that the isolation that now exists need not have occurred had he sought her help or at least confided in her:

TOBIAS: (*Numb*) I didn't want you to have to . . . you know.

AGNES: (*Laughs in spite of herself*) Oh, that was thoughtful of you! Like a pair of adolescents in a rented room, or in the family car. Doubtless you hated it as much as I.

TOBIAS: Yes.

AGNES: But wouldn't let me help you.

TABIAS: No.

AGNES: Which is why you took to your own sweet room instead.

TOBIAS: Yes.

It is interesting that while Agnes confesses to having "hated" sexual intercourse as much as he did, she earlier admitted to missing him when he left her bed: "I shall start missing you again—when you move from my room . . . if you do," she says. (They are temporarily together again because Tobias has given Julia his room while Harry and Edna remain in the house.) This seeming paradox is perhaps more widespread among "happily" married couples than might be expected. An internist, practicing in well-to-do suburbia, recently told me that the majority of his women patients, and to a lesser degree the men, ask him to write notes to their spouses requesting that for medical reasons they cease having intercourse. The reason given is that they are too tired to "accommodate" their mates. What doubly amazed me was that my friend felt this request was not symptomatic of any

serious neurosis, but an understandable, rather normal request, not at all indicating these couples no longer love each
other.

Agnes's talk of having been aware all these years of the
mutual revulsion each felt about the sex act shames Tobias
into asking just what she will do now that the truth is out.
Determined, however, to abandon her place as dominator,
she replies "Whatever you like, naturally."

Claire and Julia interrupt the colloquy but the topic continues. It is up to Tobias to make the final decision concerning Harry and Edna. Julia flatly states that she will leave the
house permanently unless the invading couple are put out.
Tobias, frustrated and in a rage, screams at his daughter that
"HARRY AND EDNA ARE OUR FRIENDS." Julia, undaunted, equals him with "THEY ARE INTRUDERS."
Tobias, very upset but still unable to commit himself to
standing by his friends without his family's support, tries to
make them realize that friendship based on any condition is
empty. Agnes responds, warning him that Harry and Edna
have brought with them a disease. The disease is terror and
if Tobias allows them to stay, the family is in danger of in-
fection. Nevertheless, it must be his decision alone. Finally
seeing that Agnes will no longer fight his battles, Tobias
summons his courage, and in the most stirring moment of
his life, he jars himself loose of old and ingrained ways by
telling Harry and Edna they may reside in his home for as
long as they wish whether his family likes it or not.

It is too late, however. The tumult within the family, the
momentous decision, were all for naught. Harry and Edna
have changed their minds. They realize now it is impossible
to alter forty years of pleasant indifference by force. Harry
feebly tries to apologize for his and Edna's presumption:

HARRY: . . . you're our best friends, but . . . I told
Edna upstairs, I said Edna, what if they'd come to us?

And she didn't say anything. And I said; Edna, if they'd come to us like this, and even though we don't have . . . Julia, and all that, I . . . Edna I wouldn't take them in. (*Brief silence*) I wouldn't take them in, Edna; they don't . . . have any right. And she said; yes, I know; they wouldn't have the right.

Tobias cannot accept Harry's realistic appraisal of their friendship and the vacuity it symbolizes; he is determined to take the interlopers in, in order to negate what both Harry and Agnes have intimated in their separate evaluations. In a three-page, orchestrated monologue, Tobias spills his guts out to Harry, first ordering him to stay, then begging him through tears of futility as he slowly realizes it is too late for any of them. A moment later Edna bleakly sums it all up:

EDNA: (*Pause. Slight smile*) It's sad to come to the end of it, isn't it, nearly the end; so much more of it gone by . . . than left, and still not know—still not have learned . . . the boundaries what we may not do . . . not ask, for fear of looking in a mirror. We *shouldn't* have come.

AGNES: (*A bit by rote*) Now, Edna . . .

EDNA: For our own sake; our own . . . lack. It's sad to know you've gone through it all, or most of it, without . . . that the one body you've wrapped your arms around . . . the only skin you've ever known . . . is your own—and that it's dry . . . and not warm.

Harry and Edna, like George and Martha, are childless and isolated. Whereas George and Martha had to create an imaginary child to appease their loneliness and in the end had to kill it and the illusion it carried, Harry and Edna, in their attempt to bring solace to the same feeling of alienation. create an imaginary depth in a life-long friendship that doesn't exist. At the end, as in *Virginia Woolf,* the illusion must be destroyed.

In talking about *A Delicate Balance,* Albee has said that it "is about the fact that as time keeps happening options grow less. Freedom of choice vanishes. One is left with an illusion of choice."[36] The experience has been as crushing for Tobias and Agnes. They too must live the remaining years without illusion. But their reality is somewhat different from learning that their closest friendship was at best superficial; what they learn is that there comes a time in every life when hope of change no longer exists. What they have made of their lives must now stand because it is too late for undoing. Tobias cannot change his skin. Even his impassioned plea to Harry is an indication not of strength but continued weakness because of its uncontrollable hysterics. Tobias a long time ago chose passivity; he must now accept its outcome.

It is interesting to read Harold Clurman's analysis of Tobias, based on his belief that the play had only to do with that "insuperable difficulty of loving one's neighbor."[37] He feels that the character of Tobias should have been played not as a little man but rather as an "outwardly imposing figure, a very 'senator' of a man, a pillar of our business community in whom the springs of sensibility have begun to dry through disuse. The welling up of his being in the play's crisis would then become more stirring and, what is more important, exemplary."[38] What Clurman has neglected to see, however, is that Tobias does not succeed in his attempt at rescuing his life from the quicksand of indifference. What is exemplary is not his sudden feelings of remorse for a life of aloofness, but his realization that despite his willingness to change, the patterns of his past are forever stamped in the anguished memories of a wasted life and in the knowledge that choice ceases to exist as we approach the termination of our lives. Tobias was, and must remain always, small. This theme is summed up rather movingly by Agnes at the end of the play:

AGNES: Time. (*Pause. They look at her*) Time happens, I suppose. (*Pause. They still look*) To people. Everything becomes . . . too late, finally. You know it's going on . . . up on the hill; you can see the dust, and hear the cries, and the steel . . . but you wait; and time happens. When you *do* go, sword, shield . . . finally . . . there's nothing there . . . save rust; bones; and the wind.

Despite the mixed reception *A Delicate Balance* received from the critics, on May 1, 1967, Albee was given the Pulitzer Prize. The next day he officially accepted the award, but remembering the controversy over the Pulitzer Advisory Board's decisions to overrule John Gassner and John Mason Brown when they proposed that Albee be given the prize for *Virginia Woolf,* he warned that it "is in danger of losing its position of honor and could foreseeably, cease to be an honor at all."[39] The following day, speaking at a news conference, he reiterated his feelings, listing exactly why he accepted the award:

> I have decided to accept the award for three reasons: First, because if I were to refuse it out of hand, I wouldn't feel as free to criticize it as I do accepting it. Second, because I don't wish to embarrass the other recipients this year by seeming to suggest that they follow my lead. And finally, because while the Pulitzer Prize is an honor in decline, it is still an honor, a considerable one.[40]

Originally underrated by the majority of New York critics, yet heralded by the Pulitzer Committee as the best play of the year, *A Delicate Balance* has shown Edward Albee at his most sympathetic, his most gentle. There is more delicateness and maturity in this play than any of his other works, and it will prevail "not only [as] a brilliant and searching play but [as] a strangely beautiful one."[41]

CHAPTER 9

ADAPTATIONS

THE FIRST of the three Albee adaptations is *The Ballad of the Sad Cafe,* based on Carson McCullers' novella of the same name. The play opened October 30, 1963, at the Martin Beck Theater to mixed reviews. Henry Hewes said: "This faithful, intelligent, and sensitive adaptation is the most fascinating and evocative piece of work by an American playwright . . . this season."[1] Martin Gottfried, however, called *Ballad* "a play of little theatre value."[2]

Notwithstanding the usual diversity of criticism a new Albee play engenders, most reviewers admitted that it was faithful to the novella with amazingly few changes in the story line. Notably, that the fight takes place out-of-doors instead of inside the cafe, and that the events of Amelia's short marriage to Marvin are not revealed to the viewer until somewhat later in the play than in the novella. To keep as close to the original prose as possible, Albee incorporated a narrator who, with minimal alterations, spoke the novella's lyrical passages. Originally, the playwright planned to use a tape recording of Carson McCullers speaking those passages, but the idea was dropped in favor of a narrator-stage manager as in *Our Town.*[3]

Much of the negative reaction to *Ballad* centered about Albee's decision to use a stage narrator. Most critics felt that his presence was alienating as well as undramatic. Walter Kerr, in particular emphasized that the novella's material, use of chorus, and incorporation of a narrator, all conspired to cause alienation.[4] In a later article he returned to the same point and said, "in the theatre we should not need hired guides."[5] Robert Brustein was even less diplomatic when he described the narrator as having only one function: "to provide the information which the author has been too lazy to dramatize."[6]

While I don't hold to the belief that use of narration

always constitutes undramatic playwrighting (we have only to look at Brecht), certain problems do arise from Albee's decision to use a narrator. Perhaps the most penetrating of these is the lack of motivation for the man to tell his story. As Albee has written it, we sense no impelling reason to listen to this grotesque love ballad. John McClain made a similar observation when he noted: "We don't, in fact, know very much about anybody in 'The Sad Cafe,' including the man who wanders through the proceedings, giving us only hints and suggestions."[7]

Miss McCullers clarifies the story for her reader early in the book by telling him what to expect. Albee, however, waits until page one hundred and sixteen before making the same point:

THE NARRATOR

> The time has come to speak about love. Now consider three people who were subject to that condition. Miss Amelia, Cousin Lymon, and Marvin Macy . . . Now, the beloved can also be of any description: the most outlandish people can be the stimulus for love. Yes, and the lover may see this as clearly as anyone else — but that does not affect the evolution of his love one whit. . . .

Thus we have had to watch most of this adaptation with no intermission, without knowing why the narrator has chosen to submit us to this unpleasant tale of freakish love. We feel dislocated from the material and unable to focus in on the play. Robert Brustein corroborated this reaction when he wrote: "Because of my unfamiliarity with dwarf-loving lesbians, [the play] was rather lost on me."[8] *Newsweek* too, wanted to "know why they behave as they do."[9] It is my contention that had Albee kept to the chronology of the novella, and not tried to build suspense by holding off thematic material until very near the end of the play, the critics would have reacted more favorably to the play's grotesqueness.

Still another reason for the narrator's inability to pull his audience into the play stems from a sociological condition less prevalent in the theatre today than when *Ballad* was first produced. As unflattering as it is to our sense of supposed sophistication, as little as five years ago the Broadway audience found it difficult to accept a Negro's omnipotence over the lives of white Southerners. They sat silent, feeling that Albee intended a sociological comment, which of course he did not.

The logical choice, it would seem, would have been to use Marvin's brother, Henry Macy, as the storyteller. Henry has a special interest in Amelia's story because it is his brother she marries. Having him step into the play and out of it, as character-narrator (much like *Our Town*) would have helped tie the two areas of the play together. Critic Whitney Bolton saw the connection between Wilder's stage manager and Albee's narrator:

> The function is all but identical . . . to describe the town, a building or buildings, the people, what happens in the town, how it came about, the state of the weather, to make commentary on events past and present. . . .[10]

Albee's narrator begins the play with an opening monologue that serves to describe the off-stage town as well as introduce Amelia to us, silently sitting at the window of her now boarded-up cafe. He takes us back eight years in time and begins the play's events:

THE NARRATOR

> . . . We are going back in time now, back even before the opening of the cafe, for there are two stories to be told: How the cafe came into being . . . for there was not always a cafe . . . and how the cafe . . . died. How we came to . . . silence.

The stage lights suggest evening, the boarded-up house once

169 |

again becomes a general store, and with the entrance of some townspeople, the dialogue begins.

Most of the talk centers about Miss Amelia's predilection for bootlegging liquor and initiating lawsuits. The only other piece of gossip we hear is that Henry Macy's brother, Marvin, is in the penitentiary. Amelia then enters, her large frame looking quite masculine in Levis and cotton work shirt. Hardly a page of conversation passes, when along the dusty road comes a hunchbacked dwarf, suitcase in hand. The dwarf declares he is "kin" to Miss Amelia and begs for shelter, offering a fuzzy photograph of his mother and half-sister as evidence that he and Amelia are, in some unexplained way, related. Never looking at the picture, Amelia contradicts her public personality and invites the little stranger in. He is not seen again for three days and rumor has it that she has murdered the ragged dwarf for whatever it was he carried in his suitcase. On the third night, determined to know what has happened to the hunchback, the townspeople congregate at Amelia's store. Just as they are about to confront her over the dwarf's disappearance, the little man makes a startlingly grand entrance:

> COUSIN LYMON descends the stairs, slowly one at a time—imperiously, like a great hostess. HE is no longer ragged; HE is clean; HE wears his little coat, but neat and mended, a red and black checkered shirt, knee breeches, black stockings, shoes laced up over the ankles, and a great lime green shawl, with fringe, which almost touches the ground. The effect is somehow regal . . . or papal. . . .

The dwarf's kingly bearing and mended clothes completely baffle the spectators into silence—broken only when the dwarf uncovers Amelia's treasured snuff-box and partakes of its contents. Eventually Lymon, whose name bears a striking resemblance to lemon and lime, confesses that the powder in the box is only sugar and cocoa because "the very teeth in my head have always tasted sour to me." The snuff-box, or rather the possession of it, anticipates Lymon's eventual reign over Amelia. It becomes his scepter, symbolically sweetening his life with power, and the barrel he is perched upon turns into his throne as he arrogantly holds court, interrogating his subjects. Two questions emerge as significant. Stumpy MacPhail is first asked if he's married and then if his wife is fat. Lymon apparently seeks to know what men are available, showing his hostility if he finds that a man is married. This sequence suggests Lymon's covert homosexuality which appears later in the pays as he unabashedly reveals his love and adulation for Marvin Macy. Even at this early juncture Albee describes him as "like a great hostess." Later clues to his womanliness will be discussed as we encounter them in the story sequence. Cousin Lymon's presence has undoubtedly changed Amelia's rather gruff disposition, for she now allows liquor to be drunk on the premises and even encourages it by giving out free crackers. Thus the transition from store to cafe is accomplished.

Four years pass and the cafe prospers, during which time Amelia and Lymon live together. The exact nature of their relationship is never fully clarified, but it appears to be asexual, again underscoring Lymon's latent homosexuality. During this interim Amelia appears happier than she's ever been, despite Lymon's growing petulence. Only when love is mentioned does she revert to her old self:

COUSIN LYMON: (*Quite coldly*) Oh, Amelia, I do love you so.

MISS AMELIA: (*With some awkward gesture, kicking the dirt off a boot maybe*) Humf! Those are words I don't wanna hear. (*Pause*) Understand?

The relationship between this giant-woman (according to McCullers she should stand six foot two) and her homunculus companion, later complicated by Marvin's return from the penitentiary, is explained by Albee and McCullers in a rather superficial way, part of which has already been quoted:

THE NARRATOR

Now, the beloved can also be of any description; the most outlandish people can be the stimplus for love. . . . Therefore, the quality and value of any love is determined solely by the lover himself. . . .

This rather vague rationale for the dynamics of this twisted triangle does not suffice for what the *Times* referred to as a relationship "perverse enough to qualify as a psychiatric case history."[11]

The asexuality of the Amelia-Lymon relationship, however, does not alter the possibility of connubial symbolism. Specifically Cousin Lymon finds a tiny velvet box hidden away by Amelia and demands to know what it contains. The box, he is informed, contains two small kidney stones which Amelia had removed years ago. Having grown within her and caused great pain at their removal, the little mementoes become the children Amelia and Lymon will never have. He asks for them as a present, and when Amelia agrees to his request, she symbolically gives him his progeny without betraying his burgeoning homosexuality.

Another interesting bit of symbolism concerns the little acorn Lymon pilfers from Amelia's curio cabinet. The cabinet, like the cafe, represents Amelia's soul — gratuitously opened whenever Lymon wants entrance. The acorn, picked the day her father died and kept all these years, is a wish to remain as little as the seed because "little" is the childhood endearment her father would always use to offset her large size. But the acorn, not having fulfilled its natural function, remains undeveloped, reminding Lymon of his dwarfishness. Once his curiosity is satisfied he refuses Amelia's offer to have it.

As the play progresses, Lymon begins to become bored

with Amelia, though she continues to try and entice him through extravagantly prepared meals. Professing no appetite, he nevertheless manages to finish what's given him—but not without assuring Amelia that he eats the fancy foods only as a favor to her. Lymon's refusal to return the love given to him by Amelia is exactly the relationship she prefers. She doesn't want her love reciprocated because then she must become responsible for someone else's emotional needs. Albee, faithful to McCullers' words, offers an explanation via the narrator:

> Therefore, the quality and value of any love is determined solely by the lover himself. It is for this reason that most of us would rather love than be loved; and the curt truth is that, in a deep secret way, the state of being beloved is intolerable to many; for the lover craves any possible relation with the beloved, even if this experience can cause them both only pain.

Amelia's story soon takes a new turn as Lymon learns of her short-lived marriage to Marvin Macy. Lymon forces Amelia to talk about "the most important fact of all in your whole life." Amelia's reluctant description of Marvin leaves the little man trembling with anticipation for the day they'll meet. Marvin soon becomes the very person whose masculinity will entice and encourage Lymon's personal fantasies. He loves the roustabout before he sees him because this hellion has the strength, the height, and the virility that Lymon can never attain. The attraction is ironically narcissistic because Marvin is really Lymon's dream of himself. There is also another aspect of Lymon's almost uncontrollable attraction to Marvin. Not having grown up with one father, Lymon continually looks for a father-substitute who will fill the emotional void this lack created. When Marvin facetiously suggests he adopt the hunchbacked dwarf, Lymon is ecstatic:

MARVIN MACY: You been followin' me around near a week now, wigglin' your ears at me, flappin'

173 |

around, dancin' . . . you don't go home 'cept for your eats an' bed. What you expectin' me to do . . . *adopt* you?

COUSIN LYMON: (*With exaggerated longing*) Oh, Marvin Macy . . . *would* you? Would you do that?

Cousin Lymon's homosexual predisposition is not as far-fetched as some critics would have us believe. Albee has already shown in several places that the midget behaves and flirts like a woman—not that effeminacy is necessarily indicative of homosexuality. There are other more substantial clues to Lymon's hidden pathological orientation. Certainly he harbors a deep-seated resentment toward his mother and hence women in general, because it was in a woman's body that he grew stunted and misshapen. Once born, he watched his mother take on two more husbands after leaving his own father. By the third husband, Lymon, too, packed his little satchel and went in search of more stable "kin." Ironically, Lymon must destroy the very person who has sheltered him because in her maternal manner, Amelia is too reminiscent of his mother. Even his opening line in the play, "Evening. I am hunting for Miss Amelia," suggests that she will be his prey.

Psychiatrist Lawrence J. Hatterer in listing some of the many underlying causes of homosexuality has included the "inability and failure to relate to women because of hostility, [or] . . . as a means of obtaining the absent or ideal father . . ., or to fulfill the need to identify with a strong male through possession of that male sexually."[12] He adds that "the core of the homosexual's attraction and choice is narcissistic."[13]

Lymon wants to know why Amelia hasn't told him about the marriage and Amelia's only answer is: "He run off; he run off years ago; I ain't married to him no more!" What Amelia doesn't tell Lymon is that Marvin ran off at the point of a gun. Why she married the ex-thief and rumored rapist in the first place, and then never consummated the marriage, is not directly explained in either the novella or the play. Even Albee was curious enough to ask Miss McCullers, only to receive a shrug and with it the enigmatic answer: "That is what she would do."[14]

Yet, after reading both the novella and the play, enough facets of her personality emerge to explain her behavior adequately. Unfortunately, the answers are not clear in the play alone, and the reader must go back to the novella for clarification. Nevertheless, we can gather from information in both works that Amelia obviously married Marvin because she wanted a husband. What she didn't bargain for was Marvin's natural inclination for sex. Her fear of having children, because her own mother died in childbirth, would not allow her to take the chance that family history would repeat itself. Marvin's incontinence panicked Amelia and she finally had to drive him from her or face her sexual phobia. Replacing Marvin with Lymon gave Amelia the opportunity to be the subservient wife without the threat of coitus. This asexual arrangement is perfectly acceptable to Lymon because his seeming conquest of Amelia gives him stature (she is taller than most men) without disturbing his homosexual orientation. In addition, Amelia could not reconcile herself to a life with Marvin because she bears too much resentment toward her father for being indirectly responsible for her mother's death. The more virile and masculine a man is, the more she is reminded of what killed her mother. Still, Amelia needs an object upon which to bestow her pent-up love, and the most appropriate recipient is the hunchback, Lymon; he is more feminine than masculine and offers no sexual threat to Amelia. Albee periodically refers to him as "Stirring, shy and coy, almost like a young girl."

Though Marvin is first repulsed by this "brokeback," Lymon is not deterred. The stunted cripple is willing to enslave himself to this symbol of masculinity in return for the privilege of remaining in his company. Marvin, seeing a way to get into the cafe—which he considers half his—allows the dwarf to befriend him. It isn't long before Marvin's plan is put into action when Lymon invites him to the cafe as his personal guest. In an ironic twist, Lymon begins to serve Marvin as Amelia had earlier served the hunchback. Marvin returns to the cafe night after night, drinking without ever paying, as Amelia, almost resigned to her fate, says nothing. Within a short time, Lymon arranges for Marvin to move into the cafe, giving the ex-husband Amelia's father's bed. Afraid of losing the dwarf, Amelia acquiesces to the arrangement:

> COUSIN LYMON: Amelia! (*She turns her sad attention to him*) Amelia, I think I told you Marvin is gonna live here with us.
> MISS AMELIA: (*Surprisingly helpless before his tone*) But . . . but, Cousin Lymon . . .
> COUSIN LYMON (*Giving orders, but taking a childish pleasure in the power of it*) Marvin Macy will sleep in your Papa's big bed, an' we will move what you have referred to as my coffin—my tiny bed—into your room . . . an' you . . . (*He pauses here for full effect*) . . . an' you, Amelia . . . well, you can pull up a mattress, an' sleep by the stove down here.

Albee's decision to put Amelia on a mattress by the stove, relegated to the status of family pet, is too degrading for her to accept. Being thrown out of her room is harsh enough. In the novella, Carson McCullers has Amelia sleep on the parlor sofa which softens the humiliation a bit. Her willingness to accept the degradation of the Albee version, is not in keeping with the personality of the woman who is about to fight with Marvin over who is to control the cafe.

The thought of the fight sends Lymon into spasms of ecstasy because in his mind they are fighting over him.

Lymon tells Marvin, while the big man greases his body in preparation for the fight, to "be real slippery so she can't get a good grip on you." The advice could easily mean that previously she had had a good grip on the ex-convict—enough to emasculate and humiliate him in front of the town. One interesting aspect of this rather disgusting fight is that Marvin is not capable of winning without Lymon's help. When it looks as if Amelia might win, Lymon jumps on her back and hangs on, choking her. It is enough to turn the tide, and Marvin regains his position, beating Amelia into unconsciousness. Symbolically, it is Lymon—because of Amelia's love for him—who effects Amelia's destruction. The narrator then sums up the play's final moments:

THE NARRATOR

(*Tableau, with* MARVIN MACY, COUSIN LYMON *together,* MISS AMELIA *sprawled on the porch*) Marvin Macy and Cousin Lymon left town that night, but before they went away, they did their best to wreck the store. They took what money there was in the cafe, and the few curios and pieces of jewelry Miss Amelia kept upstairs; and they carved vile words on the cafe tables. After they had done all these . . . they left town . . . together.

Deciding not to take over the cafe, the two men depart, never to be heard from again. Amelia, in a final moment strangely reminiscent of Lavinia in O'Neill's *Morning Becomes Electra,* retreats into the house to spend the rest of her life in despair and isolation.

What is perhaps the most surprising aspect of *Ballad* is its similarity to still another play: Sartre's *No Exit*[15]. Both plays reveal the dynamics of unfulfilled love. In the Sartre play, three rather despicable people are placed together in one room. They have been picked by the powers in control (it seems they have died and are now residing in hell) to clash psychologically with one another until the room becomes hell to live in. What kind of human triangle produces psychological hell? Sartre, puts a lesbian in with a whore who can't stomach her and seeks, instead, the solace of a man who is repulsed by her promiscuity and looks to the lesbian as a symbol of masculine triumph. *Ballad* offers much the same situation. Amelia is in love with Lymon, who rejects her in favor of Marvin. Marvin is not interested in the dwarf except to use him as a means to getting at Amelia who continues to rebuff him. Walter Kerr noticed the sado-masochistic libidinal linking and analyzed the trio's interaction: "It is clear...that each of these figures is destroyed by the one he loves. . . ."[16] An interesting note to the comparison of the two plays is that Colleen Dewhurst was chosen for the part of Amelia after being seen in a television showing of Sartre's *No Exit,* where she played the lesbian.[17]

The Sartre play works because the group is put together as punishment for certain crimes committed against society. It doesn't make any difference how personally repugnant they are; we do not have to empathize with them in order to react positively to their retribution. *Ballad,* however, creates the same hellish situation (even to its constant reference to heat) when it should have created an environment filled with compassion. The proximity of the play's characters and situation repel us, where the novella's lyric distance intrigues us. *Newsweek's* critic talked of basically the same thing when he commented that the play "is clothed in the too, too solid flesh of living actors, [making] these phantasmal beings lose the unreality that made them real."[18]

In the last analysis, the events of *Ballad* do not stand up to the intriguing concept that initiated the work; namely, that for some, the state of being loved is intolerable. What happens is that the theme becomes subverted by an overwhelming sense that what we see is not the human condition, but a freak show. It becomes impossible to identify with a petulant, vengeful dwarf, an ex-drug-pushing rapist, or a hostile, semi-ignorant, frigid woman.

Albee's ever-present concern with the outcasts of society has mistakenly led him to recreate for the stage what is, despite its haunting lyricism, essentially not engrossing dramaturgy.

His second adaptation came almost three years later, a play based on James Purdy's novel, *Malcolm*. Albee's play required a rather complicated production scheme which necessitated renting the Shubert, a theatre usually reserved for musicals. The reviews turned out to be the most disastrous of Albee's career, with all the first-nighters uniform in their condemnation of the new work. The *Journal-American* called it "a large crock of abstract and often repellent refuse."[19] *Newsweek* summed up the deluge of devastating criticism when it reported that *Malcolm* lacked "nearly every virtue drama has been known to possess."[20]

It is not my intention to beat a dead horse. There is overwhelming evidence that *Malcolm* is a bad play. Albee, himself apologized in an ad in the *New York Times* the day after the reviews had come out:

> To those who have come to *Malcolm,* my thanks. To those who were pleased, my gratitude. To those who were disappointed, my apologies. See you next play.
> Edward Albee

The play closed after seven performances and according to Richard Barr, lost $100,000. Yet, without appearing to be a scavenger over the carcass, I want to put down some thoughts in an attempt to understand why America's foremost playwright wrote a terrible play.

Albee is still unwilling, at least in public, to accept the critics' evaluation of his script, and blamed the play's failure on the director:

> I didn't like the way it was directed, particularly . . . It . . . got completely out of my hands. I let the director take over and dictate the way things should be done.[21]

While it is my conviction that the play's problem stems both from material that is basically insufficient for the stage and from a series of puzzling script changes in the adaptation, Albee does have a point about the direction. If he was referring to the overburdened production concept which necessitates the heavy-handed use of three threadmills to shift the many locales of this multi-scened play, I must wholeheartedly agree with him. Albee's structure requires thirteen scenes in act one, and twelve more scenes in act two—if one is to include what Albee refers to as his "entre-scenes." The production was so involved and intricately conceived that one stage hand said it was the "biggest show we've ever done at the Shubert."[22] Had a simple, multilevel unit set been used, the scenes could have been changed with only a shift of light, more in keeping with the fantasy world of the Purdy novel. The ultimate responsibility must rest with the director since it is his concept that a designer works with. Still the production scheme was not the sole cause of the play's failure; it only compounded problems that were already present.

In transferring the Purdy novel to the stage, Albee makes certain script changes that do not really clarify his intention or the original work. According to one source, the character of Kermit went from the dwarf of the novel to a six-foot-six Negro in rehearsals, and by the time the show opened had been changed again to the oldest man in the world wearing a Confederate uniform.[23] The metamorphosis is unexplainable except to make us wonder whether it wasn't simply that Albee did not want two adaptations to contain a dwarf as a main character. Other changes that took place are equally inexplicable. Why was the character of Estel Blanc, the Abyssinian undertaker, left out of the stage version? And why was Gus, a Negro in the novel, played by a Caucasian? Overlooking the fact that Albee inexplicably eliminated three Negro roles, the real error in judgment is that Estel's occupation as mortician (his is the first address Malcolm is given in the novel) foreshadows Malcolm's final destruction. The novel also has Gus die in the very brothel he has brought the boy to, forewarning a similar fate for the young orphan. Albee's Gus simply doesn't show up in the next scene and is never mentioned again, leaving the audience to wonder if the playwright has forgotten about him. Still another death symbol used in the Purdy work was not incorporated into the stage version: Malcolm is tattooed, first a black panther on his chest then a dagger apiece on his forearms, and finally a design of carnations just above his right bicep—all symbols of his impending extinction. Why Albee chose to omit this bizarre scene of Malcolm's initiation into death is again inexplicable.

Albee also changes Kermit's character as well as his age and stature. In the orginal work, the Girards, because of Malcolm's insistence, invite Kermit to their summer chateau. Kermit hides in his closet when they arrive to take him with them because he is afraid to associate with such wealth and splendor. A comparison of the two sections should serve to illustrate that Albee's handling of the moment is less dramatically effective than the original. Purdy has writen:

> The little man began slowly retreating backwards into the room reserved for the cats. He knew now that he could never go with them. He was too used to poverty, to the routine of deprivation, to his little empty life of complaint and irritations. . . . To be suddenly translated into a car with a monogram that looked like a vehicle from another civilization, to be surrounded by what was, in effect royalty—he could never do this. He retreated still further back, and as he did so, the movement of his back pushed open the door, and all the cats, seeing their prison opened, rushed out with cries of wildness and relief into the front room and began scratching and meowing on the pane of the tall glass door before which Madame Girard now stood.

The juxtaposition of Kermit's withdrawal and the frenzied

escape of the cats makes Kermit's action much more pitiful because we can see his deeply hidden wish to go, manifested in the cats' panic-stricken scramble to get out. The Albee treatment has so altered the same scene that it becomes both totally unrecognizable and theatrically bland by comparison. In the Albee script Kermit tells Mr. Cox that he has been invited to the Girard's chateau and that, contrary to the novel, he plans to accept. Mr. Cox, however, has other ideas:

> COX: It'd knock your eyes out, kid; you couldn't take it.
> KERMIT: Then I . . . I can't go?
> COX: Unh-unh.
> KERMIT: I can't go with Malcolm to . . . to the chateau, with Madame Girard and . . .
> COX: Unh-unh.
> KERMIT: (*Knowing it's all up*) But I'd be so happy there.
> COX: You couldn't take the splendor, kid; I'm sorry.
> KERMIT: (*As* cox *starts to leave, but not by the front door; off to one side*) I would have been so happy there, with Malcolm, and . . .

In an effort to show that Cox controls the lives of his "friends," Albee has dissipated the moment into one of un-importance. If Cox does indeed exert control over the various lives in the play as some sort of deity figure, it is better done through subtle suggestion than through a scene of silly paternalism. Cox's fastidious nature is also brought into question by this scene because Albee has abruptly changed his character, making him sound more like a New York Little League coach than the pompous pedant he is.

Speaking of deities, it has been suggested that Cox may be "Satan or . . . a messenger of the devious Divine Will?" Or that Malcolm's missing father represents "God turned away from the world or God choosing to sacrifice another son to inform and save some sinners."[24] The symbol, of course, doesn't work because as long as Malcolm is willing to die from too much coition, he will never do as a Christ image. On the contrary, Malcolm receives none of our sympathy or respect because he has no redeeming features. He may be initially innocent, but he "invites corruption. He is dumb, passive and available."[25] *The New Yorker* termed him "the boy [who was] as empty of emotion as a zombie."[26] Malcolm's character is at the heart of the play's failure. He appears stupid, not disinclined to pederasty, incapable of learning, and totally void of emotion. The audience couldn't have cared less how or why he died. And they certainly did not see the theme of the play as corruption of innocence. Perhaps it is for this very reason that Purdy's treatment of Malcolm's death is less realistic. In fact, there is a strong suggestion that the death never took place:

> The only flaw in the ceremony was the repeated insistence of the local coroner and the undertaker—later they were both silenced, it is said by money—that there had been no corpse at all, and that nobody was buried in the ceremony.

Purdy's droll description of the funeral makes Malcolm's expiration less heavy-handed, and we are able to accept the symbolism of his destiny instead of being annoyed by it.

Why then did Albee choose to adapt this ribald tale of corruption and abnormality? The answer, I think, lies in the fact that Albee, an adopted son, responded immediately and personally to the orphan boy's plight. The orphan theme has been a part of Albee's own writing from the very earliest play. The first mention of it came in *The Zoo Story* when Jerry talked of the death of both parents:

> JERRY: Good old Mom walked out on good old Pop when I was ten and a half years old. . . . We'd received the news between Christmas and New Year's, you see,

that good old Mom, had parted with the ghost in some dump in Alabama. . . . At any rate, good old Pop celebrated the New Year for an even two weeks and then slapped into the front of a somewhat moving city omnibus, which sort of cleaned things out family-wise. . . .

The theme again showed up two plays later in *The American Dream,* when the beautiful young man talked to granny about his past life:

YOUNG MAN: Then listen. My mother died the night I was born, and I never knew my father; I doubt my mother did. . . .

The orphan theme becomes paramount when in *Virginia Woolf,* George tells Nick a story, which we later find is a tale of his own adolescence. The following sequence is somewhat excised:

GEORGE: There was this boy who was fifteen, and he had killed his mother with a shotgun some years before—accidentally, completely accidentally, without even an unconscious motivation. . . .

NICK: (*Very quietly*) Thank you. What . . . what happened to the boy . . . the boy who had shot his mother?

GEORGE: I won't tell you.

NICK: All right.

GEORGE: The following summer, on a country road, with his learner's permit in his pocket and his father on the front seat to his right, he swerved the car, to avoid a porcupine, and drove straight into a large tree.

NICK (*Faintly pleading*) No.

GEORGE: He was not killed, of course. And in the hospital, when he was conscious and out of danger, and when they told him that his father *was* dead, he began to laugh. . . .

Albee's understandable sympathy for the orphan, similar to his concern for society's outcasts, has once again led him into "a straightjacket, caught in the matrix of another writer's thinking, narrative, ideas and literary style."[27]

Perhaps the best way to conclude this post-mortem on *Malcolm* is to quote Richard Watts who, upon seeing the new Albee play, reflected: "The sad, astonishing and unavoidable fact is that Edward Albee has written a simply awful play."[28]

Albee's third and latest adaptation, entitled *Everything in the Garden,* is a reworking of an earlier English play of the same name written by the late Giles Cooper. After the playwright's untimely death, producers Barr and Wilder asked Albee to Americanize it for them; Albee wasn't even to have his name on the program. Then, reported Albee:

> Something happened, and by the time I was finished with my work there was hardly a word left of the orginal. . . . Cooper's play became a catalyst and set me to working my own variations on his theme . . . the play . . . is not an adaptation of another man's work but a much more intense collaboration.[29]

The collaboration has actually produced another play, but we wonder, when we read both plays, where the original is, because the two are so curiously similar that they seem to be two translations of still a third, non-English play. Compare the following sequences, the first from the Cooper script:

JENNY: You filthy woman. It's disgusting.

LEONIE: Nothing is disgusting, unless you are disgusted.

JENNY: I am.

LEONIE: Not me.

JENNY: You!

LEONIE: Yes, me. Look, I remember when the

Nazis said I was disgusting. We were all disgusting, but we were not disgusted. Nothing you are or do yourself offends yourself. Disgust is only hate, and hate is for other people.

JENNY: You're evil. Yes you are, evil!

LEONIE: So are we all to others, but what we do is nothing.

JENNY: I shall tell the police.

LEONIE: Then they will perhaps arrest me.

JENNY: I hope they put you in prison.

LEONIE: Oh yes, they will, and I shall admit everything; how you approached me, yes, and we discussed it, yes, but the terms did not suit.

JENNY: That's not true!

Here is the same scene as Albee has adapted it:

JENNY: You're a filthy woman! It's disgusting!!

MRS. TOOTHE: (*Very calm*) Nothing is disgusting, unless one is disgusted.

JENNY: You're evil!!

MRS. TOOTH: Yes, yes . . .

JENNY: I'll tell the police!

MRS. TOOTHE: (*Stands up, stretches a little*) Good. Then perhaps they'll arrest me.

JENNY: I hope they put you in prison!

MRS. TOOTHE: Yes, they probably will, and then I shall admit everything.

JENNY: Everything?

MRS. TOOTHE: Yes, how you approached me, and we discussed it, but the terms didn't suit you. The *money* wasn't enough.

JENNY: That's not true!

One wonders why Albee bothered in the first place. The critics were equally bemused.

One reviewer called it "one of the saddest most outrageous

cop outs in recent theatrical history."[30] Richard Watts took
the minority viewpoint when he wrote that *Garden* "is the
first important American play of the season."[31] Despite the
rather poor reception, *Garden* will probably be the most
successful of the Albee adaptations because, like *Virginia
Woolf*, it has been sold to the movies.

Whether or not the new play is more collaboration than
adaptation is a moot point. What is important is that Albee
has added and changed just enough of the structure to war-
rant the new play's examination. We might begin with Cooper's description of the house, which states there are "not many
books, no pictures." Though not mentioned in the printed
version of the Albee script, the Broadway production did
have paintings (or at least prints scattered about) in addition
to a wall of books over the "optional" fireplace. Apparently
Cooper felt a lack of interest in the arts and literature in his
characters that Albee did not. I tend to side with Mr.
Cooper's evaluation of the typical middle-class suburban
home. Sociologists would agree that the American suburban
household usually lacks books, and to a lesser degree paintings, unless they were bought to match the house's color
scheme. One look at any of the typical ads for upper-middle-
class homes will quickly reveal that builders rarely advertise
a library or study. That extra room will always belong to
the maid. Affluent America would rather have a live-in maid
than a well-stocked library. Albee's sociological microscope
saw something in the American home that doesn't exist.

We see the Americanization of the script as soon as the
dialogue begins. Cooper had Jenny saving the silver from
cigarette packages; Albee's Jenny is saving coupons. In both
scripts, however, the play opens with the sound of the sub-
urbanite working on his lawn; no matter which country,
both protagonists must mow the grass. The lawnmower has
become the new symbol of suburbia. Vance Packard describes
this syndrome:

The lawn-mower industry was able to convince American males that it was somehow shameful to be seen pushing a hand mower. . . . By 1960, more than nine out of every ten lawn-mowers sold were powered. Such mowers cost from three to five times as much as hand mowers. Furthermore, having a mere motor on your mower was not enough in some neighborhoods. You also needed a seat on it. Hundreds of thousands of American males began buying power mowers with seats. These, of course, cost ten times as much as a hand mower.[32]

Albee has reflected the phenomenon quite well in the following exchange between Richard and his wife:

RICHARD: I am probably the only natural-born citizen east of the Rockies who does not have a power mower.

JENNY: Well, you cannot have one, so let it be.

RICHARD: (*Points vaguely around, suggesting the neighborhood*) Alan has one; Clinton; Mark's got one he trades *in* every . . .

JENNY: (*Surprisingly sharp*) No!

(*Silence*)

RICHARD: (*To himself*) Forty-three years old and I haven't even got a power motor.

Very near the beginning, Albee veers away from Cooper in his handling of Richard and Jenny's close friend, Jack. In both scripts Jack is an artist, but there the similarity ends. Albee's Jack talks directly to the audience, periodically stepping out of the action to comment on it. This device gives Jack a somewhat omnipotent role as he is able to stop the action whenever he wishes. On first impression it seems to work, but by the time the play ends—at least the Broadway version of it—this quasi-deified position begins to contradict the events of the last scene, leaving the audience confused as to the logic of the playwriting. But this contradiction will be better understood if discussed in its place, when the play's resolution is examined. For the moment, let us stay with the Jack of the earlier scenes who tells us he is independently wealthy and paints, not for a living (as does Cooper's artist), but simply as an amusing avocation. He likes his friends exceedingly well, enough to tell us he is going to leave them his three-million-dollar fortune when he dies.

Albee's decision to make Jack wealthy through inheritance reflects the morality of this country's citizenry who feel that income from inherited wealth deserves the highest sociological status.[33] This wealth also acts as a constant source of irritation for Richard and Jenny, even though it allows them to hobnob with the rich, because it reminds them of how really middle-class they are by comparison.

Jack soon takes advantage of his ability to stop the play and address the audience by telling us that in spite of all that money he is really quite miserable because great wealth tends to isolate. Perhaps if Albee had found a way to really show us that poor-rich Jack is unhappy, we would have believed it. At the moment, however, his confession tells us that he's just looking for sympathy, and no hard-working middle-class audience is about to feel motherly towards a self-pitying millionaire.

Mrs. Toothe, who is called Leonie Pimosz in the Cooper version, arrives and the play's exposition is over. Originally Mrs. Toothe was a Polish Jew who survived the Nazi concentration camps and is now in business for herself as lady pimp for bored middle-class housewives. Albee has changed her to a strong-willed, icy English woman, but the offer she carries is the same. This character metamorphosis bothered some of the critics. John Lahr, writing for *Evergreen Review*, asked: "Why the change? In eliminating her uncomfortable ethnic identity, he does not offend his Westchester audience."[34] I do not agree with Lahr that a presumably biased audience would be offended by learning that a

Jewess is pimping in suburbia. On the contrary, it would reinforce prejudicial views—at least until being a procuress becomes fashionable. Albee has kept Mrs. Toothe's background purposely vague in order to keep her character and its evil symbolic. If Albee had been worried about how suburbanites would receive the play, he wouldn't have written it at all. The play's events are enough of an indictment to outrage those who would be offended by its reality. One critic's reaction should be sufficient to illustrate the point:

> The idea of the sanction of prostitution by the men and the indulgence in it by their wives is unbelievable, and in another sense, ludicrous. . . . I find *Everything in the Garden* cheap and contemptuous in its point of view.[35]

That the reviewer is able to report that the events in *Garden* are "ludicrous" is in itself quite unbelievable. Hadn't he read about a similar operation blossoming in Long Island's suburbia?

There is, however, another aspect of that review that forces me to digress from *Garden* for a brief paragraph or two: It is the practice of using criticism as a vehicle for personal morality. It isn't important whether a critic likes Albee's point of view or not. That is not his job. He should only be concerned with how well Albee has communicated his intention. Critic and playwright Albert Bermel has also had some thoughts on the subject:

> In judging a given show, he [the critic] is bound to say what he thinks is wrong with it . . . but he is also bound to respect the author's intentions. He has every right to state how, in his opinion, the author has failed to rise to those intentions. But he has no business reproaching, say, Mr. Albee for not choosing some other topic, style or treatment. He is not a disgruntled customer in a restaurant. If Mr. Albee happened not to serve what he, the critic, wanted, that is too bad.[36]

According to the Cooper script, Jenny advertised for work, which brought the madam to her. In the Albee treatment, one of Jenny's friends, knowing her tight financial predicament, recommends her to the madam. The Albee version is a more realistic preparation for the later contrived denouement, where all of Jenny's friends turn out to be part of the same prostitution ring. Had Mrs. Toothe given the party and invited Richard and Jenny, the ending would have been more convincing. It is simply too coincidental that every friend of Jenny's is a whore—unless Jenny knew who the other members of the ring were and invited only them. The Albee dialogue, however, denies that possibility:

> RICHARD: (*Not quite dawn yet*) You, you all know each other?
>
> MRS. TOOTHE: Well, yes, I know all these ladies, and I've met their husbands, but I've known them, well how shall I say . . . I don't think we've all known before that we all know each other.

Returning to the plot sequence, Mrs. Toothe offers Jenny one thousand dollars—in Cooper's script the bait is fifty pounds—mentioning that rich clients would be willing to pay one hundred dollars or more for an afternoon's pleasure. In both scripts Jenny immediately rejects the proposal as disgusting, but undaunted, Mrs. Toothe leaves the money and her business card in case our heroine goes through a change of heart. Seven pages later in Cooper's version and eight pages later in Albee's, Jenny retrieves Mrs. Toothe's card from the wastebasket and silently accepts her new job.

In both plays, Richard wants to know who the strange woman is. Cooper's Jenny explains that Mrs. Toothe is a private dressmarker come to make her a dress. Richard's acceptance (he never asks how much the dress will cost) is illogical for a budget-conscious husband. Albee's solution is better. He has Jenny lie that the woman has asked her to do some charity work as a hospital volunteer. Jenny has now prepared an alibi for her planned afternoon absences.

As scene two begins, Albee introduces a bit of comic irony when Richard, boasting about his past sexual prowess, criticizes Jenny for being too prim in bed. The audience laughs at his braggadocio, knowing that it's just a matter of time before he discovers that his prim little wife is averaging better than five men a week.

The plot moves on to the next major incident when Richard receives by mail, an anonymous bundle filled with money —four thousand nine-hundred dollars to be exact. The Cooper script calls for one hundred and ninety-eight pounds, making our American girl much the more prosperous. Jack enters, and seeing all that money lying around, begins to insinuate that there is hanky-panky afoot, making a much stronger case for his murder at the end of the play. Cooper's Jack barely notices the money. Albee has Richard make Jack promise he'll not say a word about the money, and then the conversation takes a philosophical turn. Jack talks of things in their basic state as being almost valueless. A painting made of a bit of pigment stretched on plain canvas is worth about four dollars in materials; yet if it happens to be a certain Picasso, it's worth as much money as, say, twenty-five hundred cows. Even the paper that money is printed on is cheap. It's value is what we arbitrarily give it. Jack's philosophizing, while thematically tangential, holds up the action and should be cut. The play deals with the moral decay of affluent America, an idea not sufficiently connected to the evolution of the economic market place.

Richard soon finds even more money. (Jenny has been hiding it in the house since she began her new job.) Cooper's hero has been looking for his pipe cleaners (which he does periodically throughout the play) and ends up finding the money in every drawer and vase until he is "ankle-deep in the stuff." Albee's man finds the money all together in

Jenny's pocketbook, where he has gone in search of cigarettes. The resulting discovery is not quite as funny as the original. Incidentally, the need to clean his pipes constantly might suggest that Richard has a need to clean the dirt out of his house, an idea that could have been used to good advantage by Albee.

Finding the money, both Richards confront their Jennies in much the same way until finally both wives admit to being whores. After a good deal of histrionics, both men come to accept the news, with Albee's Richard melodramatically crying as the curtain descends and Cooper's hero ironically ordering champagne and brandy for an evening's celebration.

In act two, Albee's Jack returns and tells the audience that he has made good his promise and changed his will, leaving the entire fortune to Jenny and Richard. In these asides, as John Lahr has said, "Jack cajoles the audience but stops the play's action."[37] He leaves, on his way to the country club, and the next important incident is the arrival of the party guests. There is much light talk and lots of drinking, and we find out that Jenny and Richard's friends—all club members —dislike Negroes and Jews. Their club is restricted—an accurate account of "a nationwide phenomenon involving thousands of clubs."[38] Party chitchat continues until Mrs. Toothe makes an unannounced entrance. Her knowledge that all the girls would be together when the party was called on such short notice (about two hours from the time the last couple was reached by telephone) is again a weakness in both scripts. It would have been much more understandable if Mrs. Toothe had earlier asked Jenny for the use of the house to hold an important meeting. However, Mrs. Toothe does barge in and we learn that the local police are on to her and she must move to new quarters immediately. She has come to ask the help of her girls and their spouses. There follows a rather dubious recognition scene where, one by one, the neighborly wives confess to each other they are all part of

Mrs. Toothe's coterie. They then sit down with their husbands and discuss finding a way to continue their tax-exempt trade. Mrs. Toothe, always anxious to keep things businesslike, suggests that the women enjoy the garden while the men work out the problem. The men agree, and using parliamentary procedure, elect Richard as chairman.

The newly formed committee quickly settles on a new site, and all is well again until Richard's son brings Jack back from the club. Jack has been drinking and tells the news he's just received concerning the death of a club member. Jack's momentary sadness is relieved, however, when he glances up and recognizes Mrs. Toothe as a madam he used to know in London. Very quickly putting the bundle of unexplained money together with Mrs. Toothe's known past activities, he begins to laugh uproariously at the thought of all these "nice" ladies doing business in the suburbs.

Jack's recognition of Mrs. Toothe is plainly too coincidental. While it gives the party people a much stronger motivation for killing him, it is done at the expense of credence. Cooper's script comes closer to the macabre when the crowd begins to read into his actions and decides to kill him in *case* he knows about their suburban brothel. In the Cooper script, as Jack struggles to leave, he is hit over the head with a liquor bottle and evil Jenny suggests they bury him alive in her garden—which the men promptly do. The Albee variation has Mrs. Toothe decide to stop Jack from leaving, and it is her suggestion to bury him after the men smother him with a pillow. Since the play is not about Mrs. Toothe, Albee has weakened his protagonists by insisting that she control the play's events. Albee, however, does add a more realistic element to this sequence than did Cooper. In the English script the men go out, find shovels without being told where they are, dig a grave, put the body in, and cover it back up in two pages of dialogue. The feat is simply impossible. Albee solves the problem a little better when he has Richard earlier digging up the garden in search of his clogged-up cesspool. The men dump Jack in the already open trench (the shovels presumably still at the spot) and have only to shovel the dirt back within the same two pages of script.

Earlier I had referred to Jack's semi-deified position in which he was able to talk to the audience without other people on stage hearing or seeing him—much like the invisible Topper—as contradictory to the ending of the play. Since Jack, until the last scene, seems to have an extra dimension enabling him to do and see what other characters can not, being murdered by the group without his having foreknowledge of it seems not consistent with the character as originally conceived by Albee. In the stage presentation this was most apparent, and not until I had read the printed edition did I realize that part of the confusion was due to the omission of Albee's original ending. In the published script, Jack, who is dead, comes back after being buried; unseen by Jenny and Richard (who are off stage busy saying good-by to their murdering friends) he talks once again to the audience. He reminds them of the will and magnanimously assures everybody that Jenny and Richard will have to wait seven years to collect the money—unless the police find the body. He is sure, however, that the resolute couple will concoct a good story at the investigation and inherit the fortune in the end. In his continued omnipotence, we tend to believe him. Albee's ending should not have been cut because it clears up the previous inconsistency of Jack's character. Now, with the original ending in print, we can see a logical and consistent progression from beginning to end.

The murder, however, offended the critics because it was accomplished with impunity. All sorts of reasons were given as to why it should have been omitted from the play's resolution. Harold Clurman has suggested that "Albee would have done well to drop the murder, which makes the play too neat a syllogism. The man who knows the community secret would then become a mocking threat in a quizzically light-handed vein."[39] *Time* magazine made the comment that the murder "seemed an excessively melodramatic device for making the point that the corruption of values means death."[40] Albee included the murder, but handled it differently than Cooper because he wanted the work to be more than simply a "sociological play concerning itself with the morals, manners and ethics of suburban American society."[41] Albee's death scene is symbolic while Cooper's is realistic and one-dimensional. Cooper's script says murder pays. Albee's text, using a symbolic murder, allows Jack to come back and talk to us. Albee does not want his play to degenerate into an individual murder story, making all the other corruption unimportant by comparison. What Albee wants is for his public to be aware that he has indicted them for the murder of humaneness in affluent America. Unfortunately, those critics who judged the play "less effective than the London original"[42] saw a cut version of it.

Before ending this chapter, we might include Albee's defense of adaptations:

> I would agree that the majority of adaptations which arrive on our stages, be they adaptations of novels or European plays, are worthless, either through ineptitude or distortion, but it would be negligent to forget that much of the work of such pretty fair playwrights as Sophocles, Shakespeare, Racine, Giraudoux and Anouilh has been adaptation.
>
> No, the trouble with most of the stage adaptations we get in New York these years is that they are the work either of professionals who are hacks or learned men who are not theater professionals. . . .
>
> Adaptation can be a perfectly respectable occupation and more important, a valid artistic act. And naturally, no self-respecting playwright would, unless the roof were falling in on him and his, set about to adapt anything which (1) he did not respect as a work of

art (2) which he did not feel to be in line with his own aesthetic.[43]

Albee's talk of adaptation precedents is certainly historically accurate, but in other statements he has also talked about the necessity of the adaptor to submerge himself so much in the work adapted that it becomes impossible to tell where one writer left off and the other began. There is a fallacy in this thinking that is contradictory to the historical precedents cited by Albee. Those "pretty fair" playwrights used the material they found, not to reproduce something as much like the original as possible, but as a springboard for their own unique point of view. The *Electras* of Sophocles, Euripides, Giraudoux, and Hofmannsthal are each unique in their form and content. There has been no attempt at submerging one into the other so that the reader cannot tell who has written what. John Lahr, too, has commented on this misguided loyalty of Albee's to the original:

> Those artists imposed a vision on old tales. The stories they adapted were catalysts for their imaginations, not simply ends in themselves.[44]

Shakespeare owes nothing but inspiration to an Elizabethan play entitled *The True Chronicle History of King Leir,* performed, according to Henslowe, thirteen years before the Bard wrote his version. In this earlier version Lear does not go mad, and is restored to the throne to reign two or three years and then die peacefully. Had Shakespeare tried to blend his writing with the earlier play so that the differences could not be distinguished, the great tragedy would not have been written.

In all fairness to Albee, it should at least be noted that two out of the three projects were not initiated by him, but were commissioned by his producers. What Albee must learn to do is say "no" as he should have to David Merrick when the famous producer asked him to doctor-up that abortive

Breakfast at Tiffany's; or Albee must change his views on the purpose of adaptation. As Martin Gottfried observed: "If his purpose continues as being a catalytic agent for the transference of admired literary works, virtually unchanged, to the stage, he is doomed to failure."[45]

CHAPTER 10

BOX-MAO-BOX

MOM AND POP and the sequential story line are no longer
the motivating dramaturgical means for Edward Albee.
Writing still another protest play deeply imbued with social
criticism, he has changed his mode of expression again, this
time completely eliminating conventional play construction.
Reacting to the vast social changes taking place in our society
as a result of the tremendous influence of mass media communications and the electronic computer, Albee has chosen
to experiment with a theatrical form that more closely
approximates the multidimensional complexities of our age.
In constructing his new theatre piece Albee would certainly
agree with Marshall McLuhan who informs us that "the
family circle has widened. The worldpool of information
fathered by electric media—movies, Telstar, flight—far sur-
passes any possible influence mom and dad can now bring
to bear. Character no longer is shaped by only two earnest,
fumbling experts"[1]

The new theatre piece, which is really two interrelating
plays, opened prior to Broadway at the Studio Arena Theatre
in Buffalo, New York, on March 6, 1968, as part of an arts
festival. Among the literati present on opening night were
most of New York's theatre critics, proving once again that
the premiere of an Albee play, regardless of its distance from
the New York scene, is a major theatrical event.

The form in which these two new plays, separately titled
Box and *Quotations from Chairman Mao Tse-Tung,* were
presented was so at odds with conventional playwriting technique that its inception caused a furor amongst the critics.

In the program note Albee tried to prepare his audience
for the new work:

> A playwright—unless he is creating escapist romances
> (an honorable occupation of course) —has two obliga-
> tions; first, to make some statement about the condition

201

of "man" (as it is put) and, second, to make some statement about the nature of the art form with which he
is working. In both instances he must attempt change.
In the first instance—since very few serious plays are
written to glorify the status quo—the playwright must
try to alter his society; in the second instance—since art
must move, or wither—the playwright must try to alter
the forms within which his precursors have had to work.
And I believe that an audience has an obligation to be
interested in and sympathetic to these aims—certainly to
the second of them. Therefore, an audience has an obligation (to itself, to the art form in which it is participating, and even to the playwright) to be willing to
experience a work on its own terms.[2]

The first of the two plays, *Box,* opened on an almost bare
stage. The only scenery was a huge transparent cube suspended and hovering over the entire stage space. Its archi-
tectural framework was illuminated by key-lighting which
did not change for the length of the piece. No characters
appeared, nor did the cube-like skeleton move, producing a
stillness on stage tightly congruent to the play's theme. The
audience heard only a pre-recorded female voice, softly,
sweetly elegizing. Quiet lamentations drifted lightly through
the darkened auditorium as the audience stared fixedly at
the stolid cube.

What effect did this strange monody have on the opening
night audience? One critic recalled that response to the play
ranged "from admiration to outrage."[3] Martin Gottfried, not
one of Albee's admirers, but curious enough to make the
three-hundred-mile trip nonetheless, reported that he hadn't
"seen more garbage since John Lindsay last asked Nelson
Rockefeller for a favor."[4] He went on to declare that the
effect of the new work was "suffocating—as theatre, as writing,
as thought."[5] Perhaps the most indicative remark of the
evening came from Walter Kerr. "It is a good play to dress
up for because the members of the audience are going to

spend quite a bit of time looking at one another."[6] Despite Kerr's undisputed eminence as a theatre critic, his comment illustrates most profoundly the consensus of both journalistic and academic critics (expressed at the University of Chicago's 1966 Conference on the Arts) that "criticism of the arts is in a deplorable state."[7]

Clearly what was happening on stage did not hold Kerr's interest. He came to the theatre armed with traditional approaches to viewing a play, and when he was presented a theatrical experience that defied his personal criteria, he promptly rejected the evening as next to worthless. The theatre critic is still "before all else, a spectator, with a willingness to receive—not resist—new experiences";[8] we must examine Albee's new theatre piece not by the rules of another age, but as a product and creation of what I will continue to refer to in this chapter as The New Theatre.

To begin any analysis of a new theatre movement, reassessment of theatrical values is needed if we are to understand and intelligently comment upon plays of this genre. Perhaps the first such value is the traditional role played by the play's environment. Heretofore, when theatricians talked of a play's. environment they meant that area within which the actors performed. But *Box* has no corporeal actors strutting the stage; yet an environment exists. It is the huge, immobile skeleton-cube which, instead of being assigned the usual role of embellished matrix for the actor, has replaced him. The structured cube emits a disembodied voice, musingly uttering scattered cadences of sorrow and regret. The voice, which some critics rightly thought was "post-holocaust"[9] in origin, at first seems incomprehensible, until the disjointed phrases take on a distinct pattern of expression. It was *Newsweek's* critic, Jack Kroll, who connected the play's configurational thoughts and put them into the proper mosaic:

Is this a threnody being intoned by some melancholy

spirit after the holocaust that may melt and shrivel the world to a sordid blister? In effect yes—it is certainly a requiem for many of the civilized usages which are suiciding themselves throughout the human community. This "box" may indeed be a coffin for the flesh and spirit of a self-annihilated species. "Box . . . box . . . well put together," says the voice, which then proceeds to reflect with measured sadness on the decline of crafts such as carpentry and the baking of good bread, and the even more lethal decline of art which is "all craft now . . . and going further. When art begins to hurt," mourns the voice, "it's time to look around. When the beauty of art reminds us of loss rather than the attainable, when it tells us what we cannot have . . . when art hurts . . . then the corruption is complete."[10]

In his preceptive review, Kroll has alluded to certain structural elements of the play which, if considered in more detail, will shed light on the new mechanics of playwrighting. To begin with, Mr. Kroll has realized that the large cube, which Albee refers to as a box, is the symbolic coffin from which emanate the last surviving thoughts of a decimated civilization. The play, its form and content an anthropomorphic boxed frame, reminds us of Jasper John's "targets," in which the painting and the object painted become one. Similarly, Albee writes a nonillusionistic piece in which the play becomes the symbol it represents. The play becomes the coffin.

The voice, a remnant of surviving thought, not only bemoans the death of crafstmanship as it developed in the thirteenth and fourteenth centuries, and the extinction of the kind of art that somehow sought to lift man from his primitiveness, but mourns the very demise of man in such reflections as "700 million babies dead, in the time it takes—took—to knead a proper loaf of bread." With the environment no longer used to set the actor in relief, and the actor himself absent from the stage, a second esthetic emerges as indigenous to The New Theatre. Richard Kostelanetz touches upon that element in his new book, *The Theatre of Mixed Means:*

> [The] . . . heroic protagonist was once considered the pinnacle in the hierarchy of a play—he was indeed its star—so in the new theatre, in general all performers have a status equal to each other and, sometimes, to non-human elements.[11]

If it is true that Albee has given the protagonist's role over to a "box," how then does he intend to produce any empathic response in his audience? We all know that Albee realizes his audience is not about to empathize with a wooden cube; yet the play creates empathy. What Albee has done is reverse the normal audience-actor communion by writing a play that will not allow us to project our personalities on to someone else. Instead we are made to *introject* the play's thoughts and feelings into ourselves. Because we are no longer confronted with a story, because no action takes place on stage (the cube never moves), and the only emotion is lingering over and drifting through the dimly lit auditorium, it becomes clear that the play is to take place in the audience. We will not participate as an audience would participate in John Cage's silent score entitled *4' 33"* with coughs, cat-calls, or what have you. Albee is not anti-art; he is no neo-Dadaist. What happens in *Box* is that the audience has the large box fixed in its view, while the monodic voice continues its dirge. The sweet, pleasant manner of the threnody is now understood. Like the hypnotist—who may also use an object to fix our attention—the voice is amiable and reassuring, and we allow it to come into our minds. Once inside our heads, the kind-sounding words take on their mournful meaning, mixing with our consciousness until it becomes *our* voice by cuing our analogous personal remembrances. Its stream-of-consciousness gives flight to our own free assoications. The play takes place in our heads—not on the stage. We take on its emotional and intellectual characteristics by the reversed empathic response that psychologists call introjection.

As McLuhan and others before him have assured us, the seeming disconnected cadences are acceptable to the ear because, unlike the eye, it is not selective. The ear is capable of absorbing dissociated stimuli with much less trauma than the eye, which has been conditioned to receive information in a linear, sequential fashion. "We hear sounds from everywhere, without ever having to focus," says McLuhan.[12] While it is true that the brain screens out much of the surrounding sound on an unconscious level of filtration to keep us from being overwhelmed by the normal lack of auditory selectivity, we can, if we choose, use this sophisticated ability to accept and appreciate simultaneous information of the kind given in *Box*. Once the scattered bits of data are received, this "discontinuous succession of images and events . . . must be pieced together in the observer's [auditor's] mind if the piece is to be fully understood."[13] *Box*, then, properly interpreted, is a succession of assimilated thematic phrases voiced amicably enough to slip into the deeper crevices of our mind, where it reverberates and resounds until it becomes our own personal requiem for the dead.

Albee could have used a live actor to deliver his monodical lament, but he wanted the "box" to be his speaker. Also the mechanical reproduction of a human voice adds to this private contemplation of death and extinction. The presence of a living actor would have been antithetical to his purpose.

At the end of this first of two tightly interlocked plays, the voice speaks of sea gulls caught in the folds of a black net. The net, doubtlessly, represents the death of those sea birds, but the most intriguing section of that description is its mention of one bird, moving in the opposite direction from the flock, who avoids the net. This moment is really both the end of *Box* and the beginning of *Mao*, because it serves to continue the death theme as well as introduce a new, but related, second motif. Before going on to *Mao,* however, one more word ought to be said about *Box.*

Clive Barnes called Albee's new work "the first American play without the vestige of narrative."[14] This isn't quite the case as there have been many examples devoid of traditional plot presented in the Off-Off Broadway theatre—only one of which will I briefly mention. There is some similarity in form between Albee's play, *Box,* and Paul Foster's one-actor, *Balls.* In *Balls,* two ping-pong balls swing to and fro in ever-increasing then decreasing arcs, supplying the only stage activity. At the same time, voices can be heard, supposedly coming from a group of graves in a nearby cemetery close to the sea. As in the Albee play, the audience sees only inanimate objects while listening to human voice. Both plays concern death and extinction and use the sea as background sound. But Foster's play displays stage movement while the Albee piece remains visually motionless. Since Mr. Foster has been a member of the Albee-Wilder-Barr Playwrights Unit, it would seem safe to assume that the Foster play had some influence on Albee—to the degree, at least, of predating *Box* by almost four years as a non-narrative play. Because of the ocular effect of moving balls, however, the Foster play remains on the stage, while Albee's resides and rebounds beneath the cranium.

As we have said, the elegiac strains fade away—the last images concerned with that little gull and his fortunate turn from the net. Refusing to go along with his fellow creatures —all flying toward their death—he opposes the group and lives. This simple maxim prepares the audience (while the stage lights dim and the previously suspended cube is lowered onto the stage floor) for *Mao,* "an outgrowth of and extension of the shorter play," says Albee in the program notes.

The stage lights come back up and we find ourselves on

the deck of an ocean liner. There are four passengers in view: a long-winded lady, and old woman, a minister, and Chairman Mao Tse-Tung. During the course of the play the characters (with the exception of the minister who never moves out of his chair) sit, stand, and walk through and around the giant frame of the cube, which has been integrated into the ship's structure to stand unseen as it symbolically covers the entire deck.

The first words spoken in this second play are by Mao Tse-Tung, whose speeches, Albee says, are taken directly from his little red book *Quotations From Chairman Mao Tse-Tung;* and so, the adage about the sea gull tells us that death, and now its counterpart—revolution—are the topics under Albee's sociological scrutiny.

Chairman Mao initiates the piece with a Chinese fable, too long to relate, which ends with an analogy between Imperialism and Feudalism, the two mighty mountains which God will help the Chinese people destroy. All through the play this interpolated, contrapuntal, voice speaks of the necessity to destroy the United States by war and revolution. Mao never talks to the other passengers—only to the audience—periodically leaving the stage to saunter smilingly up and down the theatre aisles, delivering his insidious Communist tautologies: "Whoever sides with the revolution in words only," he preaches, "is a revolutionary only in speech." At one point in the piece he sits in an empty seat and watches the play. Though a character listed in the *dramatis personae,* he is totally outside the event, closer to the members of the audience than to the other passengers on board the luxury liner.

Why does Albee do this? Why does he create an event and then pull a major character out of it periodically to roam the auditorium? The message that Walter Kerr did not get in his review titled "Mao—But What Message," is quite clear. Mr. Albee is forcing us to take a good long look at this

Communist leader. We are compelled to recognize his existence because he is the only one in the play who talks directly
to us. While it is true that the old woman, who keeps repeating verses out of sequence from an old doggerel attributed
to Will Carpenter, faces the audience in her recitation, there
is a subtle attempt at retaining some esthetic distance.

Mr. Albee is trying to tell us that this man, spouting his
platitudinous homiletics, is not a make-believe character. He
exists, and his reality should be recognized in diplomatic
affairs and world politics. After twenty years of government
stability, it is absurd to perpetuate the belief that the real
China is based on Formosa, preparing one day to invade the
mainland. This kind of politics tends to minimize Mao's
threat in the eyes of our citizenry. By reading directly from
Mao's book, Albee plops the despot in our laps, making it
impossible to ignore his intentions. The man is not a figment
of someone's imagination; he is real and simplistically clear.
"Political power grows out of the barrel of a gun," he says
benignly, repeating this theme again and again with such
variations as "only with guns can the whole world be trans-
formed." He is out to destroy the United States, and banning
his writings is a misguided form of protection.

Mirroring most of the free world's refusal to admit to
Mao's right to rule China, the other characters in the play
remain unaware of his presence. This, of course, is the first
clue that the rest of the cast are political and, in the case of
the minister, religious symbols—all floating upon the sea,
which has a long literary history as a death symbol. Our
characters, then, are riding the precarious crests and dips of
a possible ocean death—a striking symbolism for a world
population continually threatened by nuclear annihilation.

Another traveler on this symbolic journey is the long-
winded lady who talks incessantly to an indifferent minister,
prattling on while he tries to snooze inconspicuously. It is
this lady and what she represents—not Mao—that most inter-

ests Albee. She begins to speak, continuing what appears to be shipboard chitchat, but her conversation soon takes on an outright candor. Unfortunately these early monologues are so filled with abstraction that her thoughts defy comprehension. Suddenly, in the midst of this one-sided conversation, the incorporeal voice of *Box* returns over the theatre's public-address system and begins all over again, running with, and in counterpoint to, the action aboard ship. The recorded voice still laments the extinction of art and the demise of man; Mao preaches the destruction of Capitalism and the United States; the bereft old woman recites a poem about the removal and extinction of old people from the society; and the tourist lady's abstruse monolgue makes it clear that communication is also dead. Albee has created a dramatic polyphonic poem whose individual voices thematically relate in their separate tales of death and revolution.

It may be of some interest to note that on opening night, according to Walter Kerr, *Box* was not played simultaneously but after *Mao* had been completed:

> After about 10 minutes of 'Box,' the cube is occupied by four intercut, noncommunicating people who speak the lines of an hour-long recital called 'Quotations from Chairman Mao Tse-Tung.' When they have finished, the stage is emptied and 'Box' is repeated.[15]

When this viewer saw the play—ten days later—*Box* was running along with the last part of *Mao;* both finished at approximately the same time, and to my mind the juxtaposition is a much more insightful concept. The recent Broadway presentation has adhered to this change, referring to the new theatre piece as *Box* and *Quotations From Chairman Mao Tse-Tung.*

At the start of this chapter, I stated that with the advent of *Box-Mao-Box* new dramaturgical formulae must also emerge so that the critic will not judge The New Theatre by outworn criteria, and in so doing, relegate himself to obsolescene and deny himself the opportunity of deciphering the essence of a new generation of artists. Recently, Robert Corrigan, speaking at the University of Chicago convention, argued the same point when he stated that the basic problem in the arts today "is how to goad our scholars, critics, and educators into catching up with what's going on, with what the artists are doing."[16] Walter Kerr, in his review of *Box-Mao-Box* did make mention of new theories of communication when he reported:

> Some feel that linear sequence is out, circuitry in—and the theatre had better catch up. Some feel that narrative itself is now disposable tissue and are really trying to shred it into fine bits that will never come together again.[17]

But this rather casual summation of Marshall McLuhan's linear-sequential theory only attempts to nullify the tremendous insight McLuhan shows in explaining the modern artist's obliteration of standard and unquestioned theatrical forms. Kerr also draws the wrong conclusion when he proposes that The New Theatre playwrights destroy the narrative with no intention of putting it together again. The emphasis on who shall put it together has changed, that is all. First, however, let us examine McLuhan's premise a bit less cursorily before talking of its application to the non-narrative play. Marshall McLuhan's hypothesis might best be explained by first quoting him directly:

> Western history was shaped for some three thousand years by the introduction of the phonetic alephbet [sic] . . . a construct of fragmented bits and parts which have no semantic meaning in themselves and which must be strung together in a line, bead-like, and in a prescribed order. . . . The line, the continuum became the organizing principle of life. . . . Rationality and logic came to depend on the presentation of connected and sequential facts and concepts.[18]

Kerr's comment that the counterpointed voices "join verbally, not logically,"[19] is an example of the sequential rationality syndrome McLuhan refers to. Because the events were not in a cause-effect relationship, Kerr apparently didn't realize that each character was logically connected by the overall theme of death and revolution, the structural extrapolation of which I will discuss in more detail later.

McLuhan points out that the invention of the printing press made the linear-sequential narrative available to the public which consequently allowed for private reading and an individual point of view. With the emergence of computer technology and electronic circuitry, information can be gathered and disseminated at such fantastic speeds that the public (which he now calls the mass audience) can no longer remain isolated and retain the rugged individualistic attitudes of the industrial revolution. Information that used to be received on an individual, sequential basis (teacher-student, reader-book) has given way to the multifaceted, multifocused means of mass communication in an electronic age. So much information is received each day that the mass audience is literally *massaged* with data. This computerized knowledge has moved man from the world of "data classification," to the era of "pattern recognition."[20] According to McLuhan, we live in a society that can have instant vision of a complex process; yet we continue to think in fragmented and single planes. Areas of data are becoming so interrelated that it is almost impossible to break them down into their components. Because of the power of mass media (It is conceivable that a man voting late in California can be informed of the outcome of a national election before he has cast his ballot.), the peoples of the world have become irrevocably involved and interlocked with one another.

How then does McLuhan's hypothesis relate to The New Theatre and Albee's play in particular? To begin with, he feels that a society educated and run by instant data processing "simply has no time for the narrative form, borrowed from earlier print technology. The story line must be abandoned."[21] Corroborating McLuhan's position is the following statement from critic Richard Kostelanetz:

> . . . so my experience with the new theatre leads me to find conventional theatre and movies needlessly confined in space; and because the miniscule space allows so little to happen, the action in these old media also seems rather slow.[22]

Speed, of course, is not the only consideration in trying to formulate new dramaturgical esthetics, but the plot is dead by almost any new playwright's standards. Theatre critic Albert Bermel has said that the theatergoer "has watched so much television, so many ancient movies, that he can predict the outcome of almost any Broadway plot. If there are five possible endings, he knows them all in advance."[23]

A society that obtains such instantaneous coverage of the war can literally be informed about it before the war department. Think about the parents who see their wounded son on television before the information has reached Washington. A populace that is instantaneously informed in detail about the worst atrocities man can devise has already seen anything a realistic play can create. Recently, the editors of a publication that was based on the University of Chicago symposium on the arts and the public, summed up one of the speeches whose subject was the modern audience. The editor's summary referred to the audience as "a participant in today's violence on such immediate and intimate terms, that fact has indeed transcended fiction, contemporary history deposed drama, startling actuality dwarfted the impact of fiction—so that modern man may well ask, Who needs art?"[24] Another speaker at the same symposium added this depressing thought:

> Is it possible that total communications have a subtle power that even censorship lacked—the power to excommunicate art? To silence and dilute it with *communi-*

cations—a jamming of the air waves, the sight waves, the thought waves.[25]

In reaction to the ever increasing competition between the real, more exciting stories brought to us through mass media communications, The New Theatre playwrights write surrealistically, abandoning the traditional rules of realism and the well-constructed plot. They have gone on to other areas of experience to conceive the new forms their material will take. McLuhan's concept of pattern recognition, for instance, which has already become helpful in understanding modern optical painting, can be very helpful in analyzing the new Albee play. Before discussing this concept as it pertains to *Box-Mao-Box,* it might be well to explain briefly its application to modern painting.

The optical art that is currently being displayed in most contemporary art museums around the country is based on the principle of total viewing as opposed to the more traditional fragmented perusal of the painted area. With the incorporation of mathematically created optical effects or color combinations, it becomes impossible for the viewer to focus his attention on a small section of the canvas (data classification) ; his eye "jumps" when he attempts to view the picture in fragments, and he is forced to contemplate the picture as a whole (pattern recognition) . The entire design must be absorbed at once.

In *Box-Mao-Box* Albee has done much the same thing. In fact, Clive Barnes' review likened the players to "colors on a painter's canvas."[26] From the very inception of the play, its concept was not linear. Instead of writing out the speeches one after the other, Albee has said he "wrote each speech for each character on a different page,"[27] which is tantamount to saying he wrote four separate sections of the play, with an overall playing pattern in mind that would only take shape when the separate speeches came together. In creating a play that would discourage sequential viewing, Albee came upon a concept of vocal polyphony, which he then set about to develop into a play. In working out the design of this play for contrapuntal voices, it must have occurred to Albee that its presentation would tend to ward off direct audience empathy because there is no story line. Consequently, a new form of empathic response had to be evolved if the play was to catch the conscience of its viewer-auditors. Clive Barnes became aware of this when he noted, "we are not, I think, intended to be engaged by the characters, even though the two monologues reveal once more Albee's great skill for capturing the actual sound of speech."[28]

As we have already shown, Albee's first piece, *Box,* reversed the natural direction of audience empathy and created, in its stead, a form of introjection. The polyphonic, non-narrative structure of *Mao* also demanded a change in the traditional actor-audience empathic relationship. The technique of Albee's second piece was a more sophisticated and complex form of the same psychological theory of introjection. Whether the technique came intuitively or consciously is a matter of conjecture, but the fact is the play operated on a new level of empathic participation.

Perhaps the best way to analyze the play's effect on the audience is to acquaint the reader with a recent concept in the behavioral sciences known as "cognitive dissonance." The term was coined by Dr. Leon Festinger in his book, *A Theory of Cognitive Dissonance*. Dr. Festinger explains dissonance to mean "the existence of nonfitting relations among cognitions,"[29] and cognition as "any knowledge, opinion, or belief about the environment, about oneself, or about one's behavior."[30] According to Festinger, and those behavorial scientists influenced by him, two cognitive elements that are perceived not to correspond in conjunction with a certain accepted and accustomed reality will impinge upon our psychological equilibrium and create dissonance or imbalance. In other words, if I am standing in the rain unprotected and do not get wet, my experience-set is impinged upon and I feel dissonance. "The existence of dissonance, being psychologically uncomfortable, will motive the persons to try to reduce the dissonance and achieve consonance."[31] Dissonance occurs when a smoker continues to smoke knowing that prolonged use of tobacco can cause lung cancer. In trying to reduce the dissonance he may stop smoking, or repress the problem, or find literature and personal testimony negating the *Surgeon General's Report*. Although psychologist Roger Brown has written that "the principles of cognitive dissonance are probably the most influential ideas in social psychology,"[32] Festinger's theory is not entirely without precedence: It is an outgrowth of both W. B. Cannon's famous theory of homeostasis and Freud's theory of ambivalence. Of course, Cannon was mainly concerned with physiochemical stability, and Freud's thesis dealt primarily with emotional pathology. All these men, however, were deeply involved with the problems of human stability, whether on a chemical, pathological, or behavorial level.

What I propose, in my analysis of The New Theatre and specifically of Albee's play, is that these contemporary plays create a form of cognitive dissonance in the viewer because they produce cognitions that do not correspond to a learned rationality-set. We go to the theatre expecting to see a sequential plot replete with exposition, development, climax, and resolution. We expect to have the chaotic and complex elements of life sifted, selected, modified, and ordered. This traditional and expected arrangement has always attempted to show what the artist has discovered; without more than passive participation, we have been able to empathize, purge ourselves, and leave the theatre emotionally cleansed—free to concentrate on other matters.

The New Theatre, reflecting a society that is exposed to the Electric Circus, The Beatles, LSD, stereophonic sound, computer technology, a changing sense of time that permits instantaneous viewing of a man shot to death half-way around the world—even extraterrestrial probes—has finally broken out of the confines of the realistic play and begun to reflect the surrealistic events of our space age. This New Theatre stands in direct opposition to the current conglomeration of obsolescence available on the Broadway stage. Gordon Rogoff, in commenting on the present state of the theatre, wrote in a recent article: "The theatre commonly presented is obsolete, removed from current sense of reality, lodged firmly in the conceits of irrelevant forms, and slavishly enthralled by the old views of character, time, place, and action."[33]

The theatergoer who views and audits a New Theatre play feels dissonance because the old familiar plots are gone. He sees and hears the play but does not immediately understand it all. This partial comprehension disorients him; the spectator finds that his accustomed passivity is no longer enough to produce an empathic response. He has difficulty relating to what he experiences because instead of viewing a succession of events occurring in a cause-and-effect pattern, he is bombarded with simultaneous stimuli presented configurationally—the parts to be put together at another time. This technique, as one critic has observed, "effectively discourages the most recalcitrant habits of narrow focus."[34]

In *Mao* Albee has constructed a non-narrative polyphony of symbolism that does not resolve itself or allow for immediate empathic response. The playgoer leaves the theatre with his expectation of emotional involvement not satisfied. A psychological state of unrest then builds up, which impells him to try to piece together the disconnected fragments of his theatrical experience in an effort to reduce dissonance and evoke a delayed catharsis. I use the word catharsis here in the sense that John Gassner used it to mean intellectual enlightenment. Professor Gassner described the process as a search for emotional balance:

The ultimate relief comes when the dramatist brings the tragic struggle to a state of rest. This cannot occur so long as we are left in a state of tension. . . . Only enlightenment, a clear comprehension of what was involved in the struggle, an understanding of cause and effect, a judgment on what we have witnessed, and an induced state of mind that places it above the riot of passion—can effect this necessary equilibrium.[35]

There are some major differences, however, between what Professor Gassner referred to as the initiator of catharsis and what I am led to believe originates it in The New Theatre. Gassner limited his argument to tragedy as the only form of theatre that produces catharsis, stating that only when an intellectual judgment has been made, based on the cause-and-effect outcome of the protagonist's struggle, will enlightenment occur as the final outcome of "pity and fear."

The New Theatre differs on exactly these traditional points. Modern catharsis, or intellectual enlightenment, can occur without tragedy because the struggle involved is no longer between characters on stage. Identification, which is the usual method of projecting oneself onto one of the play's characters and thus vicariously participating in his struggle, now takes on a different empathic object. There is still struggle in the plays of The New Theatre, but it is an internal one, residing in the minds of the audience as it tries to piece together the simultaneous, configurational stimuli offered by the new medium. This new struggle is difficult and cannot be fully resolved until the play is over and the spectator has had a chance to review the experience in whatever sequence he chooses. Consequently, the basic difference between Professor Gassner's theory and mine is that while he talked of spontaneous enlightenment based on witnessing the play's tragic resolution, I am considering a technique of playwrighting that is not concerned with individual conflicts, is more sociological in its orientation, and seeks to delay catharsis in an effort to force the theatergoer into a more active and lingering intellectual and emotional participation.

By creating dissonance, the play forces the spectator to reduce the psychological imbalance either by rejecting the play outright as meaningless, repressing it out of consciousness, or if he intuitively feels that the play has merit, by attempting to discover for himself its final pattern. He does this by reviewing the data assimilated during the theatrical experience. Impelled by a disquieting sense of unfulfillment, he examines and re-examines the experience—only now he can choose to analyze the dramaturgical elements one at a time, shifting and interpolating them until a clear, understandable pattern emerges.

When this pattern is recognized as meaningful, the spectator has taken on a new role as creator by collaborating with the playwright on the play's final design, but he is still an audience because he experiences enlightenment. This feeling of intellectual discovery or catharsis reduces his dissonance, returning him once more to a state of consonance. It is at this precise moment of insight that he also experiences identification. Before The New Theatre, identification occurred between audience and player as the spectators empathized with one or more of the actors. Now, however, the moment of insight sets up an empathic connection between playgoer and playwright—usually long after both have left the theatre. This identification creates empathy, and the theatregoer experiences the psychological state of mind that the playwright was in when he wrote the play. Psychologist Robert Katz describes the process in his excellent book on the empathic response:

> Empathy ultimately is vicarious introspection — We *introject* [italics mine] the other person into ourselves and it is our own imagination that is active, having been stimulated by the preceptual cues that came to us from the other person via our own eyes and our own ears.[36]

How long he remains with that state depends on whether he agrees with what his mental probing has discovered—that is, the playwright's point of view. Disagreement after insight is achieved will result in a repetition of cognitive dissonance; and the spectator will be able to extricate himself from this second state of psychological discomfort only by negating whatever disturbing insight he may have received or by finding a way to overcome his resistance.

Clive Barnes was quite correct when he said that the play "does not call for normal responses."[37] Walter Kerr, writing about his personal response to the play, unknowingly described the cognitive dissonant process at work:

> In a way, we have been saved from drowning as the woman has. Whether out of his instincts or his intentions, Mr. Albee has thrown us a life preserver, a story not just to keep us afloat, but to make us wish to keep afloat.
> We've had to grab at ourselves, very nearly at random; we've had to tie strings together, and not too securely. But we have been supported. And have remained interested in going on.[38]

Apropos these remarks, let us go on to a further discussion of the play's thematic implications. We can start by challenging Kerr's earlier statement on non-narrative plays. When he complains that the cut-up narrative will never come together again, his prophecy implies two conclusions: first, that a separated narrative will not communicate, and second, that the only form of thematic transmission is through the sequential plot. As to the first of these assumptions, we have already seen that it *is possible* for the out-of-sequence plot to be put together in the spectator's head and still communicate the playwright's intention. Supporting this proposition is theatre critic Richard Kostelanetz who observes:

> Whereas the old theatre, as well as the old music and the old film, imitated the formal character of print by

offering a line of development, the new theatre presents
a discontinuous succession of images and events, which
must be pieced together in the observer's mind if the
piece is to be fully understood.[39]

Secondly, there are other equally effective means of communication besides the story, or for that matter, the word.
McLuhan, in analyzing television communication, says that
"by surpassing writing we have regained our wholeness, not
on a national or cultural, but cosmic, plane. We have evoked
a supercivilized sub-primitive man."[40] Kostelanetz, too, in
taking about nonliterary methods of communication in the
theatre, has referred to an awakening of our other senses:

> The ultimate meaning of an event can be nothing
> more than the form it offers—the medium of multiple
> means can be the entire message—just as the complete
> effect of a piece may be the enhancement of the audience's sensory perception.[41]

In *Box-Mao-Box,* however, the revolutionary form of the
piece is not its only meaning. Because Albee still chooses to
use the word as his major means of expression, the play's
innovative form only underscores its basic theme in that
both the form and the content of this piece are concerned
with death of the old through revolution. This is not to say
that Albee has written a propaganda play condoning the
Communist revolution. On the contrary, we will see that he
is out to awaken other forms of revolution in us—forms that
will incite an assault on the societal *status quo,* the cold
war and the theatre being only elements of that stagnant
condition.

Those contrapuntal theses of death and revolution in *Mao*
can best be elucidated by returning to a discussion of the
long-winded lady casually seated in her deck chair, prattling
comfortably on about her private life to a sleepy minister.
As we listen to her private confessions, the abstract comments
suddenly turn into a concrete tale of a recent, rather trau-

matic incident, bringing this matronly woman into sharp
focus. She relates an episode she witnessed in which a taxi
went out of control, leaving dead pedestrians strewn all over
the street, grotesquely marking out the automobile's path.
Her first thoughts, she tells the cleric, were that someone was
making a movie because "the mind works that way." She was
not able, or willing, to conceive of real death when it was
happening. Her attitude is essentially no different from the
way the United States watches the Vietnam war via television.
The populace of this country observe the atrocities with the
same detachment they would give to a war movie playing
for the tenth time on the early, late, or late late show. The
difference is that these players really die—but much of the
viewing public doesn't believe it. The long-winded lady only
reflects her country's condition when she cannot believe it
is really death that she sees. The constant year-in and year-
out coverage of the war has dulled most people's minds to
its horror. Hence, it doesn't take much of a logical jump—
now that we know Mao is on board ship—to realize that this
matronly lady, like the statue she passed leaving New York
harbor, is a symbol for the United States.

She appears to be a very lonely lady, at the age of retirement; having outlived her husband, she now contemplates
the imminent coming of her own demise. She is in need of
talk, solace, and reassurance from the Church, but all she
gets is a sleepy-eyed minister out to avoid any involvement
that might wake him up.

The lonely lady is the last stage of Mom. Reflecting the
census accurately, Mom has outlived Dad. Daddy is dead and
the country is in Mom's shaky hands. Avoiding any direct
confronation with problems at home, she has decided to
leave and cruise away her retirement, in self-imposed isolation. The problem of retirement for senior citizens is an old
theme of Albee's. Ostensibly, the concern he has shown for
those in their declining years, as dramatically echoed in *A*

Delicate Balance, and before that in *The Sandbox* and *The American Dream,* stems from a constant preoccupation with that time in a citizen's life when he has outlived his usefulness to the society. In a recent interview, Albee highlighted this personal concern when he talked of a childhood book he still remembered. It was a "book about a fire engine. It was about to be retired and didn't want to be, or wasn't about to be—whatever it was, it affected me greatly."[42] While Albee was only half serious in mentioning a book that affected his childhood, the long remembrance of it, to the exclusion of so many others he must have read, suggests he still carries that little story and its message with him in adult life.

The phlegmatic minister, not aroused by this woman's fear for her future, is obviously symbolic. Abandoning its historical role of spiritual leader, the Church, according to Albee, has fallen asleep in the face of the problems of modern society. In a world threatening to double its population within the next forty years, Pope John XXIII made a plea for large families as late as 1960.[43] And, according to the latest encyclical of Pope Paul VI, the church still will not approve of any artificial means of birth control for the world's half-billion Roman Catholics. Not wanting to underscore the symbolism any further than he has, Albee suggests still another interpretation of the silent clergyman. He has said: "There is a Protestant minister who doesn't say anything. He keeps falling asleep. I suppose he's sort of a critic, except that he's sober."[44] Albee's facetious attempt to shift the symbolism is backing away from his original intention. Presumably, the connection he would like to make is that both professions have fallen asleep to what is happening.

Mom goes on with her story, admitting that dad died of a spreading cancer, which ostensibly reflects the present malignant conditions in this country. The woman is afraid of being next, and she confesses to the minister that she is in fear of falling—even dreams of it. If the long-winded lady

223 |

does indeed represent the United States, what Albee is insinuating is that this country is rightly in fear of falling from its place as world leader. It could also mean we are about to fall from grace, since the recipient of the lady's confession is an ecclesiastic. In viewing her present life she remarks that there's "nothing to hold on to. So you lean on your imagination and over one goes." The "aged lady," as she refers to herself, tells of the time she fell, or jumped, overboard on another cruise: "When you're in the water, boats move away with astonishing speed." The woman is worried that the supports of her life are slipping away, and she is in fear of falling over. Her observation of the speed with which a boat moves away (unnoticed while on board) is her way of saying how fast the older generation is left behind. The last time it happened, the ship stopped to pick her up. She fears it will happen again, and this time she will be left alone to die while the new generation goes on. She feels abandoned and isolated, a useless relic waiting to die amongst a new generation she does not understand. Her dilemma is paradoxical. Earlier she talked of the loneliness a rebellious daughter has brought her (the girl is off somewhere with two Mexicans, an illustration of the next generation's break with tradition); yet she deliberately seeks the isolation of a ship's voyage. She wonders, still talking to the dozing cleric, why she hasn't killed herself. Her only answer is "I have nothing to die for."

Albee's comment relates to the uncommited generation—those who go through life unwilling to stand or die for a cause they believe in. It is a country of great compromisers who will bend with the wind to get ahead, or to avoid a socially unacceptable position.

The long-winded lady's concern with her impending demise in the face of this generation's revolutionary fervor is echoed and magnified by an older woman's incessant, out-of-sequence recitation of a long-forgotten poem attributed to William Carpenter: "Over the hill to the poorhouse I'm trudgin' my weary way I, a woman of seventy, and only a trifle gray." This monotonous rhyme scheme stands in grotesque counterpoint to the long-winded lady's predicament. Some critics have felt the old woman is a symbol of Europe or even England,[45] but I prefer to see her as a second, more macabre parody of this country. It is a droll reflection which predicts a possible future path for the nation.

There is only one more aspect of *Box-Mao-Box* that needs clarification. It is the connection between the play's structure and musical form. In the program notes, Albee has revealed that "I have attempted, in these two related plays, several experiments having to do—in the main—with the application of musical form to dramatic structure. . . ." Albee has also been quoted as saying that he has organized the play "to make the proper contrapuntal effect."[46] The critics, in their eagerness to dispense with the Albee experiment, have jumped on the musical band wagon and used the analogy to nullify the play. One critic compared it to the A,B, (A), A sequence of a Bach partita and, in doing so, said of the Albee piece: "There is nothing of any artistic quality in it either. Not even remotely."[47] Evidently the reviewer, so busy figuring out what musical form Albee used, never listened to the words. Walter Kerr also took Albee to task for writing a play whose structure is based on musical form. His opinion is that since "music is not meant to be looked at"[48] the play cannot be sustained. His logic is wrong; Albee's play is not music; it is based on music, therefore the rules of music do not apply. Kerr might also want to know that there are modern composers around town, *a la* the action-and-gesture theatrics of John Cage, who would disagree with his supposition. In all fairness to Mr. Kerr, I should mention that when he saw the plays a second time six months later, he admitted "liking them better."[49]

Theatre and the other arts are changing at such a rapid

pace, cross-fertilizing one another, that the old lines of demarcation have been eradicated. New hybrid forms are emerging in the performing, as well as the fine arts. In today's exceedingly complex and interrelated society, The New Theatre is seeking to reflect contemporary life and create meaningful communication in a world besieged by a plethora of communication systems. The job of the critic is to approach the event without preconceived notions as to what the theatrical experience should be. Criticism must not be used to entrench or affirm one's ideas; nor should the critic set himself up as arbiter of public morality. His job is to interpret, encourage, and generate ideas so that creative thought will always prevail. As to *Box-Mao-Box,* I feel much as Clive Barnes did when he wrote:

> Personally, I welcome it and look forward to seeing it again. It may well be one of Albee's best plays; it is unquestionably his most adventurous.[50]

CHAPTER 11

TWO INTERVIEWS WITH EDWARD ALBEE

RUTENBERG: I'd like to discuss something that was mentioned by you in another interview and pursue it further here because I think it has relevance to understanding your work—particularly the structure of your plays. You once stated, "I find play construction and musical composition enormously similar . . . I can carry on an analogy between musical form and play structure all night if you'd like me to." What I would like is for you to relate the analogy specifically to your own plays, using whatever examples would make the comparison clearer.

ALBEE: I'm sorry that I ever said I could run on about it all night if I wanted to. I can only talk about the feeling I have about it, prefacing that by saying first that when I was eleven, I decided I wanted to be a composer. I started listening to serious music when I was around nine, and by the time I was eleven—eleven and a half—I decided I wanted to be a composer but found that I was either too lazy or too inept to learn to play the piano or to learn to read music so that was all that came to. But since that time—since I was nine years old—which is over 25 years now—I have been listening to serious music with maybe something more than the amateur's ear and have, among my friends, a surprising number of composers. Now I said that play structure and musical form seem to me to be similar, but that is primarily something that I intuit, rather than anything that I could show by graph. But a play, though it does exist physically on the stage, and can be read, is enormously aural. And the structure of a play is apprehended, in the mind, by the ear, very much the way that a musical composition is. I don't know if I can be more explicit than that. But quite often when I read a play of my own, I do notice that there's counterpoint here, or the themes are returning the way they will in a sonata allegro form. When I'm writing my own play, I don't set out consciously to imitate musical structure—it's just that when my plays are going well, when I'm writing them and the writing seems to be going well, they seem to me very much to relate to musical form.

RUTENBERG: In the *New York Times,* as early as February 15, 1960, you made this statement about work on *Virginia Woolf*: "The older couple have created a fantasy child . . . whom they drag out to advance their divergent viewpoints." Did your idea of the child change by the time you finished the play?

ALBEE: I don't believe so. The way I write plays primarily is to discover that I'm with an idea, that I have been thinking about the idea, then I spend anywhere from six months to two years letting the idea develop without doing any work at the typewriter. Which is why I could have said that I was writing the story of *Virginia Woolf* in 1960 when actually I didn't start writing it, I believe, until—when—until the summer of '62, I guess—yes '62. It seems to me that the child has remained a fantasy child. But with a sensitive, intelligent couple like Martha and George in *Who's Afraid of Virginia Woolf* the fantasy child can be just as real as any real child. There was some notion in my mind, while I was working on the play, and it's not terribly important, but it was there, which is the reason actually that I named the couple Gorge and Martha—after General and Mrs. Washington. There might be an allegory to be drawn, and have the fantasy child the revolutionary principles of this country that we haven't lived up to yet. I don't think the nature of the child changed very much in the course of thinking about writing the play. I've a very great argument with a number of critics who said that the fantasy child was a weak point in the play. It struck me as being a rather important development.

RUTENBERG: Don't you think that the child is used to solace their loneliness, besides advance divergent viewpoints?

ALBEE: Well doubtless because they were childless they created the child. I would imagine that would be more an unconscious use, or certainly using the child as an intellectual weapon is more conscious than the emotional weapon and the emotional need.

RUTENBERG: Did the child also symbolize or represent the false illusions we all seem to carry with us, and the subsequent exorcism suggest a new state of emotional honesty?

ALBEE: Well certainly—the exorcism of the non-existent child—that was the point I was trying to make about the exorcism of the non-existent child—sure.

RUTENBERG: What do you think of this particular interpretation forwarded to me recently: The child is really a symbolic Christ child, and when George, who represents (possibly) the Protestant Church six centuries younger than "Martha," the Catholic Church, exorcizes their baby, it is a sign that religion is no longer needed to fill our lives with illusion. Nick does say two times, "Jesus Christ, I think I understand," after the exorcism.

ALBEE: That is a lot of Christian nonsense. But this is something interesting. I begin to suspect that I put an awful lot more Christian symbolism into my plays than I am consciously aware of Lord knows people have been finding a great deal of Christian symbolism in *Tiny Alice*. And a woman once sent me a paper that she had published on *The Zoo Story*, pointing up rather beautifully I thought, that Jerry in *The Zoo Story* was Christ. And it is true, in *The Zoo Story*, for example, that Peter does deny Jerry three times. He says, I do not understand the whole point of the dog story three times; and I guess it is also true in *Who's Afraid of Virginia Woolf*. Nick says that he does understand three times—which is another form of denial perhaps. But no deliberate Christian allegory.

RUTENBERG: Did you have Nikita Krushchev in mind when you named Nick—Nick?

ALBEE: Yes, but not very importantly, only to the extent that I named George and Martha after George and Martha Washington. It's not a major point.

RUTENBERG: *The Catholic Transcript* on January 1, 1963, said that it seemed (we're talking about *Virgiina Woolf*) that the only motivation for Martha's verbal lacerations and humiliations in addition to her alleged promiscuity was that, "George has been content with a subordinate position at the college." Does that seem in keeping with your idea of Martha's motives?

ALBEE: That would be an over-simplification certainly—an enormous over-simplification.

RUTENBERG: Richard Watts has said that Nick's character, as written, is "somewhat underdeveloped." Would you agree with him?

ALBEE: I'll grant that the concentration was on George and Martha, with Nick and Honey as a motivating audience. But, then again, if you've got a man like Nick, who's in a power situation where he's got to tread very carefully, and speak very carefully, and be reticent, and be quiet, and find out exactly what he's supposed to say, he's not going to be terribly loquacious.

RUTENBERG: Had you ever considered a less realistic setting in order to give the play more of a sense of universality? Or at least a more multi-area arrangement?

ALBEE: Its never semed to me that the abstraction of the set leads to greater universality of the play. No I hadn't ever thought of the more abstract set. I know a lot of other people have. Harold Clurman kept saying that he thought it should have been done with a more abstract set. And I do believe that the production that Ingmar Bergman did in Stockholm had an abstract set. I saw the play in Princeton which was done with basically the set we did in New York except that you could see through it, to a certain extent, and it didn't seem to change the entire thing very much to me.

RUTENBERG: Since so many critics have tried to understand *Tiny Alice* on all its many levels would you mind commenting on the following interpretation. It's rather long but we may get to something at the end of it. Julian, a lay brother who has always wanted to be of service to God, is suddenly offered a unique chance. He can become the instrument through which millions will be granted to the Church, provided he sacrifice his vow of celibacy and marry a Miss Alice, the woman who has made this financial offer. Thinking this request the will of God and somewhat motivated by subconscious sexual repression which can now be fulfilled, he accepts the proposal. However, as soon as the wedding ceremony is over, he is told that he has not really married Miss Alice, for she is only the surrogate for Tiny Alice, a Deity of some kind, and that in reality it was the Deity he married through Miss Alice. Julian is then asked to accept this Deity as an act of faith by remaining with her while the others, including his wife-surrogate, depart for other ends of the earth, presumably to start the cycle again. Refusing to accept this new God as an act of Christian faith, mainly because he can't see her (though he can't see his own God either), and also because he will not allow himself to worship any God-symbol whether it be Tiny Alice or any religious relic of his own God in the place of God himself, he is killed and left to die at the foot of Alice who, if she exists, lives in the replica and elsewhere. In other words, he must remain with her one way or another, in order for the original bargain to be consummated. Julian, near hysteria, does not know why he must die; and so, in order not to negate an entire life of devotion to the Church and have his life made a mockery, he finally chooses to accept Tiny Alice as an act of faith—as God—just before he dies. As soon as he does this, the abstraction which up to now he was not able to see, becomes apparent and real to him. That is, whether God is real or not doesn't matter; once we accept Him on faith, he becomes real. The audience is then left with this to think about. If Tiny Alice is not God and Julian has deluded himself at the last moment of his life by swearing allegiance to a false God, he has betrayed his own God and in so doing has destroyed his own soul, which ironically will still benefit the Church because of the millions granted through Julian's marriage. On the other hand, if Julian is right and Tiny Alice is really God in a form he had never thought of or conceived of, then what happens at the end of the play is the transfiguration and union of a Christian martyr with his God.

ALBEE: I think that's absolutely lovely. Who did that?

RUTENBERG: I wrote it.

ALBEE: You did! Indeed that is a good deal of what the play is about, and very succinctly put.

RUTENBERG: You probably have read Philip Roth's review in *The New York Review of Books* in which he says, "Tiny Alice is a homosexual daydream in which the celibate male is tempted and seduced by the overpowering female, only to be betrayed by the male lover and murdered by the cruel law, or in this instance, cruel lawyer. . . . In the end the playwright likens him to Jesus Christ—and all because he has had to suffer the martyrdom of heterosexual love." What validity has Mr. Roth's analysis?

ALBEE: I read Mr. Roth's piece with a good deal of morbid

interest, and I suppose as much as anything it proves once again that promising writers are not necessarily good critics. Naturally—I shouldn't say naturally—but the fact is that Mr. Roth's hysteria is his own and has no basis in fact whatever. If Mr. Roth feels threatened, I'm sorry for him. But there's certainly no validity whatever that I can find in his article— I won't call it a review—to the hysterical charges that Mr. Roth raises. I really don't know what was bugging the poor man.

RUTENBERG: I've heard of two alternate endings to *Tiny Alice* that were once considered. The first was to have Julian die inside an attic closet. The second, that he would be tied to the model with rope, to die slowly. Why were these endings abandoned?

ALBEE: Originally when I was thinking about the play, before I got to writing it down, I was going to have him tied to a large table, a leg of which would break, and then he would be, as the leg broke and the table angled out onto the floor, in a crucifixion position. As for the thing about the attic closet, what I meant by that was that the last scene of the play should seem as though he is in the attic closet, enclosed, as a child in the dark, and that no one would come. There are a number of things you can't do on the stage. I suppose, ideally, Julian would have been thrust right into the lap of the audience for the last scene. After the fact, I even considered, or rather thought about, how nice it would have been if I could have had some of the play on film, in order to bring Julian much closer.

RUTENBERG: If the heartbeat and breathing at the end of the play are supposed to represent a larger dimension of Alice, either in Julian's hallucinations or as a further personification of her, why then did the majority of the audience take it to mean Julian's last dying breath? Do you think the production should be clearer on this point—or the play-writing?

ALBEE: I was astonished that the audience thought it was Julian's breath. I expected the audience to think one of the two other things—either that it was Julian's total hallucination or that it was the personification of the abstraction. I'm totally startled. Obviously it must be either a fault in the production, or in the playwriting, or just as likely, and probably even more likely, it must be the unwillingness or inability of the audience to make that further jump.

RUTTENBERG: This question may be irrelevant, but I'm curious to know: What do you think happens to Grandma after she walks out on Mommy and Daddy in *The American Dream?*

ALBEE: Well, Grandma is outside of the situation by that point. I suppose you could use the word and say that she died, and I guess in a sense that she did die. Just as in *The Sandbox,* where she dies specifically. She really doesn't die; she merely departs from a form of life that is a great deal more dead than anything else. I guess I meant her specifically to die, but not in a sense that we understand "die"; to move out of the death within life situation that everybody else in the play was in.

RUTENBERG: We'll move on to your adaptation of *Ballad.* Did you confer with Carson McCullers?

ALBEE: Sure, I talked to Carson a lot.

RUTENBERG: What were some of the questions you asked her?

ALBEE: One question I finally asked here—since the majority of the story seemed quite clear to me—I did ask her this one point, and that is why Miss Amelia married, and indeed since she did marry, exactly why she rejected her husband sexually? I was curious, really, because I couldn't give any answers to the actors or really even to myself as to why specifically she married and having married, rejected her husband. I couldn't give any psychological answer, and since we're stuck with the theatre in which both the directors and the actors demand psychological explanations for everything they do, I thought I should be able to provide one. I understood it intuitively. It didn't raise any problems for me. I couldn't get an answer from Carson. She merely shrugged and said: "That is what she would do." So I tried to leave it at that. It seemed to me quite natural that it is what Miss Amelia would do. However, it did not solve the questions of either Alan Schneider or of Colleen Dewhurst, or of the majority of the critics, unforunately.

RUTENBERG: How did you come to the idea that a Negro actor should play the narrator? If no other Negroes were used in the cast did this tend to alienate the narrator from the people in the play instead of bringing him closer? Alan Lewis has said that the "race problem was . . . needlessly introduced." How do you feel about that in retrospect?

ALBEE: I didn't want the race problem introduced into the play at all. I wanted the narrator to be removed from the remainder of the action of the play. I didn't want him to be one of the town folk. I wanted him to speak Carson's words which were beautifully written. I wanted a removal and that's why I chose a Negro for it. It didn't seem to me to make any particular comment on Negro-White relations. And the removal (maybe it was the fact that he was a Negro) seemed to remove him sufficiently from the action to be an objective voice.

RUTENBERG: Edward Parone in the Los Angeles production of *The Death of Bessie Smith* used her recordings to help tie the play together through her vocal presence. Why had you decided not to use the records in the New York production? It would seem a very natural part of your play.

ALBEE: The reason I did it may have been the wrong reason, but I didn't want to capitalize on the sensational aspects. It seemed to me that it would have been cheating, that it would have been getting an audience emotional response by cheap methods. I would have loved to have seen the Los Angeles production to see whether or not it didn't do that. I can't imagine that Parone did it for sensational reasons or to get a cheap reaction, but it seemed to me that it wouldn't have allowed the play to stand on its own feet as much as I wanted it to.

RUTENBERG: I understand you were commissioned to write *The Sandbox* for the Spoleto Festival, but that it was never performed there. What happened?

ALBEE: That was the season at Spoleto when Gian-Carlo Menotti asked fifteen or twenty writers and composers and other people to do things for a project he had for Spoleto called "Album Leaves," which was meant to be a serious revue. Aaron Copeland wrote a piece; Ionesco wrote a short play. Lots of people did things, and then, with the usual chaos that goes on at the Spoleto Festival, practically nothing was done.

RUTENBERG: Would you say that the play is an attack on society that no longer has any use, respect, or patience for its old people?

ALBEE: That's safe enough thing to say, I suppose.

RUTENBERG: On February 15, 1960, in the *New York Times* you said that *The Zoo Story* is not a nihilistic or pessimistic play because as Jerry dies he passes on an awareness of life to Peter and that the play "therefore is obviously not a denial of life." But Jerry didn't just die, he committed suicide. Isn't that a denial of his life?

ALBEE: Christ did something of the same sort of thing.

RUTENBERG: You think it was a suicide?

ALBEE: Well, what is the nature of suicide? There are all forms of suicide. Christ perfectly well knew what was going to happen to him. He was told to stop. He did not stop. It's a form of suicide. The word suicide shoudn't be used, actually, nor do I think that Jerry necessarily did commit suicide either, anymore than Christ did.

RUTENBERG: Isn't Jerry out to destroy the complacency he sees in Peter, and when he fails to penetrate Peter's neatly ordered world, decides the only way to get any recognition from him is to have Peter participate in his death.

ALBEE: Indeed! Had Peter understood, had he not refused to understand, then I doubt the death would have been necessary. Jerry tries all through the play to teach and fails. And finally makes a last effort at teaching, and I think, succeeds.

RUTENBERG: Is there any validity in this statement from *Contact,* October 1963, issue. *"The Zoo Story* describes an unsuccessful homosexual pass."

ALBEE: I don't think so. I get rather upset sometimes by all these references to homosexuality in my plays. I'm trying to think if I've ever written about a homosexual at all in any of the plays I've written so far. I don't believe that I have.

RUTENBERG: Peter has been referred to by Harold Clurman as society's "average representative." Is that what you had in mind?

ALBEE: He's a little average. When I first wrote the play, before I did my revisions on it, he was much more of a stereotype. The play was practically all Jerry, and Peter was much more of a figure of fun, and I tried to make him more of a three-dimensional human being. But he certainly does have an awful lot of the half-awake, half-asleep, safe attributes. The way most people manage to get through life certainly.

RUTENBERG: Do you think an average man is capable of holding down a job that will pay him $18,000 a year as an executive?

ALBEE: What do you mean by that?

RUTENBERG: He must be doing something beyond the average for a company to pay him $18,000 a year. That is quite a bit of money for Mr. Average to make.

ALBEE: Oh! Average in attitudes.

RUTENBERG: Robert Brustein said that "*The Zoo Story* lacked a convincing antagonist." Do you think that despite your continued work on the play before it was produced, Peter is not developed as he might be?

ALBEE: I disagree with practically everything that Brustein says. Brustein is fairly bright, but terribly limited. I find it very difficult to go back to my plays and see how I would have done them differently. I find it almost impossible to do that, so I can't say. He seemed to be three-dimensional enough to me.

RUTENBERG: Why doesn't Peter just walk away and let Jerry have the bench?

ALBEE: That's an interesting question, isn't it? One—there wouldn't have been a play—would there? But that's not the real reason. It struck me that Jerry is intelligent and clever enough to keep Peter there. Now naturally Robert Brustein wouldn't have stayed, Jerry Talmer wouldn't have stayed, and the majority of other nervous critics who say that per-haps Peter wouldn't have stayed wouldn't have stayed either —but these men, perhaps, throw themselves into the play too much—see too much of themselves in Peter.

RUTENBERG: Let's go to some general questions on playwriting. What, as you see it, should be the function of the playwright?

ALBEE: I guess you can divide playwrights into two basic categories—aside from the good ones and the bad ones. There is the playwright who feels that he's basically a manufacturer who constructs entertainments for a buyer's market. A lot of very good plays, to their intention, have been written by this kind of man. There is also the kind of playwright who really, outside of the pressures that come about, is totally his own man. He writes the plays basically for the audience of himself and is delighted if other people like the plays as well. And I suppose, then, if he starts thinking about it after the fact of each piece that he writes, he sort of sees himself as a social critic. As a man out-of-step with his society. A man who feels primarily that his play should not have had to have been written.

RUTENBERG: Do you feel yourself as a social critic?

ALBEE: I've been called one often enough. I don't set out to write plays as a social critic, however, but that would seem to be the effect that I have.

RUTENBERG: Has periodically teaching, or rather "refereeing," playwriting classes helped you in your own writing?

ALBEE: It's forced me to think a little more clearly—to think on my feet, to intellectualize some things that I usually apprehend intiutively. I suppose it hasn't hurt.

RUTENBERG: Do you ever work from a written plot outline?

ALBEE: No; never. I find part of the joy of writing in discovering what is going on with the characters and getting out of my system what is filling it.

RUTENBERG: What is the outlook for the American

Theatre? Where are new playwrights coming from in a situation that does not allow failure from its artists?

ALBEE: The new American playwrights have been coming from Off-Broadway and are being assimilated usually, and destroyed, by the commercial theatre uptown. Off-Broadway at this moment is very unhealthy. The theatre is quite sick, and the commercial theatre is in worse shape than it ever was. But it seems to me that every other kid in Greenwich Village, for example, is carrying a play under his arm that he has written. There are more young playwrights functioning in New York alone, for example, today than ever have been in this country before.

RUTENBERG: Can they be produced? Can they get their plays done?

ALBEE: They get them done. The critics are quarrelsome and unpleasant about it, but the kids keep writing. I don't really know how to answer the question whether or not a theatre can support, to use the awful word, serious playwrights or not.

RUTENBERG: Do you think that the New York theatre is going to decentralize more than it has, and, if so, where will the theatre go?

ALBEE: I doubt that it will decentralize, or if it does decentralize more of the worst aspect of it will be decentralized, I suspect.

RUTENBERG: Can young playwrights develop in a nonprofessional environment? Say, a college theatre?

ALBEE: I suppose a young playwright could develop in a college theatre if the people who are running the college theatre were free-swinging and adventurous. Otherwise it would be just as dead as working in a commercial theatre.

RUTENBERG: What do you think of the formation of

the American Playwrights Theatre? The purpose of the organization is to give the colleges a chance to produce an original play by a well-known writer.

ALBEE: I don't really know what good that does. I can't understand the whole point of it.

RUTENBERG: The point of it is that the colleges are always producing tired revivals and this doesn't encourage young artists to write original scripts. It also offers the professional writer a chance to get his play done prior to Broadway and to work out some of the kinks without the fantastic expense. It may also help break the reticence we have to accepting new plays before the New York critics tell us it is a hit.

ALBEE: Maybe that would be fun for a kind of playwright who likes to do a lot of revisions. A playwright who doesn't feel that once he's seen his work that he's had it. For myself if I had a play done, let's say at a university, I can't imagine that I'd be terribly interested in having it put on commercially—just because the play would be over for me. I would have seen what I'd done and I'd be hard pressed to care about having it done commercially.

RUTENBERG: Would you say, then, that writing for you resembles an emotional catharsis?

ALBEE: Oh, indeed it does.

RUTENBERG: Julian Beck wrote a letter to his friend which was published in the *Times* in which he said that he predicted more "will be seen and heard of and about . . . the Theatre of Cruelty." He said that "if we could at least feel pain, we might turn towards becoming men again instead of . . . callous automata." Do you agree with this prediction?

ALBEE: Well, one has to, because he's merely talking about the same thing that everybody's been yapping about for the longest time. That the audiences prefer re-affirmation of their own values; that they want to see comforting things; that they don't want to be upset and disturbed. It is the play-wright's function, or at least the function of a number of playwrights, to keep hammering at this point.

RUTENBERG: Do you have any other comments to make in closing?

ALBEE: One thing does please me. When I went to school, when I was in Prep School (the only time I spent in college was a year and a half), plays weren't taught, and now they are. It's fascinating and wonderful. I find that plays by Becket, Genet, Brecht, and Ionesco are taught as part of modern literature courses in schools and colleges. It's an extraordinary development. I think it's wonderful.

August 7, 1968

RUTENBERG: I understand that Albarr productions has signed a multiple picture contract with Universal. Since it will be your first attempt at writing for the cinema, can you say something about the project?

ALBEE: In theory it's a multiple picture deal. You never know how multiple a picture deal is until you've made your first one. The first picture that we are going to make, that I'm going to write the screenplay for and co-produce with Dick Barr, is my play *The Death of Bessie Smith*. That's the first project. Whether we'll go beyond that I've absolutely no idea. That depends upon whether or not I enjoy writing screenplays, whether or not I enjoy my relationship with Universal, and whether I find it possible to work in the film medium. But anyway, that's the first thing we're going to tackle. There are a couple of others set up after that, but I want to get that one out of the way first before I make any predictions.

RUTENBERG: Will Bessie Smith be absent, or at least not portrayed, in the film?

ALBEE: I haven't made up my mind yet. I'm told you have to open things up and make films very visual. But I don't think I'd like to have anybody portraying Bessie Smith. She's really a symbol as well as a reality, and how you picture a symbol on the screen I don't know.

RUTENBERG: I read that you're interested in Topar's *The Tenant,* is that true? For a film adaptation?

ALBEE: Theoretically that is the second film that I'll be doing. As I say, let's get through the first one first to find out if there is going to be a second one.

RUTENBERG: I'd like now to move on to your stage plays. In *Box-Mao-Box,* the program note mentioned you had attempted to do several experiments having to do in the main with application of musical form to dramatic structure. Could you be more specific as to what musical form, if any, you based your play on?

ALBEE: No. Musical form in general. Not a specific form like a toccata or a passacaglia or anything like that, but the general application of musical structure to dramatic form. Yes. Or the other way around.

RUTENBERG: What else besides musical form did you experiment with—because you mentioned several experiments.

ALBEE: Well, within the framework of musical form the use of counterpoint and the relationship between musical and dramatic structure. Several linking experiments in the relationship of musical and dramatic structure, plus of course the usual experiments in dramaturgy.

RUTENBERG: Do you intend to do any rewrites for its

Broadway debut which I am told will be sometime in the Fall?

ALBEE: I don't think so. I made a few clarifications—not clarifications, disclarifications—of the play after the Buffalo production to fragment it a little bit more, make the counterpoint more evident. Maybe I cut about three or four minutes from the entire hundred minute length. I don't think I plan to cut anymore. No.

RUTENBERG: In our last interview, you said that "If I had a play done, let's say at a university, I can't imagine that I'd be terribly interested in having it put on commercially because the play would be over for me"; yet *Box-Mao-Box* which was done in Buffalo will have its Broadway debut this Fall. Have you changed your mind about seeing your plays done commercially after the initial premiere?

ALBEE: *Box-Mao-Box* is still in flux, I think. I am doing a little work on it, as I said, and learning something from it for future work. Therefore, the experience isn't exhausted for me in this particular instance. Then again, the Arena Theatre in Buffalo isn't a university. I would imagine that if it were a pure, straight, naturalistic play I might be quite fed up with it by now. But since the play is, for me at least, fairly adventurous, there's still something to be learned.

RUTENBERG: Does the silent minister suggest that you mean to say that the church has fallen asleep to the modern needs of society?

ALBEE: I suppose anybody could put whatever symbolism they want to it.

RUTENBERG: One critic said that you had used the AABA of a Bach partita. Is that correct?

ALBEE: That's surprisingly perceptive for a critic.

RUTENBERG: It had occurred to me that the first piece,

Box, happens not on the stage, but in the spectator's head. It's so constructed as to mix and key off our own stream-of-consciousness based on analogous personal experiences.

ALBEE: Very good. True.

RUTENBERG: Is the long-winded lady a symbol of this country, and is her fear of falling indicitive of our own foreign policy?

ALBEE: Again we get into the area of symbols. Right there I plan to be absolutely no help. I think it's about time that audiences and critics and just everybody in general, including playwrights, get rid of this whole notion of the conscious symbolism in realistic or symbolic plays and begin to understand that the use of the unconscious in the 20th Century theatre is its most interesting development. Whatever symbolic content there may be in *Box* and *Quotations from Chairman Mao Tse-Tung,* both plays deal with the unconscious, primarily. That's where it is, and it must not be pigeonholed, examined, and specified. That's wrong.

RUTENBERG: Are you saying then that you aren't particularly aware or conscious of what the long-winded lady represented, and you worked it out purely on an intuitive level?

ALBEE: I'm always a good deal more aware of what I'm doing than half the critics think I am—or than sometimes I even let on myself. People will read signposts into anything because they seem unwilling to suffer an experience on its own terms and let their unconscious come into full play. That is what is supposed to happen in a play. This pigeonholing and symbol-hunting is merely an attempt not to suffer the experience the playwright wants the audience to suffer.

RUTENBERG: Do you mean to say that the intellectualization process is really a defense against an emotional experience?

ALBEE: It's not a process of intellectualization curiously enough, it's a process of trying to find superficial hangers to hold on to. There is a certain process, I suppose, of trying to intellectualize an emotional experience that makes people feel terribly smart. But it avoids the dramatic experience certainly.

RUTENBERG: Let's talk about your latest adaptation, *Everything in the Garden*. Why change Mrs. Toothe from a Polish Jew with a concentration camp background to a rather mysterious English lady. John Lahr in *Evergreen* said it was because you didn't want to offend your Westchester audience.

ALBEE: John Lahr is a very confused young man. I'm trying to remember why I changed Mrs. Toothe from Mrs. Pimosz who in the English version was a Polish Jew. Why did I do it? It certainly wasn't from Mr. Lahr's theory. That may be why he would have done it, but it certainly wasn't why I did it. As I remember, I wanted a symbol of something that Americans would be terribly impressed by. Since Americans *are* terribly impressed by money and by the English, it seems that the offering of money should come from the British. It amused me. God knows there was enough of an attack on the Westchester type anti-semitism in that play so that Mr. Lahr's remarks are ridiculous.

RUTENBERG: More than one critic complained that Jenny and her friends were just not up to the kind of call girls men are willing to pay $100 an afternoon for. *Show Business* said: "I couldn't honestly think of any of those suburban matrons as possibly being a $100 girl," and the *Telegraph* described Jenny as "ill-combed hair, uninteresting wool skirts, flat shoes and oversized droopy grey pull-over sweaters;

a result about as glamorous as crushed apple pie." Did you intend Jenny to be played so unglamorously? And if so, for what reason?

ALBEE: Because this play was much more interested in the reality sex life of the American male than the fantasy sex life of the American male. Most men, when they cheat on their wives, think they're going to be cheating with some stacked eighteen-year-old number and they usually don't. They usually end up with their neighbor's wife. So the play was absolutely accurate and factual, and if the critics don't like it, it's because they prefer their fantasy sex life to their real one.

RUTENBERG: Why did you cut the original ending of your play for the Broadway presentation?

ALBEE: It was a last desperate moment because the way the play had been directed up to that particular point, the end wasn't working. I think that with a different directorial concept, the ending would have worked. You *will* notice that the published version of the play has the original ending, and the productions being done in stock and amateur and in Europe have my original ending.

RUTENBERG: Why did you decide to have Madame Toothe make the decision to stop Jack from leaving and also bury him after the murder? Cooper, as you remember, had Jenny come up with the idea.

ALBEE: I'm not quite sure that I remember now. It's about a year, at least a year, since I wrote the American version of that particular English play. I do understand, by the way, that the screenplay is being written by John Osborne. This may not be true, may be true, which is interesting. Maybe it will go exactly back to Giles Cooper's script, in which case our present critic for the *New York Times* can become a little less hysterical about the whole matter. I don't quite remember why I did all that; it seemed proper and right at the time.

RUTENBERG: The reason I mentioned it is that if Richard and Jenny are the protagonists, and not Mrs. Toothe, then it would seem they should make the decision.

ALBEE: Acquiescence to any form of moral structure is as active, it seems to me, as presenting the alternatives to such a decision.

RUTENBERG: Don't you feel that Jack's recognition of Mrs. Toothe as an old madam friend from London is a bit contrived, or at least coincidental, especially since the murder hinges on this recognition?

ALBEE: Certainly no more contrived or coincidental than the majority of the events in the play—both Mr. Cooper's version and my own.

RUTENBERG: I'd like to discuss *A Delicate Balance* with you. Most of the critics felt that *Balance* had to do with the responsibility of friendship versus the rights of privacy. But I had always felt that the play goes deeper than that into destroying illusions. Specifically, the illusion that in this society we have true friends, and the illusion that it's never too late to change what we are. Would you agree?

ALBEE: Well, I would certainly hope, and I would definitely agree with you that *A Delicate Balance* does go a trifle deeper than the majority of critics claim to see. As I recall it—again now it's two years since I wrote that play—as I recall, the basic premise of that play was the perpetuation of the illusion that freedom of choice remains after a certain time. The point of the play was that we lose . . . we develop a kind of arthritis of the mind, of the morality, and change becomes impossible finally, as one of the characters does say in the play: "Everything becomes too late, finally." That was the basic point of the play, not whether or not we live up to our responsibilties of friendship. After a while it doesn't matter because we become helpless again.

RUTENBERG: After you accepted the Pulitzer Prize for *Delicate Balance* and warned the committee that the prize is an honor in decline, critic John Simon said you should have refused it outright, as Sartre refused the Nobel prize. Mr. Simon's reasons were the play was "neither a critical nor an audience success." Any comment on his evaluation of your work or the motives for your acceptance?

ALBEE: I wrote what was I thought was rather a good reply to Mr. Simon, which was published in the *New York Times.*

RUTENBERG: Excuse me, it will be included in the chapter on *Balance.*

ALBEE: Good. I phrased it rather carefully, much better than I could do off-the-cuff now.

RUTENBERG: In *Malcolm,* why did you leave out Estel Blanc, the Abyssinian undertaker? It would seem an excellent beginning for a play that ends in Malcolm's death.

ALBEE: Why did I leave out Estel Blanc, the Abyssinian undertaker? Again I don't remember. As I recall the stage finally became so cluttered with characters, all of whom I was enjoying enormously but everybody else was sitting there with stony disregard, that one or two of them had to go. Yes, Estel Blanc vanished quite early. I think I thought he was a blind alley in some particular fashion. He was an interesting one-scene grotesque, but I thought the play had too many one-scene grotesques in it.

RUTENBERG: According to the novel, Malcolm's death is left uncertain or at least it's uncertain as to whether anyone was buried in the cemetery. Why did you feel it necessary to make his death so definite?

ALBEE: I don't think I made his death any more definite than Purdy did. Poor boy was fucked to death, both in the book and in the play.

RUTENBERG: Ruth White has said you had written an epilogue which took place five years later in which Madame Gerard called all the people together to attend a belated funeral for Malcolm. The reaction is, "Who is Malcolm?" What made you decide to cut it from the production and the printed version of the play?

ALBEE: Because I thought it was wrong.

RUTENBERG: Why didn't it work?

ALBEE: Again you're taking me back—what, four years, three-and-a-half—to remember something which is a rather unpleasant experience to begin with. It struck me at the time, as I remember it, that I preferred to leave the audience with the death of Malcolm and the vacant gold bench fading into darkness. That struck me as being a more poignant ending and the other perhaps a more literary and intellectual comment that probably would have taken away from the apparently minute emotional involvement the audience had anyway.

RUTENBERG: In one interview you said, "I didn't like the way it was directed. It got completely out of hand." What went wrong?

ALBEE: I think in that same interview I clarified the point further. I believe I said that it was the one experiment that I made, letting the director have his head completely. And I did whatever the director wanted. Alan Schneider and I do seem to have survived the experience quite nicely together.

RUTENBERG: Why did you leave out the tattooing scene from the Purdy novel?

ALBEE: Why did I leave out the tattooing scene? Again, if I'd kept every single thing in, every single scene in Purdy's book including many that I enjoyed enormously, we would have had a play that was nineteen hours long. I did have to make some selection.

RUTENBERG: Why did you change Gus from the original Negro boy to a Caucasian for the play?

ALBEE: Change who?

RUTENBERG: Gus. He was Melba's first husband—or at least sexual partner—and he was played by a Caucasian. In the book he's a Negro.

ALBEE: I think it was a matter of casting, as I recall. God knows it wasn't a question of trying to clear the stage of Negroes. As a matter of fact, we went into rehearsal with at least one Negro in the cast. Then I changed the nature of that character and unfortunately he couldn't play it.

RUTENBERG: In the novel Gus dies at the brothel and is found by Malcolm; yet in the play there's no mention of this. It seems as if you had simply forgotten about him. I understand that there was mention of his death in an earlier version where Melba says: "He's been dead for years." Why was this sequence cut?

ALBEE: Again, you can do in a novel many things that you can't do in a play. In a play you've got to simplify just a little bit, because an audience is capable of following just so many strands—and remembering so many things. Because they also have to watch when they're at a play, as well as listen and pay attention. Those are very difficult things for audiences to do. When you're reading a book you can go back for one thing; you can read at leisure. You read much more slowly than you hear in a play. Again, it was a question of making choices.

RUTENBERG: You don't think that an audience could remember? You don't think that Gus's unexplained disappearance would bother them?

ALBEE: It didn't bother me. Maybe it bothered you.

RUTENBERG: It certainly did.

ALBEE: I'm trying to recall. I think I would have had to go into something rather elaborate about time sequences, and I didn't want to do that.

RUTENBERG: The last time we talked about *Tiny Alice* I asked you why you felt the heartbeat at the end did not work for the audience and why they thought it was Julian's heartbeat? You felt it was either a fault in the production, or in the playwriting, or the inability of the audience to make the further jump. Had you considered that the heartbeat was simply too human to be thought of as coming from a deity. Perhaps some less anthropomorphic sound should have been used, unless it's Julian's image and not the real God at all.

ALBEE: Well, that's the whole basis of the play: the creation of God in the image of man.

RUTENBERG: Bernard Dukore, writing in *Drama Survey*, informs us that "tiny alice" is homosexual argot for a man's anus. Was that pun intended when you titled your play?

ALBEE: I don't know where half these people get their arcane information from. It's fascinating information and perhaps I'll be able to use it in a play some day.

RUTENBERG: The same writer makes a comparison of your "Alice" to Lewis Carroll's "Alice" because both seem to grow large and small. Had you the Carroll tale in mind when you wrote the play?

ALBEE: No, I had very little in mind except my own imaginaion.

RUTENBERG: Concerning *Virginia Woolf,* Martin Gottfried has written: "The reason George and Martha cannot have children is that they are really men, homosexuals." Ingmar Bergman, in talking about how he'd like to have directed the show, made the same comment. Is there any validity in this interpretation? Are the couple really disguised homosexuals?

ALBEE: Apparently they are from Martin Gottfried's point of view. And apparently Mr. Bergman heard about the possibility and thought it would be an entrancing way to do a play. I worry for Martin Gottfried. He's one of the homosexuality-hysterical critics along with Jerry Talmer who's sitting at the *Post* waiting for Dick Watts to retire. They seem to find homosexuals under every bed, including their own. I worry for them terribly. No, the play was written about men and women, for men and women. It is interesting that what's-his-name (I'm not going to mention his name, since I've mentioned it elsewhere—if you want to mention it you can find it, a film critic for a weekly magazine) wrote in his review of the film version of *Virginia Woolf,* that it was obviously a disguised homosexual play. I wrote this man a letter, or rather I didn't—I had somebody else write him a letter. And he wrote back and said that what he meant was that was the only way he could accept the validity of the relationship. This man whose name I won't mention, J.M. are the initials, and he writes for a news magazine which is not *Time.* I worry about critics. They should try harder to clarify in their own minds and for their readers the distinction between an author's disturbances and their own.

RUTENBERG: You mentioned in our last interview that the exorcism of the nonexistent child suggested a new state of emotional honesty. Yet, I have read in an interesting book called *Pragmatics of Human Communication* that the myth of the alive child has now only been replaced by the myth of the dead child, and that the original illusion remains intact.

ALBEE: No. I don't think so at all. Certainly they're left with the core of the memory of having created a myth and having destroyed it. The awareness of that is the important thing that they're left with. They're not self-deluding people by the end. They're not even self-deluding people at the beginning of the play. They are always totally aware that they are dealing with a myth and not reality.

RUTENBERG: Are you still planning an adaptation of Knowles' *A Separate Peace?*

ALBEE: No, he has sold that to the movies now, and I don't see any point in making a play of it now that it's going to be a movie.

RUTENBERG: Any other adaptations being considered for the stage?

ALBEE: No conscious ones.

RUTENBERG: I read you're working on a very different kind of musical. What's it about and are you really at work on it at the moment?

ALBEE: In theory I am, not in actuality. I would like to tackle a musical one day, but I'd have to write my own music and my own lyrics and my own book. I do have sort of ideas for it, but I want to keep them very secret.

RUTENBERG: I understand you are also working, or at least thinking, about a play called *Seascape*. Can you say something about it?

ALBEE: As little as possible. I am about half way through it. It was going to be one of two short plays, each one an hour long, under the overall title *Life and Death*. *Seascape* was to be the first one, and an hour-long play called *All Over* was to be the second one. However, *Seascape* seems to have gotten out of hand and is going to be at least two and a half hours long—maybe infinitely longer so it's not going to be the first of two plays on a double bill. It's, I suppose, about evolution, really. Two of the characters are people and two of the characters are not.

RUTENBERG: What are they—these non-human people?

ALBEE: I'm not saying they're not human; they're not people. See the play and find out.

RUTENBERG: And what about the other work you mentioned—*All Over?*

ALBEE: That's still going to be about forty-five minutes or an hour long. I'm about a third of the way through that. I'm always working on about three or four things at the same time.

RUTENBERG: I've read that you were busy at one point reading books on apes. Is that research in preparation for a new play, or a pleasant diversion?

ALBEE: Well, it's certainly not a pleasant diversion since we are on the way down hill, are we not? Partially research, but everything I do is a combination of pleasure and research.

RUTENBERG: Does the book on apes have anything to do with your evolutionary play *Seascape?*

ALBEE: I wouldn't be surprised.

RUTENBERG: What happened to the play you had been thinking about called *Atilla?*

ALBEE: I'm still thinking about it, as I'm still working on another play, in one way or another for the past four or five years, called *The Substitute Speaker.* I always have lots of things going. I never know which is going to come out first.

RUTENBERG: Anything on paper concerning *The Substitute Speaker?*

ALBEE: Yes. Every one of them has something on paper—if its nothing more than a promissory note to myself.

RUTENBERG: Will you have a new play ready for the Fall season?

ALBEE: I don't know. I suppose *Box* and *Quotations from Chairman Mao Tse-Tung* are reasonably new. Those are the only ones I plan to have on Broadway this year or anywhere. The only new ones.

RUTENBERG: What about an opera entitled *Ice Age* with music by Bill Flanagan? How far have you gotten with that?

ALBEE: Well, I've gotten the first act of the libretto written. I understand he's got part of the first act music written. He and I are at sort of a stand-off. I want to hear the rest of the first act music before I write the rest of the libretto, and he wants to see the rest of the libretto before he writes any more music. We'll get there.

RUTENBERG: In *Newsweek,* you made the statement that playwrights make better critics. Could you explain what you meant?

ALBEE: Better critics than what?

RUTENBERG: Better critics than professional theatre critics.

ALBEE: It's always been my notion, if we're to judge from the excellence of the music criticism that we've had in this country—especially when the *Herald Tribune* was alive and Virgil Thompson was the lead critic and had fellow composers as music critics—we had the best music criticism we've ever had in the United States. I do believe that if our better playwrights were our drama critics, we'd have better drama criticism, more informed audiences, and a better theatre.

RUTENBERG: What about a critic who might be a director such as Harold Clurman?

ALBEE: Well there are always one or two people around who are very excellent critics; people of the theatre who are involved in the theatre. But if we can possibly rid ourselves from what Harold Clurman refers to as the Jewish Mafiia, this group made up of Simon and Brustein and that very sick man from *Women's Wear Daily*, what's his name?

RUTENBERG: Gottfried.

ALBEE: Gottfried. These people who are trying to overthrow the theatre as it exists and recreate it in an image that they and their analysts can live with. If we can possibly get some people who *can* do something in the theatre as critics rather than these appalling men, anything like that would help.

RUTENBERG: Would you comment on the following evaluation of your work written by Martin Gottfried: "Albee is not a real intellectual having neither the patience nor the humility for education, and his discussion of philosophical material is hampered by a weakness of vocabulary."

ALBEE: I think that applies beautifully to Martin Gottfried.

RUTENBERG: I haven't read anywhere of your impressions of Russia during your State Department trip. Could you say a few words about how you felt, and what took place and your evaluation of the country and its people?

ALBEE: When I got back from my first trip to Russia about five years ago, after being in Russia for a month and in some of the satellite countries for another month, I decided, after I'd evaluated the whole experience, I could indeed sit down and write a very long book about it. And after I'd thought about that for a while, I decided not to. One, because I'd only been there once, and secondly because I'd met so many very nice people whose lives and reputations I didn't want to damage by repeating the conversations that we'd had. I found it best to keep my thoughts about my trip to the Soviet Union to myself. I still feel that's pretty true. I've been once again. It's a huge a complex and rather exhilarating and frightening subject. It would take a very long time. It would take a book.

Chronological list of premieres

THE ZOO STORY ....September 28, 1959, Schiller
Theater, Germany.

January 14, 1960, Provincetown
Playhouse, New York City.

THE SANDBOX ....April 15, 1960, The Jazz
Gallery, New York City.

FAM AND YAM ....August 27, 1960, The White
Barn, Westport, Connecticut.

THE DEATH OF BESSIE   April 21, 1960, Schlosspark
SMITH ....Theatre, Germany.

March 1, 1961, York Playhouse,
New York City.

THE AMERICAN DREAM ....January 24, 1961, York Playhouse
New York City.

WHO'S AFRAID OF VIRGINIA   October 13, 1962, Billy Rose
WOOLF? ....Theatre, New York City.

THE BALLAD OF THE   October 30, 1963, Martin Beck
SAD CAFE ....Theatre, New York City.

TINY ALICE ....December 29, 1964, Billy Rose
Theatre, New York City.

MALCOLM ....January 11, 1966, Shubert
Theatre, New York City.

A DELICATE BALANCE ....September 12, 1966, Martin
Beck Theatre, New York City.

EVERYTHING IN THE   November 16, 1967, Plymouth
GARDEN ....Theatre, New York City.

BOX-MAO-BOX ....March 6, 1968, Studio Arena
Theatre, Buffalo, New York.

September 30, 1968, Billy Rose
Theatre, New York City

Notes

INTRODUCTION

[1] Jean Gould, *Modern American Playwrights* (New York: Dodd, Mead & Co., 1966), pp. 273-277.

[2] *New York Times*, July 15, 1968.

[3] Marver H. Bernstein, Robert K. Carr, and Walter F. Murphy, *Essentials of American Democracy* (New York: Holt, Rinehart and Winston, Inc., 1968), pp. 484-485.

[4] Harold Clurman, "The Theatre of the Thirties," *TDR* T6 (Winter, 1959), 3-11.

[5] Gerald Rabkin, *Drama and Commitment* (Bloomington: Indiana Univ. Press, 1964), p. 6.

[6] Ibid., p. 7.

[7] "The Theatre in American Political Life: A Symposium," *yale/theatre*, 1968, II. 14-15.

[8] Interview by Richard Schechner entitled "Reality Is Not Enough," *TDR* T27 (Spring, 1965), pp. 118-152.

CHAPTER 1

[1] *Die Welt*, Sept. 29, 1959.

[2] *Darmstädter Echo*, Sept. 29, 1959.

[3] For an interesting study of conformity within the Big Business Organization, the reader is referred to W. H. Whyte's *The Organization Man* (New York: Doubleday & Co., Inc., 1957).

[4] Edward Albee, *The American Dream* and *The Zoo Story* (New York: Signet Books, 1963), p. 19.

[5] Vance Packard, *The Pyramid Climbers* (New York: Crest Books, 1964), p. 96.

[6] James C. Coleman, *Abnormal Psychology and Modern Life* (New York: Scott, Foresman and Co., 1950), p. 183.

[7] *New York Times*, Feb. 15, 1960.

[8] George E. Wellwarth, *The Theater of Protest and Paradox* (New York: Univ. Press, 1964), p. 276.

[9] Harold Clurman, "Theatre," *Nation* (Feb. 13, 1960), pp. 153-154.

[10] Ibid.

[11] Rose A. Zimbardo, "Symbolism and Naturalism in Edward Albee's *The Zoo Story*," *Twentieth Cent. Lit.*, VIII (April, 1960), pp. 10-17.

[12] *New York Herald Tribune*, Jan. 25, 1961.

[13] Robert Brustein, "Krapp and a Little Claptrap," *New Republic* (Feb. 22, 1960), pp. 21-22.

[14] Vance Packard, *The Waste Makers* (New York: Pocket Books, Inc., 1963), pp. 25-34.

[15] Coleman, pp. 119-120.

[16] Alfred Chester, "Edward Albee: Red Herrings and White Whales," *Commentary* (April, 1963), pp. 296-301.

[17] Mary Lukas, " 'The Death of Bessie Smith' and 'The American Dream'," *Catholic World* (Aug. 1961), pp. 335-336.

[18] *Daily News*, March 14, 1964.

[19] Richard Kostelanetz, "The Art of Total No," *Contact* (Oct., Nov., 1963), pp. 62-70.

[20] Tom F. Driver, "The American Dream," *Christian Century* (March 1, 1961), p. 275.

[21] *New York Times*, Feb. 15, 1960.

[22] Clurman, pp. 153-154.

[23] Zimbardo, pp. 10-17.

[24] Ibid.

[25] Henry Hewes, "Broadway Postscript," *Saturday Review* (Feb. 6, 1960), p. 32.

[26] Kostelanetz, pp. 62-70.

[27] Brustein, pp. 21-22.

[28] Zimbardo, loc cit.

[29] *New York Times*, Jan. 15, 1960.

[30] Personal interview with John Gassner, March 16, 1965.

[31] *New York Times*, Feb. 15, 1960.

[32] *New York Herald Tribune*, Jan. 25, 1961.

CHAPTER 2

[1] Allen Lewis, *American Plays and Playwrights of the Contemporary Theatre* (New York: Crown Pub., Inc., 1965), p. 85.

[2] David Reisman, Nathan Glazer, and Reuel Denney, *The Lonely Crowd* (New Haven: Yale Univ. Press, 1963), p. 57.

[3] Philip Wylie, *Generation of Vipers* (New York: Pocket Books, Inc., 1962), pp. 204-205.

[4] Reisman, pp. 56-57.

[5] Wylie, p. 186.

CHAPTER 3

[1] *New York Times*, February 25, 1968.

[2] Ibid.

[3] Julian Beck, "Notes from the Underground," *Evergreen Review*, May, 1968, vol. 12, no. 54, p. 14.

CHAPTER 4

[1] *New York Herald Tribune*, Jan. 25, 1961.

[2] *New York Post*, Jan. 25, 1961.

[3] *Variety,* Feb. 15, 1961.

[4] Edward Albee, *The American Dream* and *The Zoo Story* (New York: Signet Books, 1963), p. 53.

[5] Martin Esslin, *The Theatre of the Absurd* (New York: Doubleday & Co., 1961), p. 227.

[6] Esslin, p. xix.

[7] Albert Camus, *Le Mythe de Sisyphe* (Paris: Gallimard, 1942), p. 18.

[8] Mary Lukas, loc. cit.

[9] Wylie, p. 49.

[10] Wellwarth, pp. 279-282.

[11] Henry Goodman, "Edward Albee," *Drama Survey,* II (Spring, 1962), pp. 72-79.

[12] Wylie, p. 199.

[13] Reisman, p. 56.

[14] Wylie, pp. 192-193.

[15] For an interesting study of the emancipated woman, read Betty Friedan's *The Feminine Mystique* (New York: Dell Pub. Co., Inc., 1963).

[16] Whitney Balliett, "Off Broadway," *The New Yorker* (Feb. 4, 1961), pp. 63-66.

[17] *New York Herald Tribune,* Jan. 25, 1961.

[18] *Theatre Arts,* March, 1961.

[19] Personal Interview, March 17, 1965.

[20] Henry Hewes, "Broadway Postscript," *Saturday Review* (Feb. 11, 1961), p. 54.

[21] Reisman, p. 56.

CHAPTER 5

[1] Personal Interview, March 17, 1965.

[2] James Baldwin, "Theatre: The Negro In and Out," in John A. William's ed., *The Angry Black* (New York: Lancer Books, 1962), p. 21.

[3] *New York Herald Tribune,* March 2, 1961.

[4] *New York Times,* March 2, 1961.

[5] Wellwarth, p. 278.

[6] Lewis, pp. 84-86.

[7] Robert Hatch, "Arise Ye Playgoers of the World," *Horizon* (July, 1961), pp. 116-117.

[8] Goodman, loc. cit.

CHAPTER 6

[1] John Gassner, "Broadway in Review," *ETJ* (March, 1963), pp. 77-80.

[2] Wellwarth, pp. 282-284.

[3] *New York Mirror,* Oct. 15, 1962.

[4] *New York Post,* Oct. 15, 1962.

[5] *New York Times,* May 7, 1963.

[6] L. E. Chabrowe, "The Pains of Being Demystified," *Kenyon Review*, XXV (Winter, 1963), pp. 145-146.

[7] *Saturday Evening Post*, Jan. 18, 1964.

[8] Spurgeon O. English and others, *Intro. to Psychiatry* (New York: W. W. Norton & Co., Inc., 1957), pp. 24-25.

[9] *Catholic Transcript*, Jan. 1, 1963.

[10] Personal Interview, March 17, 1965.

[11] Henry Hewes, "Broadway Postscript," *Saturday Review* (Jan. 30, 1965), pp. 38-39, 65.

[12] *Theatre Arts*, Nov., 1962.

[13] Lewis, pp. 90-91.

[14] *New York Herald Tribune*, Oct. 15, 1962.

[15] Henry Hewes, "Broadway Postscript," *Saturday Review* (Oct. 27, 1962), p. 29.

[16] *Catholic Transcript*, loc. cit.

[17] *New York Times*, Oct. 15, 1962.

[18] *Time*, Oct. 26, 1962.

[19] Robert Brustein, "Albee and the Medusa-Head," *New Republic* (Nov. 3, 1962), pp. 29-30.

[20] *New York Times*, Oct. 15, 1962.

[21] *Literary Times*, Dec., 1964.

[22] Personal Interview, March 16, 1965.

[23] Personal Interview, March 17, 1965.

[24] Chester, pp. 296-301.

[25] Gassner, *ETJ* (March, 1963), pp. 77-80.

[26] Chester, loc. cit.

[27] *New York Post*, Oct. 15, 1962.

[28] Personal Interview, March 17, 1965.

[29] For analysis of contemporary undergraduate morals, turn to Gael Greene's *Sex and the College Girl* (New York: Dell Pub. Inc., 1963).

[30] R. H. Gardner, *The Splintered Stage: The Decline of the American Theatre* (New York: MacMillan Co., 1965), pp. 146-153.

[31] Lewis, pp. 81-98.

[32] Ibid.

[33] *Time*, Oct. 26, 1962.

[34] Chester, pp. 296-301.

[35] John Gassner, "*Who's Afraid of Virginia Woolf?* On LP," *Saturday Review* (June 29, 1963), pp. 39-40, 55.

[36] Richard Duprey, " '*Who's Afraid of Virginia Woolf?*'," *Catholic World* (Jan., 1963), pp. 263-264.

[37] "The Loser," *Documentary Film*, WCBS TV, March 30, 1965.

[38] *New York Times*, April 26, 1963.

[39] Personal Interview, March 17, 1965.

[40] Ibid.

[41] *Life*, Dec. 14, 1962.

[42] *New York Herald Tribune*, Jan. 24, 1965.

[43] Erich Fromm writes about man's dislocation and aloneness in his *The Heart of Man: Its Genius for Good and Evil* (New York:

Harper and Row, 1965).

[44] Albert Camus, "Absurd Freedom," in *Inquiry and Expression,* ed. by Harold G. Martin and Richard M. Ohmann (New York: Holt, Rinehart and Winston, Inc., 1963), p. 346.

[45] Henry Hewes, "Broadway Postscript," *Saturday Review* (Oct. 27, 1962), p. 29.

[46] *New York Times,* April 26, 1963.

[47] *Saturday Evening Post,* Jan. 18, 1964.

[48] Julian Beck, "Thoughts on Theater from Jail," *New York Times* (Feb. 21, 1965), p. 3.

[49] *Psychology Today,* July, 1968.

[50] Gassner, *ETJ* (March, 1963), pp. 77-80.

CHAPTER 7

[1] Robert Brustein, "Tiny Alice," *New Republic* (Jan. 23, 1965), pp. 33-36.

[2] *Time,* Jan. 8, 1965.

[3] *Newsweek,* Jan. 11, 1965.

[4] *Newsday,* Dec. 30, 1964.

[5] *Nation,* Jan. 18, 1965.

[6] *Daily News,* Dec. 30, 1964.

[7] *New York World-Telegram and Sun,* Dec. 30, 1964.

[8] *New York Herald Tribune,* March 23, 1965.

[9] *Nation,* loc. cit.

[10] Martin, *Inquiry,* pp. 797-798.

[11] Stuart W. Little, "Theater News," *New York Herald Tribune* (Dec. 31, 1964), p. 7.

[12] *Long Island Press,* Dec. 30, 1964.

[13] Philip Roth, "The Play that Dare Not Speak Its Name," *New York Review of Books* (Feb. 25, 1965), p. 4.

[14] Abraham N. Franzblau, "A Psychiatrist Looks at 'Tiny Alice,'" *Saturday Review* (Jan. 30, 1965), p. 39.

CHAPTER 8

[1] *Women's Wear Daily,* Sept. 23, 1966.

[2] *New Republic,* Oct. 8, 1966.

[3] *Daily News,* Sept. 23, 1966.

[4] *Nation,* Oct. 10, 1966.

[5] *New York Times,* Aug. 16, 1966.

[6] *Herald Tribune* (Paris) Sept. 23, 1966.

[7] *Vogue,* Nov. 1, 1966.

[8] NBC-TV News, 11:15 PM, Sept. 22, 1966.

[9] John Gassner, "Broadway in Review," *ETJ* (Dec., 1966) pp. 450-452.

[10] *Herald Tribune,* loc. cit.

[11] Gassner, *ETJ,* loc. cit.

[12] *Village Voice,* Sept. 29, 1966.

[13] Gassner, *ETJ,* loc. cit.

14 *New York Times,* Oct. 2, 1966.

15 *Newsweek,* Oct. 3, 1966.

16 Geoffrey Gorer, *The American People: A Study in National Character* (New York: W. W. Norton & Co., Inc., 1964), p. 54.

17 Ibid., p. 49.

18 Erik H. Erikson, *Childhood and Society* (New York: W. W. Norton & Co., Inc., 1963), pp. 290-291.

19 *New York Times,* Aug. 16, 1966.

20 *New York Times,* Oct. 2, 1966.

21 William Ernest Hocking, "Thoughts on Death and Life," in *Inquiry and Expression* ed. by Harold C. Martin and Richard M. Ohmann (New York: Holt, Rinehart and Winston, Inc., 1963), p. 582.

22 WINS Radio, Aug. 23, 1966.

23 Gorer, p. 131.

24 *Saturday Review,* Oct. 8, 1966.

25 *Toronto Daily Star,* Sept. 24, 1966.

26 *New York Times,* Sept. 23, 1966.

27 Hocking, p. 580.

28 Harold Clurman, "Introduction," *The Playwrights Speak,* ed. Walter Wager (New York: Delacorte Press, 1967), pp. xx-xxi.

29 Erich Fromm, *The Sane Society* (New York: Holt, Rinehart and Winston, Inc., 1962), p. 204.

30 Ibid., p. 160.

31 Ibid., p. 139.

32 *New York Post,* Sept. 23, 1966.

33 *Commonweal,* Oct. 14, 1966.

34 *World Journal Tribune,* Oct. 2, 1966.

35 Erikson, p. 295.

36 *Newsweek,* May 29, 1966.

37 *Nation,* loc. cit.

38 Ibid.

39 *New York Times,* May 2, 1967.

40 *New York Times,* May 3, 1967.

41 *New York Post,* Oct. 8, 1966.

CHAPTER 9

1 *Saturday Review,* Nov. 16, 1963.

2 Martin Gottfried, *A Theatre Divided: The Postwar American Stage* (Boston: Little, Brown and Co., 1967), p. 268.

3 *New York Herald Tribune,* Sept. 30, 1963.

4 *New York Times,* Oct. 31, 1963.

5 *New York Herald Tribune,* Nov. 17, 1963.

6 Robert Brustein, *Seasons of Discontent* (New York: Simon and Schuster, 1959-65), p. 157.

7 *New York Journal American,* Nov. 10, 1963.

8 *Brustein,* loc. cit.

9 *Newsweek,* Nov. 11, 1963.

10 *Morning Telegraph,* Nov. 6, 1963.

[11] *New York Times,* Nov. 10, 1963.

[12] Lawrence J. Hatterer, M.D., *The Artist in Society: Problems and Treatment of the Creative Personality* (New York: Grove Press, Inc., 1965), p. 139.

[13] Ibid.

[14] Personal Interview, March 17, 1965.

[15] Jean-Paul Sartre, *No Exit and Other Plays* (New York: Vintage Books), pp. 1-47 [No pub. date].

[16] *New York Herald Tribune,* Nov. 17, 1963.

[17] *New York World-Telegram and Sun,* Oct. 29, 1963.

[18] *Newsweek,* Nov. 11, 1963.

[19] *Journal American,* Jan. 12, 1966.

[20] *Newsweek,* Jan. 1966.

[21] The Paris Review Interviews, *Writers at Work* [introd. Alfred Kazin] (New York: Viking Press, 1967), p. 326.

[22] *WPAT Gaslight Revue Program Guide,* Feb. 1966, p. 31.

[23] *New York Herald Tribune,* Jan. 10, 1966.

[24] *New York Times,* Jan. 12, 1966, and *Newark Evening News* Jan. 23, 1966.

[25] *Time,* Jan. 21, 1966.

[26] *The New Yorker,* Jan. 22, 1966.

[27] *Show Business,* Jan. 22, 1966.

[28] *New York Post,* Jan. 1, 1966.

[29] *New York Times,* Nov. 26, 1967.

[30] *Westside News and Free Press,* Dec. 7, 1967.

[31] *New York Post,* Nov. 30, 1967.

[32] Packard, *The Waste Makers,* p. 29.

[33] Packard, *The Status Seekers,* p. 218.

[34] John Lahr, "The Adaptable Mr. Albee," *Evergreen Review,* May, 1968, pp. 37-39, 82-87.

[35] *Villager,* Nov. 30, 1967.

[36] Albert Bermel, "The Unprincipled, Inconsequential Critic," *The Arts & The Public* ed. by James E. Miller, Jr. and Paul D. Herring (Chicago: The University of Chicago Press, 1967), p. 111.

[37] *Westside News,* loc. cit.

[38] Packard, *The Status Seekers,* p. 165.

[39] *Nation,* Dec. 18, 1967.

[40] *Time,* Dec. 8, 1967.

[41] *Morning Telegraph,* Dec. 1, 1967.

[42] *Saturday Review,* Dec. 16, 1967.

[43] *New York Times,* Jan. 9, 1966.

[44] Lahr, p. 37.

[45] Gottfried, p. 272.

CHAPTER 10

[1] Marshall McLuhan and Quentin Fiore, *The Medium is the Massage* (New York: Bantam Books, 1967), p. 14.

[2] Program note to *Box-Mao-Box.*

[3] *Christian Science Monitor,* March 11, 1968.

[4] *Women's Wear Daily,* March 11, 1968.

[5] Ibid.

[6] *New York Times,* March 17, 1968.

[7] James E. Miller, Jr. and Paul D. Herring, eds., *The Arts & The Public* (Chicago: The University of Chicago Press, 1967) p. 5.

[8] Albert Bermel, p. 121.

[9] *Buffalo Evening News,* March 7, 1968.

[10] *Newsweek,* March 8, 1968.

[11] Richard Kostelanetz, *The Theatre of Mixed Means* (New York: The Dial Press, Inc., 1968), p. 37.

[12] McLuhan, p. 111.

[13] Kostelanetz, loc. cit.

[14] *New York Times,* March 8, 1968.

[15] Ibid.

[16] Robert W. Corrigan, "Where the People Are," in *The Arts & The Public* ed. by James E. Miller, Jr. and Paul D. Herring (Chicago: The University of Chicago Press, 1968), p. 131.

[17] *New York Times,* March 17, 1968.

[18] McLuhan, pp. 44-45.

[19] *New York Times,* March 17, 1968.

[20] McLuhan, p. 63.

[21] Ibid., p. 126.

[22] Kostelantz, p. 285.

[23] Bermel, p. 123.

[24] Miller, p. 6.

[25] Wright Morris, "How Things Are," in *The Arts & The Public.* ed. by James E. Miller, Jr. and Paul D. Herring (Chicago: The University Press, 1968), p. 39.

[26] *New York Times,* March 8, 1968.

[27] *New York Times,* February 25, 1968.

[28] *New York Times,* March 8, 1968.

[29] Leon Festinger, *A Theory of Cognitive Dissonance* (California: Stanford Univ. Press, 1957), p. 3.

[30] Ibid.

[31] Ibid.

[32] Roger Brown, *Social Psychology* (New York: The Free Press, 1965), p. 584.

[33] Gordon Rogoff, "The Fourth and Endless Theatre," *yale/theatre,* no. 1 (Spring, 1968), 78-87.

[34] Kostelanetz, p. 37.

[35] John Gassner, "Catharsis and the Modern Theatre," *European Theories of the Drama* revised by Henry Popkin (New York: Crown Pub., 1965), pp. 514-518.

[36] Robert L. Katz, *Empathy Its Nature and Uses* (London: Collier-Macmillan Limited, 1963), pp. 93-94.

[37] *New York Times,* March 8, 1968.

[38] *New York Times,* March 17, 1968.

[39] Kostelanetz, p. 37.

[40] Marshall McLuhan, [cited by] Richard Kostelanetz, *The Theatre of Mixed Means* (New York: The Dial Press, Inc., 1968), p. 34.

[41] Kostelanetz, p. 41.

[42] *New York Times,* February 25, 1968.

[43] Vance Packard, *The Waste Makers,* p. 246.

[44] *New York Times,* February 25, 1968.

[45] *Buffalo Evening News,* March 7, 1968.

[46] *New York Times,* February 25, 1968.

[47] *Toronto Daily Star,* March 7, 1968.

[48] *New York Times,* March 17, 1968.

[49] *New York Times,* Oct. 13, 1968.

[50] *New York Times,* March 8, 1968.

Selected Bibliography

Albee, Edward. *A Delicate Balance*. New York: Atheneum Pub., 1966.

————. "Creativity and Commitment." *Saturday Review*, June 4, 1966, p. 26.

————. *Everything in the Garden*. New York: Atheneum Pub., 1968.

————. *Malcolm*. New York: Atheneum Pub., 1966.

————. *The Ballad of the Sad Cafe*. New York: Atheneum Pub., 1963.

————. *The American Dream* and *The Zoo Story*. New York: Signet Books, 1963.

————. *The Death of Bessie Smith* and *The Sandbox*. New York: Signet Books, 1963.

————. *Tiny Alice*. New York: Atheneum Pub., 1965.

————. "Who's Afraid of the Truth?" *New York Times*, II (Aug. 18, 1963).

————. *Who's Afraid of Virginia Woolf?* New York: Pocket Books, Inc., 1963.

Baldwin, James. "Theatre: The Negro In and Out." *The Angry Black.* ed. by John A. William. New York: Lancer Books, 1962, p. 21.

Balliett, Whitney. "Off Broadway." *The New Yorker* (Feb. 4, 1961), pp. 63-66.

Bagdikian, Ben H. "It Has Come to This." *Saturday Evening Post,* August 10, 1968, pp. 21-22, 80-83.

Baxandall, Lee. "The Theatre of Edward Albee." *TDR* T28 (Summer, 1965), 19-40.

Beavin, Janet Helmick.; Jackson, Don D.; and Watzlawick, Paul. *Pragmatics of Human Communication: A Study of International Patterns, Pathologies, and Paradoxes*. New York: W.W. Norton & Co., Inc., 1967.

Beck, Julian, "Theater and Revolution." *Evergreen Review,* May, 1968, pp. 14-15, 88.

—————. "Thoughts on Theater from Jail." *New York Times* (Feb. 21, 1965), p. 3.

Bermel, Albert. "The Unprincipled, Inconsequential Critic." *The Arts & The Public*. ed. by James E. Miller and Paul D. Herring. Chicago: The Univ. of Chicago Press, 1967.

Bernstein, Marver H.; Carr, Robert K.; Murphy Walter F. *Essentials of American Democracy*. New York: Holt, Rinehart and Winston, 1968.

Berton, Pierre. *Voices From the Sixties*. New York: Doubleday & Co., 1967.

Brustein, Robert. *Seasons of Discontent*. New York: Simon and Schuster, 1959.

Buffalo Evening News.

Catholic Transcript.

Catholic World.

Chabrowe, L. E. "The Pains of Being Demystified." *Kenyon Review*, XXV (Winter, 1963), pp. 145-146.

Christian Century.

Christian Science Monitor.

Chester, Alfred. "Edward Albee: Red Herrings and White Whales." *Commentary* (April, 1963), pp. 296-301.

Clurman, Harold. "Introduction." *The Playwrights Speak*. ed. by Walter Wager. New York: Delacorte Press, 1967.

—————. "The Theatre of the Thirties." *TDR* T6 (Winter, 1959), 3-11.

—————. "Theatre." *Nation* (Feb. 13, 1960), pp. 153-154.

Coleman, James C. *Abnormal Psychology and Modern Life*. New York: Scott, Foresman and Co., 1950.

Commonweal.

Cooper, Giles. *Everything in the Garden*. London: Evans Bros. Ltd., 1963.

Corrigan, Robert W. "Where the People Are." *The Arts & The Public*. ed. by James E. Miller and Paul D. Herring. Chicago: The Univ. of Chicago Press, 1967.

Darmstäder Echo.

Daily News.

Davison, Richard Alan. "Edward Albee's 'Tiny Alice': A Note of Reexamination." Modern Drama, Vol. II (Summer, 1968), pp. 54-60.

Die Welt.

Digby Diehl. "Interview with Edward Albee." *Transatlantic Review* 13 (Summer, 1963), pp. 57-72.

Downer, Alan S., ed. *The American Theatre.* Voice of American Forum Lectures, 1967.

Dukore, Bernard F. "Tiny Albee." *Drama Survey,* Vol. V. #1 (Spring, 1966), pp. 60-66.

English, Spurgeon O., and Stuart M. Finch. *Introduction To Psychiatry.* New York: W.W. Norton & Co., Inc., 1957.

Erikson, Erik H. *Childhood and Society.* New York: W.W. Norton & Co., 1963.

Esslin, Martin. *The Theatre of the Absurd.* New York: Doubleday & Co., Inc., 1961.

Frankel, Max. "Why the Gap Between LBJ and the Nation." *New York Times Magazine,* Jan. , 1968, pp. 26-7 ff.

Franzblau, Abraham N. "A Psychiatrist Looks at 'Tiny Alice'." *Saturday Review* (Jan. 30, 1965), p. 39.

Frenz, Horst., ed. *American Playwrights on Drama.* New York: Hill and Wang, 1965.

Friedan, Betty. *The Feminine Mystique.* New York: Dell Pub. Co., Inc., 1963.

Fromm, Erich. *The Heart of Man: Its Genius for Good and Evil.* New York: Harper and Row, 1965.

————. *The Sane Society.* New York: Holt, Rinehart and Winston, Inc., 1962.

Gardner, R. H. *The Splintered Stage: The Decline of the American Theatre.* New York: MacMillan Co., 1965.

Gassner, John. "Broadway in Review." *ETJ* (March, 1963), pp. 77-80.

————. "Broadway in Review." *ETJ* (Dec., 1966), pp. 450-452.

————. "Catharsis and the Modern Theatre." *European Theories of the Drama*. ed. by Barrett H. Clark, revised by Henry Popkin. New York: Crown Pub., 1965.

—————. " 'Who's Afraid of Virginia Woolf?' on LP," *Saturday Review* (June 29, 1963), pp. 39-40, 55.

Gilman, Richard. "The Stage." *Commonweal* (Nov. 9, 1962), pp. 175-176.

Glazer, Nathan. "The New Left and Its Limits." *Commentary*, July, 1968, pp. 31-39.

Goodman, Henry, "Edward Albee." *Drama Survey* II (Spring, 1962), pp. 72-79.

Gorer, Geoffrey. *The American People: A Study in National Character*. New York: W.W. Norton & Co., 1964.

Gottfried, Martin. *A Theatre Divided: The Postwar American Stage*. Boston: Little, Brown and Co., 1967.

Gould, Jean. *Modern American Playwrights*. New York: Dodd, Mead & Co., 1966.

Greene, Gael. *Sex and the College Girl*. New York: Dell Pub., Inc., 1963.

Hatch, Robert. "Arise Ye Playgoers of the World." *Horizon* (July, 1961), pp. 116-117.

Hatterer, Lawrence J., M.D. *The Artist in Society: Problems and Treatment of the Creative Personality*. New York: Grove Press, Inc., 1965.

Hentoff, Nat. "The War on Dissent." *Playboy*, Sept., 1968, pp. 155, 170, 228-252.

Hersh, Seymour M. "The Secret Arsenal." *New York Magazine*, August 25, 1968, pp. 26-7, 82-87, 90, 92.

Himelstein, Morgan Y. *Drama Was a Weapon: The Left-Wing Theatre in New York 1929-1941*. New Jersey: Rutgers Univ. Press, 1963.

Hocking, William Ernest. "Thoughts on Death and Life." *Inquiry and Expression*. ed. by Harold C. Martin and Richard M. Ohmann. New York: Holt, Rinehart and Winston, Inc., 1963.

Journal American.

Katz, Robert L. *Empathy*. London: Collier-Macmillan, Ltd., 1963.

Kaufman, Walter. *The Faith of a Heretic*. New York: Doubleday & Co., 1963.

Kerr, Walter. *The Theatre in Spite of Itself*. New York: Simon and Schuster, 1963.

————. "O'Neill's Day Dream vs. Albee's Truth." *New York Herald Tribune* VII (Jan. 24, 1965), p. 1.

Kostelanetz, R. "The Art of Total No." *Contact* (Oct.-Nov., 1963), pp. 62-70.

————. *The New American Arts*. New York: Collier Books, 1967.

————. *The Theatre of Mixed Means*. New York: The Dial Press, Inc., 1968.

Lahr, John. "The Adaptable Mr. Albee." *Evergreen Review*, May, 1968, pp. 37-39, 82-87.

Lewis, Allan. *American Plays and Playwrights of the Contemporary Theatre*. New York: Crown Pub., Inc., 1965.

Life.

Literary Times.

Little, Stuart W. "Theater News." *New York Herald Tribune* (Dec. 31, 1964), p. 7.

Lukas, Mary. " 'The Death of Bessie Smith' and 'The American Dream'." *Catholic World* (Aug., 1961), pp. 335-336.

Mannes, Marya. "The Half-World of American Drama." *Reporter* (April 25, 1963), p. 48.

Marcus Thomas B. " 'Tiny Alice' and Tragic Catharsis." *ETJ* XVII (Oct., 1965), pp. 225-233.

Martin, Harold C., and Richard M. Ohmann. *Inquiry and Expression*. New York: Holt, Rinehart and Winston, Inc., 1963.

McCarten, John. "Mystical Manipulations." *The New Yorker* (Jan. 9, 1965), p. 84.

McLuhan, Marshal, and Fiore, Quentin. *The Medium is the Massage*. New York: Bantam Books, 1967.

Meehan, Thomas. "Edward Albee and a Mystery." *New York Times* (Dec. 27, 1964), p. 1.

Miller, Jorden. "Myth and the American Dream: O'Neill to Albee." Modern Drama Vol. VII, #1 (Sept., 1964), 190-198.

Morgan, Thomas B. "Angry Playwright in a Soft Spell." *Life*, May 26, 1967, pp. 90-99.

Morning Telegraph.

Morris, Wright. "How Things Are." *The Arts & The Public.* ed. by James E. Miller and Paul D. Herring. Chicago: The Univ. of Chicago Press, 1967.

Nadel, Norman. "The Theater." *New York-Telegram and Sun* (Dec. 30, 1964), p. 1.

Nannes, Casper. *Politics in the American Drama.* Washington: The Catholic Univ. of American Press, 1960.

New American Review #4. Signet Books, New York: The New American Library, 1968.

New Republic.

Newsday.

Newsweek.

New York Herald Tribune.

New York Mirror.

New York Post.

New York Times.

New York World-Telegram and Sun.

Oglesby, Carl, and Shaull, Richard. *Containment and Change.* New York: The Macmillan Co., 1967.

O'Hara, John. "The Talk of the Town." *The New Yorker* (Dec. 19, 1964), 31-33.

Orzel, Nick., and Smith, Michael., eds. *Eight Plays from Off-Off Broadway.* New York: The Bobbs-Merrill Co., Inc., 1966.

Packard, Vance. *The Status Seekers.* New York: Pocket Books, Inc., 1961.

———, *The Waste Makers.* New York: Pocket Books, Inc., 1963.

———, *The Pyramid Climbers.* New York: Crest Books, 1964.

Purdy, James. *Malcolm.* New York: Avon Books, 1959.

Rabkin, Gerald. *Drama and Commitment.* Bloomington: Indiana Univ. Press, 1964.

Report of the National Commission on Civil Disorders. New York: Bantam Books, 1968.

Reisman, David, Nathan Glazer, Ruel Denney. *The Lonely Crowd.* New Haven: Yale Univ. Press, 1963.

Roth, Philip. "The Play that Dare Not Speak Its Name." *The New York Review of Books* (Feb. 25, 1965), p. 4.

Samuels, Charles Thomas. "The Theatre of Edward Albee." *Massachusetts Review* (Winter, 1961-2), pp. 187-201.

Saturday Evening Post.

Saturday Review.

Schechner, Richard. "Reality Is Not Enough." *TDR* T27 (Spring, 1965), pp. 118-152.

Show Business.

Stewart, R. S. "John Gielgud and Edward Albee Talk About the Theater." *Atlantic Monthly* (April, 1965), pp. 61-68.

Taubman, Howard. "Enigma That Runs Down." *New York Times* II (Jan. 10, 1965), p. 1.

Theatre Arts.

The Paris Review Interviews. *Writers at Work.* Introd. Alfred Kazin. New York: Viking Press, 1967.

"The Theatre in American Political Life." *yale/theatre.* II (summer, 1968), 12-16.

Time.

Toronto Daily Star.

Trotta, Geri. "On Stage: Edward Albee." *Horizon* (Sept., 1961), p. 79.

Variety.

Weales, Gerald. *American Drama Since W.W. II.* New York: Harcourt, Brace & World, Inc., 1962.

Wellwarth, George E. *The Theater of Protest and Paradox.* New York: New York Univ. Press, 1964.

Westside News and Free Press.

Wise, David. "When Spies Get Caught: Perspectives on the 'Pueblo'." *New Republic,* Feb. 10, 1968, pp. 9-10.

Women's Wear Daily.

World Journal Tribune.

WPAT Gaslight Revue Program Guide. Feb., 1966.

Wylie, Philip. *Generation of Vipers.* New York: Pocket Books, Inc., 1962.

Zimbardo, Rose A. "Symbolism and Naturalism in Edward Albee's *The Zoo Story.*" Twentieth Cent. Lit., VIII (April, 1960), pp. 10-17.